The Names of Minimalism

The Names of Minimalism

*Authorship, Art Music,
and Historiography in Dispute*

Patrick Nickleson

University of Michigan Press
Ann Arbor

Published in the United States of America by the
University of Michigan Press
Manufactured in the United States of America
Printed on acid-free paper
First published January 2023

A CIP catalog record for this book is available from the British Library.

Library of Congress Cataloging-in-Publication data has been applied for.

https://doi.org/10.3998/mpub.10207791

ISBN 978-0-472-13328-4 (hardcover : alk. paper)
ISBN 978-0-472-03909-8 (paper : alk. paper)
ISBN 978-0-472-90300-9 (Open Access e-book)

The University of Michigan Press's open access publishing program is made possible thanks to additional funding from the University of Michigan Office of the Provost and the generous support of contributing libraries.

Cover: Tony Conrad pickets La Monte Young's concert in Buffalo, New York (April 1990). Photo by Chris Hill. Design: Seita Goto.

Contents

Digital materials related to this title can be found on
the Fulcrum platform via the following citable URL:
https://doi.org/10.3998/mpub.10207791

Illustrations

Acknowledgments

It is likely true of all books, but it bears stating here right up front: if I had started writing today, this would be a very different book. During its initial research and writing at the University of Toronto, its submission as a proposal to University of Michigan Press, and the four years that I spent rapidly or slowly revising it for publication, my thinking about the content went through innumerable changes. What never budged for me, perhaps to my own detriment, was the initial formal idea: three pairs of composers, held in tension through their early collaborative practices but forever represented, in music histories, for their disputes. I liked the way they buzzed together, and I never broke with that image.

Throughout all of that rewriting, I worked closely with many friends, collaborators, colleagues, artists, composers, and mentors who left their mark on this book or, when things felt distant from minimalism, my thinking more broadly. Before anyone else I want to thank Dylan Robinson, whom I have not yet managed to get to say a single word about minimalism in ten years of friendship and collaboration, but who kept me busy, motivated, open-minded, and indeed employed through many of the years of researching and writing this book. Another mentor largely disinterested in minimalism, Sherry Lee, advised the original thesis project and has remained consistently available and supportive in the years since. Benjamin Piekut generously pushed me to make this project better at every step, and I hope it meets some of his very high standards. Tamara Levitz marked up drafts with extensive comments, suggestions, and corrections. She then nearly immediately called to speak through her ideas and ensure it didn't read as anything other than enthusiasm for where I was taking my ideas. No one is as extradimensionally smart and generous as Kerry O'Brien. She has been a partner in the most exciting, critical, and thoughtful conversations I have had about and around music, and she consistently pulls out a remarkable anecdote or connection from her extensive archival expertise in the weirdest corners of American experimentalism. These are the people I set out to impress whenever I paused to share a new draft, and they have been my models for generous, creative, critical, engaged scholarship.

Toronto will forever be home thanks to the people there. I was very lucky to join a cohort of colleagues who evaded, at all turns, any singular disciplinary or methodological orientations. Jeremy Strachan guided me throughout grad school and beyond; we collaborated on many projects and drank many more pints. I hope both continue. All my thanks and all my love to Ed Wright, Yun Emily Wang, Caitlin Martinkus, Gabriela Jiménez, Rebekah Lobosco, September Russell, Hilary Donaldson, Alia O'Brien, and Scott Hanenberg. Joshua Pilzer, Jeff Packman, and Ken McLeod each had a lasting impact on this project, and are inseparable from how I understand teaching and mentorship. Ken passed away from cancer in spring 2022; I will never forget the last time I saw him: in person at a pub in Toronto, on the very literal eve of Covid-19 lockdowns, as we enthusiastically chatted about the impact and methods of the ongoing rail blockades at Tyendinaga in support of Wet'suwet'en pipeline resistance.

Too many others provided generous feedback on drafts or influenced my thought over drinks or Covid phone calls. Jeremy Grimshaw and Branden Joseph wrote brilliant books on La Monte Young and Tony Conrad that were the major music-historical reference points throughout my writing, and each has provided generous insight along the way. I have learned lots from David Cecchetto, including that it's often better to have interesting ideas than correct ones. Sumanth Gopinath assigned the book to his Minimalism seminar at the University of Minnesota in the final moments of proofreading, and provided invaluable last minute commentary and correction for which I am deeply grateful. Jamie Currie demands that writing about music be an artistic practice. As does Tanya Lukin Linklater, who taught me that method means holding things in relation. Will Robin has been a model of generosity and public engagement in scholarship. Vincent de Roguin provided invaluable access to Terry Riley's archive, as well as a comfortable floor to sleep on amid one of the best personal libraries I've seen. Jaime Jones, Tomas MacAuley, Ciaran Crilly, and the rest of the faculty at University College Dublin gave me an institutional home in the final months of revisions. Chris Stover and João Pedro Cachopo were brilliant collaborators through another book project in the midst of this one. Dan DiPiero contributed to that project, and has been an excellent source of support-at-a-distance as we worked through the publication process in parallel. I relearned everything I thought I knew about music in two years working with the faculty and students in the Conservatory of Music at Mount Allison University in 2017–2019. They join landmarks like the Walker Road woods, my neighbors on Allison Avenue, and all the regulars and bartenders at Thunder & Lightning for making Sackville, New Brunswick feel like home for two years. Mary Francis gave me faith that people might have interest in this work, and Sara Cohen expertly guided me through the process of getting it into readers' hands. Tony Conrad let me come interview him in his Buffalo apartment one morning in 2016 before taking me out for coconut soup and spent the afternoon into the late evening speaking about his work. Tony Oursler, Jeff Hunt, Tyler Hubby, Arnold Dreyblatt, Chris Hill, and the others who knew Conrad closely during his life have been incredibly generous with anecdotes, insights, and archival materials. My good friend Seita Goto got stuck on our couch in Dublin after a Covid-soaked road trip through Northern Ireland, which resulted in this book's beautiful cover, for which I'm very grateful.

My family—Mom and Dad, Sara and Brian, Sean, Karol, Luke and Jake—have been equal parts supportive of and baffled by my career in academia so far, and I thank them for their patience and faith. Justin Quenneville and I can hold a conversation forever, and we basically have since I began writing this book; he, Kendell, and Topher offered stability and sanity during the worst parts of a pandemic lockdown, and even offered our family a new member, Ethan. Ryan, Kat, and Luka flip effortlessly between great friends at a great distance to London roomies whose spare bed I can claim for months at a time without batting an eye. Jamie and Pete took me in without question on the first of many trips to the British Library; they have the world's greatest couch. Lastly and most importantly, my partner Laura and our dog Backgammon-dash-Rockstar have been my world outside this and all other books from its very earliest development. I would not have finished without their constant love and encouragement, or without the excitement I felt to take breaks to walk, cook, travel, or watch movies with them.

Throughout its long development, this book was supported by funding from the Social Sciences and Humanities Research Council of Canada, and from an Irish Research Council Postdoctoral Fellowship. Several archives provided important access and permissions. I am thankful to Terry Riley, the Estate of Tony Conrad, University of California San Diego Library Special Collections and Archives, the British Library, and the Paul Sacher Stiftung.

Dublin, April 2022

Introduction

"La Monte Young Does Not Understand 'His' Work"

————

What can we make of this claim, printed on a lone picketer's placard outside Hallwalls Art Gallery in Buffalo, New York, in early April 1990? Certainly La Monte Young, one of the leading figures in contemporary experimental music, is well aware of what he's doing. For many listeners, Young's music is the epitome of a particular idea of complexity: not a rigid formalism, but a music grounded in esoteric ideas about the interrelation of tuning and time, duration and attention, and, in collaboration with his partner Marian Zazeela, light and space. Nevertheless, when concertgoers arrived at Hallwalls they encountered "La Monte Young Does Not Understand 'His' Work" in large, typed letters across the top of a particularly wordy protest placard. Passing Buffalo residents and concert attendees might have recognized the lone picketer as Tony Conrad, a local artist, media studies professor, and, most recently, activist in ongoing local disputes over media access, free speech, and public discourse (Figure 1).[1]

It was not Conrad's first time picketing a concert of experimental music.[2] In 1964 he joined a slightly larger protest, led by Henry Flynt, of a performance by Karlheinz Stockhausen at Town Hall in New York City during which they expanded upon Cornelius Cardew's argument that Stockhausen's music serves global, bourgeois imperialism.[3] At that time, Young and Conrad worked together in a group called the Theatre of Eternal Music, devising a daily practice of long-duration, collectivist, just intonation drones (see Chapter 2). Decades later, at some point in the mid-1980s, Young asked Conrad and their bandmate John Cale to sign release forms acknowledging Young as the sole composer of a mass of tapes the ensemble had recorded together. Conrad was shocked; he refused permission and began a nearly three-decade

Figure 1. Tony Conrad pickets La Monte Young's concert in Buffalo, New York (April 1990) . Photo by Chris Hill, courtesy of Jeff Hunt and Tyler Hubby.

argument against Young that took many forms both discursive and performative. On this occasion, he picketed.[4]

In contrast to the Town Hall show, now Conrad was out front of a much smaller venue, as part of a much smaller protest, in a different era in which the celebrity or even the public relevance of experimental musicians could not be taken for granted. Conrad disputed Young's (mis)understanding of his authorial propriety, and, more generally, the normative authorial conventions in Western art music to which Young appealed. What Young heard as reified, enclosed property under his authority, Conrad heard as the sounding result of egalitarian, collective labor. What Young failed to understand about his music, in Conrad's mind, was not its rigorous harmonic complexities or its use of long durations. It was rather that he understood the Theatre of Eternal Music's practice as *his own* music. Conrad's claim was not about the form of the music, but the forms of relationship, organization, and collectivism undertaken by the ensemble during their years of performance and rehearsal. Young's misunderstanding was not formal, it was political: he didn't misunderstand his *music*; he misunderstood it as *his* music.

Indeed, one might say the (mis)understandings here were *political* rather than *musical*, but Conrad himself would have dismissed this interpretation as too neatly delimiting music's porous territories. The lines demarcating what is and is not music play a key role in how Young and Conrad each (mis)understood their earlier collaboration. Conrad insisted at the time that Young could only hear Conrad's arguments as mere "interpersonal bickering," where Conrad considered the protests part of or equivalent to "Music."[5] Where Young had made a career of bringing into composition social relationships, the sound of butterflies and fire, or the noise of dragging tables and chairs, he was rather skeptical of such expansions when they were undertaken by others. "What I'm trying to say," Conrad told an interviewer in 1996, "is that both the message conveyed through my picketing, and the picketing itself, were not communications primarily intended for La Monte Young personally. They were communications which took place on the public level, which is the level of culture, of symbolic statement. These were symbolic or formal statements, which are as much a part of 'Music' as this interview is."[6]

Conrad's protest introduces a new fault line into our conceptual relationship to La Monte Young's compositional authority, without simply reallocating musical propriety from one party to another. Rather, the newly drawn line redistributes the relative possibility of musical propriety from its impossibility. Or perhaps we could say it redistributes ideas of private property in opposition not to other private properties, but to faith in public spaces and the very notion of a commons; "music" not in opposition to noise or unmusical sound, but to the various "outsides" it prefigures and the methods by which they are enclosed. More importantly, the dispute between Young and Conrad marks how we allocate value and resources to each side of such binaries, and the concomitant (mis)understandings that come into play when lines are being consistently redrawn.

This book is about the recurrence of such disputes between the best-known figures of what we retroactively call "musical minimalism" as they redistributed not authorial propriety, but the (im)possibility of authorship, normative modes of claiming property in music, and their historiographic inscriptions and policings. I begin with Conrad's picket—a topic I will return to in more depth in Chapter 2—because, of all the stories in this book, it best stands in for my methodological and political concerns. Three such concerns are worth introducing up front. First, I am less interested in understanding minimalism through its music—though it does play an important part—than in thinking through minimalism's politics of authorship, organization, and propriety as each has been staged in music historiography. Second, Conrad arguing that Young does not "understand" *his* work draws me toward recognizing dissonant (mis)understandings of this music that are frequently in play: not just the disagreement between Conrad and Young, but the notion that they in fact (mis)understood different things about their collaborative work. I hear in questions of (mis)understanding questions of pedagogy, transmission, intelligence, historiography, and egalitarianism. Such (mis)understandings draw us into relation not specifically with historical actions or their historiographic account, but rather with how we stage the gap between them. Not right and wrong through appeal to universal judgments, but a recognition of speaking, working, and living at incommunicative or incommensurate cross-purposes.

Third, and most importantly, I am excited by where Conrad's protest draws our story: not into a concert hall or onto the musical page, the supposed "proper" locations of art music historiography, but onto the street and outside an art gallery. These have quite often been the proper locations of minimalism's historical impropriety. The terrain of critical reflection and historiography in play throughout this book is not composers seated at their desks silently inscribing sounding forms, but pairs of composers as they found themselves together in shared spaces: upholding sound collectively over long durations or unending repetitions in lofts, art galleries, and garages; discussing the nature of their collaborative relationships; or in dispute over whether or not they meant the same thing by how they have understood those sounds and relationships. In response to all of these, how do I, as a historian, stage such moments of dispute? Are they a necessary terrain of human interrelation? An inevitable step toward interpersonal failure? A contentious moment in an otherwise peaceable relationship? Representative allegory of an infinite struggle over resources, capital, and power?

These recurring disputes over, about, and within authorship between minimalist composers point backward to their earlier and close collaborations. To hold in dissonant, proximate tension the relationship between the earlier collaborations and the later disputes, I propose the term *(early) minimalism*. I mean for this formulation to capture, under one term, the homonymic collision of the collaborative authorial politics of early musical minimalism and its refraction through music histories eager to confiscate that politics by recasting it as naive, failed, or ignorant—in a word, to cast early minimalist music and its politics as *early*. Productive of the most canonically famous minimalist music, the music that I call "early minimalism" was the result of collaborative practices through which composers refused recording their music to scores, instead valorizing magnetic tape (as archival medium, compositional technology, and ontological site of "the work"), organizing their own bands, and performing live in lofts and art galleries rather than in concert halls.[7] Each of these local practices was taken up as a critique of the normative, material work engaged in by composers of their teachers' generation. Under the heading of early minimalism we can think of the collective drones of the Theatre of Eternal Music (Chapter 2), the tape-phasing interactions of Terry Riley and Steve Reich, organ-driven music like *Four Organs* and *Two Pages* performed by the ensemble Reich and Philip Glass shared (both Chapter 3), and the ringing harmonics of Rhys Chatham's and Glenn Branca's electric guitar music (Chapter 4). Other musics could fit here, to be sure, but I choose these artists precisely for the historiographic value of staging the minimal gap between collaboration and dispute. Early minimalism was a radical challenge to compositional convention and normative practices of art music authorship. It has been acknowledged as such but is always very carefully circumscribed if not outright denied in its efficacy (see Chapter 1). These disputes and their collaborative geneses have too often been pruned away to leave behind a scored, concert hall tradition that we today call minimalism, written down by composers who join up with, rather than continuing to challenge, a longer trajectory of modernist authorship.

That *(early) minimalism* is marked as "early" is also central to my dissensual proposal. By "early" I mean the historiographic politics through which the music of early minimalism has been cast as ignorant, naive, and failed. In such a rendering, the music is the product of formal ignorance, its authorial politics is naive, and it was already "dead" by the early 1980s because of the inevitable failure of that ignorance and naivete. These collaborations are not only early chronologically in the various composers' careers, but also in being rendered as guileless moments of youthful rebellion, the inevitable failure of which is indexed through the subsequent disputes over authority. "Early" captures a homonymic gap between the politics of the formative music and the historiographic poetics of the later disputes. I call this relationship, following the philosopher Jacques Rancière, one of *dissensus*, "a conflict over homonyms."[8] For example, I place in close tension *minimalism* and *(early) minimalism*—with its doubled *early* registers—to consider the mechanism by which the collaborative authorial politics of early minimalism have been confiscated toward reproducing yet another art musical-ism operating under the same old authorial politics. I imagine this on the order of a calculation. Existing histories have taken the statement "early minimalism was early" and reduced its terms to produce, simply, "minimalism" free from any considerations of changing authorial politics and proprieties. In contrast, I insist that these two *earlies* are homonyms deserving detailed attention and emphasis. Thus, (early) minimalism.

While the homonymic trajectory of various minimalisms is key to telling the story, another homonym in dispute here is *authorship*. Indeed, salvaging *authorship* more or less as conventionally defined has been the motivating concern, I argue, of existing music-historical writing on minimalism. (Early) minimalism is further made *early* through insistence on minimalism's place within teleological assumptions about the movement from simplicity to complexity, youth to maturity, or ignorance to knowledge. More broadly critics, historians, and the composers have consistently called upon a facile reading of early minimalism's naive kinship with 1960s radicalism to insist that the politics of early minimalism was always doomed to fail.[9] (Early) minimalism thus aims to capture discursive slippages in musicological, political, and historiographic realms as the music of minimalism is rendered representative of formal ignorance and political naivete, and then subsequently turned into an allegory of the necessity of authorship in art music. In this sense, I am tracing the construction of what Branden Joseph criticized as the "metaphysical history of minimalism," a narrative that, in failing to question "the tropes of authorship, influence, expression, linear progression, and disciplinary specificity," recreated, over and over, an unchanging essence of minimalism that carried on from Young's early work and primordial drones through to the 1980s. As Joseph writes, "Within the larger history of minimalism, this originary content, variously modified and inflected, continues through the canonic lineage connecting Young to Riley to Reich to Glass, a trajectory that is presented, both collectively and in each individual case, as illustrative of the increasing sophistication and establishment of minimalism, a trajectory that ends in opera and appearances at the Brooklyn Academy of Music."[10]

The Names of Minimalism examines the history of early minimalism along authorial lines traced by art historians, through the narrative and ethical concerns of historians and philosophers of equality and revolt like Rancière, and building from the invaluable primary work of historians, theorists, composers, and performers of minimalism. The limiting frames of my investigation are nevertheless the figures, music, documents, and concepts that music historians will recognize as minimalism: the lives and work of the "big four" minimalists—La Monte Young, Terry Riley, Steve Reich, and Philip Glass—as they developed their most prominent works from the early 1960s to the early 1980s, in San Francisco and, more importantly, New York City. I do little to trouble the normative "content" of musical minimalism, and as a result, present what will likely seem like an archaic repertoire list for those dedicated to an updated and revivified minimalism.[11] The protagonists of my disputes are all white American men. The most important scholarship on minimalism in the last two decades has recognized the presence of people of color, queer folks, and members of communities traditionally marginalized by art music histories as having been contributors to what minimalism is from its very beginning. In turning to dispute I want to recognize that we are firmly in the zone of white, heteropatriarchal masculinity.[12] These authorship disputes are, for lack of a better term, pissing contests. I view this closed territory of consideration not as a failure but as an opportunity. In returning minimalism to the "founding fathers" whose dominance most scholarship aspires to escape,[13] I want to take stock of the absent causes of this hegemonic framing and the modalities of its exclusions. I do this rather than expand the terms of inclusion because, as Donna Haraway has noted, discourses of inclusion are often the means by which white, heteropatriarchal discourse sustains itself.[14] Rather than inclusion of other voices, then, I want to dig deep into the pissing contests to examine how minimalism was constructed as, and to many audiences remains, the purview of white dudes bickering over who did what first.

My inclination is that this is not a club into which we should relegate new voices, or voices whose contributions were not appreciated in the first place. The recent concern for "white racial frame" in music studies has produced the most exciting disciplinary critique in recent years; following those claims, I think it is key that we do not enliven a saggy, dying discourse like "minimalism" through diversifying its repertoire lists as if it wasn't definitively and problematically very white all along. I want instead to rethink how we hold the "classic" repertoire in its place. What are the authorial, political, and historiographical concerns that have either gone unspoken or been actively elided to uphold minimalism as one more -ism in the history of white, twentieth-century, Euro-American, patriarchal, "literate" composition? Minimalism had many important political successes, I argue throughout; the displacement of racial biases in the downtown music scene was absolutely not one of them. This is not to say that we should only continue to center or tell the stories of prominent names; far from it. It is simply that in digging into the history of minimalism, I was consistently struck by how its key contributions were elided in music histories, and how, rather than addressing that, contemporary work has tended to introduce new figures without rethinking the originary problematic that, as I understand it in this book, has to do with modes of authorship and historiography in the 1960s and 1970s that should have fundamentally displaced the macho, white, property-oriented conception of art music that musicology seems always to rediscover hiding behind challenges to its centrality. I dread the either/or proposal that this might outline—either inclusion of new voices or critique of foundational figures. Such a choice need not be made.

The reigning question is then a methodological one. How can we pressure that canonic content so as to break the framing devices (authorship, historiography, disciplinarity, privilege, property), that have always benefited university-trained, white, male composers who were able to play with the institutional privileges upheld by musical literacy as signaled in notation (or its safe refusal)? Even beyond the privileges maintained through the act of refusal, in the coming pages I focus on how that refusal was policed or treated as a youthful misstep. This treatment then later allowed central protagonists like Steve Reich to reclaim the products of that refusal as an individual, proprietary privilege. As Cheryl I. Harris, Aileen Moreton-Robinson, and others have argued, we should understand whiteness in such contexts as a form of property—one that pays out interest in social and economic capital and historiographic import.[15] Even as I praise the collaborative politics and critiques of authorship practiced within (early) minimalism, I am simultaneously attentive to the mechanisms by which that shared terrain is once again made property, through appeal to scholarship, priority, pedagogy, and critical press. Moments of interauthorial dispute, in their tensions both between disputants and between the dispute and the period disputed-over, provide volatile pressure with which to break out of historiographic norms that hold together property, authority, and whiteness. Moreover, I contend that these disputes have *always* held the musicological concept of minimalism together precisely through being repeatedly elided. As I discuss in Chapter 4, "minimalism" was often clearly intended as a distinguishing marker that was necessarily about a musical practice that prioritized rhythm, repetition, and collectivist white appropriations of Black musical culture and, indeed, Black voices. Disputes over, within, and about authorship have been the unspoken terrain—the absent cause—that motivates and coheres musical minimalism as a valuable concept in contemporary histories of Western art music. I worry that simply diversifying that field with new subjectivities who had been initially marginalized, as if we are now in possession of a better, inclusive, twenty-first-century minimalism, risks letting art music historiography off the hook for problems that we continue to replicate and that, I argue, are endemic to the very notion of a literate, Western art music. We cannot simply maintain the same genres, concepts, priorities, properties, and relationships while introducing supplementary names to repertoire lists. Perhaps minimalism, imagined as an "art music," is little more than the discursive alibi through which white, radical authorship and its privileges can be maintained as a historical property explicitly in its appropriations of Black musical legacies.

Why then propose a method founded on examining disputes between white authors? This is a complex question, and as such I would like to take a few stabs at an answer. We can note first that authorial *disputes*, more than any particular *dispute*, are a recurring fact of the development of musical minimalism. The art historian Branden Joseph provided me with a first motivation when he wrote that the history of minimalist music is "to a surprising degree a history of authorship disputes."[16] While less concerned with music, James Meyer similarly argues that minimal art should be understood "not as a movement with a coherent platform, but as a field of continuity and conflict, of proximity and difference."[17] Historians and critics of music, attached to a less reflexive critical discourse of authorship, have been hesitant to acknowledge the recurrence of authorial disputes as a positive, cohering frame. Instead, writing on musical minimalism is haunted by the implicit danger that such dispute was the inevitable, negative outcome of what is rather universally considered a fundamental element (or flaw!) of minimalism's emergence: its ties to, differently articulated, 1960s counterculture, politics, radicalism, and revolt. Its dominant figures' interest in interauthorial collaboration and performance registers a generational rejection of heteronomous impositions of authority.[18] The dominant narrative "emplotment" of minimalism's historical destiny fits neatly into histories of the 1960s from the vantage point of the 1990s and beyond. I borrow "emplotment" here from Davide Panagia, who uses it to name how the Aristotelian *muthos* of a well-ordered plot becomes mapped onto historical writing in terms of necessary destinies through the "proper" interrelation of action, character, and normative sequence.[19] For scholars writing in the 1990s, there is a clear narrative trajectory from 1960s origins to the present: an allegory of youthful radicalism narrated from the perspective of mature recantations of early affiliations (Chapter 3). It was only through and paired with such retractions that early minimalism could be made recognizable as an event within normative music histories. The "lesson" of minimalism, in such discursive framing, can be little more than a high-visibility allegory of the impossibility of collaborative authorship in art music.

When the nineteenth-century ideal of "Western art music" is the disciplinary frame, the narrative capture of collaboration is simultaneously *very* carefully proscribed (the hierarchical dynamics assumed in relationships between performers, audiences, conductors, spouses, and so on), and largely unthought. As such, the disputes so recurrent among minimalist composers have never been addressed head on. Throughout the early years of this project, I was told more and less explicitly that such investigation could only be an airing of gossip and private intrigue, irrelevant to critical work in music studies. Art music composition is a solitary pursuit; authorship precedes it, and collaboration follows along carefully prescribed lines defined by genre, historical period, institutional associations, and so on. Dispute, this line of thought insists, is the inevitable result of some failure—whether utopian or cynical, naive or reckless, structural or interpersonal—to recognize that inexorable chronology.[20] It is precisely for this reason that digging into these disputes seemed important, and indeed why the case study structure wound up so focused on white, male authors. Is it possible, I began to wonder, that the reason we are supposed to bracket out authorship disputes is that they are the messy part of the process that must—to uphold a fantasy of strong, singular authority—be kept outside?

My first answer, then, to "Why authorial disputes?"[21] is that they are taken for granted in musicology, and they're taken for granted because they are assumed to be inevitable when collaboration is introduced in the wrong way and at the wrong point in the process of narrative emplotment.[22] Disputes, I argue, always point to moments of indistinction and uncertainty—not necessarily in the dispute itself, but in the moment recounted. Thematizing dispute insists upon a whole different narrative temporality as we find ourselves in a buzzing gap between event and its account. Toward recognizing this tension, I refuse here any sense of resolving the disputes. When we abandon the normative criteria for judgments—for example, ownership in property, historical priority, authorial paternity—we find ourselves not in the well-regulated bounds of a courtroom dispute between preconstituted parties, but rather in a situation in which the first responsibility is for participants to stage, through the tools of narrative, the logic through which they can be party to a dispute in the first place. In short, the first task of these disputes is not to present evidence, but to constitute oneself as a valid disputant. The major figures of early minimalism have drawn attention to their formative radicalisms and collaborations precisely to dispel their efficacy and utility for subsequent generations of composers.

Periods of dispute, revolt, uprising, rebellion, and uncertainty more generally are difficult to historicize because they are so often tied to their "inevitable" destiny. Historians of leftist and radical politics—at their utopian best—have long addressed this issue by highlighting the possibility of other outcomes.[23] The October Revolution of 1917 was a moment of radical uncertainty; but for any historian not directly and outspokenly dedicated to radical historiography, Stalinist crimes tend to be folded back onto the revolutionary moment as its inevitable telos. The same could be said of other periods of revolt, when historical events are proleptically predicated on their eventual outcomes. The historian Allan Greer notes that the genre distinctions between *revolt, rebellion,* and *revolution* in historiography have precisely to do with attaching the founding actions to their "destiny": where revolutions succeed, revolts and rebellions are labeled as such because they *had* to fail. "They were not simply overwhelmed by superior force"—Greer is caricaturing this historiographic impulse—"they were justly chastised by the god of History."[24] Kristin Ross shows that the Paris Commune is only acknowledged as an event at all by radical historians, from Marx and Engels to the Situationists. But even they tend to temper their readings with paternalistic tips on failed strategy: *if only* the Communards had taken the Bank of France rather than playing at "symbolic games" like tearing down the Vendome Column, these writers implore, the Commune might have held![25] Historians like Ross and Greer build on the model of E. P. Thompson, who began his history of the English working class by insisting, against all prior writing, that the men and women of that class were present at and active in the birth of their own movement, and were not just following, as if automatons, broader cultural and political dictates. For Thompson, the way that individual members of the working class were written out of the history of their own appearance is one symptom of a broader historiographic tone that he calls "the enormous condescension of posterity," the narrative mode of treating historical agents as ignorant dupes merely carried along by the inevitable and teleological flow of time.[26]

How can we link such moments of revolt with minimalist historiography? The student revolts of May '68 in France (and around the world) were roughly contemporaneous with the beginnings of minimalism and provide relevant historical and conceptual reference. Historians of the May revolts have often been its most repentant partisans, those eager to apologize for their youthful ideals. Kristin Ross describes a "police order of history" that chronicles the memory of May as its repentant partisan-historians insist that a "generational we" announced affiliation with the "trajectory of a once lived drama that has become destiny." The narrative line for these repentant figures, in television interviews commemorating May, was always "We didn't know then what we know now." Ross draws on a simple point about the fictional and narratological dimension of historical writing when she reminds us that such a perspective can be inverted to insist, without logical contradiction, that "maybe 'we' did know then what 'we've' forgotten now."[27] These partisan-critics add a new dimension to the critique of revolt, as the issue of whether or not students led the revolts (chronologically, yes) was brought into conflict with the Marxist-Leninist orthodoxy that workers *must* be the spark of revolution. A convicted belief in the Leninist emplotment—the future-myth of communism claimed as a science—led writers like Louis Althusser to label the students "infantile" in their misguided, egocentric, and bourgeois faith in their own efficacy.[28] Critics at the time could narrate the revolts among white, middle-class students and artists as fitting within the broader historiographical archetype of a mature narrator looking back on turbulent youth from a position of comfortable maturity.[29] Once again, the dominant narrative emplotment—how a link is forged between character, action, and necessity—suggests that May cannot enter proper history until it has been renounced. Instead of a present event of (effective) negation and critique, it is made into a "lesson of history." A well-framed historiographic question entirely breaks this hegemonic narrative for Ross. How can one measure or prove the inevitability of movement from ignorance/youth to knowledge/maturity? Is it not possible that the younger selves had a receptivity to the world, to knowledge, empathy, and action that has been lost or hardened?

Jacques and Danielle Rancière, in the moments after May, addressed a parallel political question: by what mechanisms does it pass that the same figures who were most willing to become leaders of revolt are also often subsequently the ones eager to be apologetic spokesmen and leaders in politics, business, and media?[30] Is the goal of history really to stage pedagogic engagement of the (ignorant) past from the position of the (knowing) present? The Rancières were members of Les Révoltes Logiques, a collective of radical historians working in Paris in the 1970s on traditions of revolt who insisted that the purpose of history was to "recognize the moment of a choice, of the unforeseeable, to draw from history neither lessons nor, exactly, explanations, but *the principle of a vigilance toward what there is that is singular in each call to order and in each confrontation.*"[31] In setting up a framework of radical, archival historiography, they needed to break with the stultifying notion that history, via historians, should be about a paternal logic of lessons learned; it instead had to be understood as a practice of narrative *vigilance* toward both concrete moments of confrontation and the tenor of the subsequent calls to order. In their various archival investigations, collective members found that both the confrontation and the call to order were often framed through homonymic appropriations of the same language. Under such a realization, excavating past instances of even "unsuccessful" revolt meant providing precedents and traditions to contemporary radicalism where before they had only paternalistic lessons on the inevitability of failure.

Minimalism was not a collective revolt. But early minimalism marked such a confrontation because of its turn to authorial collaboration in relation to normative art music authorial practice. Collaboration and dispute are placed in a causal relationship through which music historians have been able to argue for (or, more often, imply) the inevitability of failure of collaboration as *registered in the disputes* rather than investigating the material, historical ramifications of the minimalists' break with conventional authorship in their early collaborative exchange. Building from the Révoltes Logiques model—which can very unfairly be caricatured as inverting the polarity such that youthful enthusiasm and rebellion are sources of knowledge, after which settles in an aged, hardened impermeability concerned only for posterity and power—I want to insist that early minimalism, which produced all of the canonic works of minimalism, has much to tell us about how authorship is policed in music historiography. The various breaks between these early minimalist collaborators have had many ramifications, all rounded off by historians pointing to their inevitable arrival in dispute; but I contend that postwar music histories are hindered by reframing the break with normative authorship politics as its exact opposite, the reconstitution of genius, singular, star composers by centering popular figures like Steve Reich and Philip Glass.

The minimalists were not alone in this historical moment; if this were a history of effective 1960s challenges to authorship in music, I would be remiss not to highlight collaborative challenges to conventional authorship among rock musicians, free jazz performers, and the self-organizing and liberation politics of soul, funk, and R & B. I do not intend to suggest here that early minimalism is exceptional or alone in reframing authorial politics during this period; if anything, it provides a relatively low-stakes context within which we can nevertheless watch radicalism defanged. Early minimalism built upon organizational developments in the band-concept of figures like Ornette Coleman and John Coltrane as much as it did upon the compositional model of John Cage. In this sense, early minimalism is not exceptional but instructive. My goal here is to track the close interplay between authorial radicalism (confrontation) and its effective confiscation in narrative history (call to order) as highlighted in a musical style that has become, in the context of white, Euro-American metanarratives of twentieth-century composition, an allegory of the utopianisms and inevitable recantations of the 1960s counterculture. As I will show in Chapter 1, which focuses on Reich's 1968 essay (or is it a manifesto?) "Music as a Gradual Process," too many music historians take too much pleasure in casting minimalism as doomed to fail. The list of figures calling Reich to order and insisting that he repent for his earlier radicalism, ignorance, or naivete includes not only historians but Reich himself. Early minimalism benefits from the same historiographic attention as put forward by radical historians like Ross and Rancière in that it attempts to extract, from those events that induce the most frothing about political irrelevance from historians (the key concern in Chapter 1), a counterhistory or set of precedents for contemporary thought and action in music. As Ross wrote of the "symbolic game" of tearing down the Vendome Column during the Paris Commune, "the strength of the gesture as antihierarchical act can be gauged by the hysteria registered" among contemporary writers.[32]

We should return to the question: *Why authorial disputes?* Let's answer again as such: because they are a recurring fact of musical minimalism that have been written off as an inevitable destiny, the repentant correction, or the sign of youthful ignorance that would imagine authorial collaboration as a possibility in art music. Even more, the inevitability of this destiny has meant that it barely needs commentary as we all nod along in recognition of one of the master teleologies of twentieth-century political thought: radicalism recanted. In the case of minimalism, as I will show, this narrative emplotment folds in conservative assumptions about the destiny of revolt drawn from the most classist, bourgeois elements of art music's historical apparatus, dedicated as it is to the concert hall tradition and literate art music broadly, but also more specifically to liberal individuality and its metaphysical foundation in the logically questionable and ethically suspicious property claims that began with Rousseau's "This is mine" in his *Discourse on the Origin of Inequality* (1755). Musicology's narrative frames and confiscatory practices are oriented toward saving sole authorship's (white) property-function in music history and its attendant claims to genius, originality, delegation, and hierarchy. It is because collaboration and interpersonal dispute are treated as irrelevant to the history of early minimalism that it is drawn into the generic and institutional affiliations of "art music," and thus nearer to comparisons with a Cagean history than one marked by Coltrane's or Coleman's influence. Another answer to "Why authorial disputes?" is, in brief: because we think we know all too well why there were authorial disputes.

My metanarrative concerns grow out of what Rancière calls the poetics of knowledge or, more plainly, a radical politics of historiography. (Rancière, if it isn't already clear, will be another key protagonist in this book.) In brief, when we refuse the teleological assumption of dispute as inevitable, authorial disputes can then hold us in a space of indistinction. Our critical and disciplinary tools are guided by the imperative to mark, enclose, and classify indistinctions, thus rendering distinct relata. I want to avoid at all costs the liberal, consensus-oriented conception of dispute that can only imagine dispute as a rocky patch on the way to amenable resolution for all parties. As Davide Panagia tells us, antagonism is not always dialectic.[33] I am not concerned with settling the disputes that I investigate. My model of dispute holds us in a space of historiographical dissonance, the sustenance of which requires vigilant narrative attention. My method is not only indistinct and impure, but *indistinguishing* and *impurifying*.[34] I think here of the clashing, resonant beating of small intervals held over long durations, and the *more-than* of resonance and buzzing difference tones. I think of La Monte Young's *Drift Studies* for how their droning pitches create distinct, resonant pockets in the corner of my living room when played on my stereo or how, when humming along while I listen through headphones, my voice entirely changes sonic relationships audible between the recording and my ears. Or I think of Tony Conrad's (always insufficient) practice of maintaining precise manual dexterity while bowing double stops on his violin, drawing our attention to the unwavering sustenance of highly amplified difference tones. I similarly hear those moments of slippage in a tape phase process when, prior to arriving at new, recognizable rhythmic orientations, the listener is held in a suspended slippage of echoes and doublings. I hear *Pendulum Music* as a process in which distinct microphone-swooping *whoomps* indistinguish themselves by becoming humming-feedback. None of the processes audible in this music includes distinct parts that can be made to stand metaphorically in for the whole. What is *minimal* in early minimalism, I insist, is not the list of musical materials animated, but the space of indistinction between them, and the way they feed-back and feed-forward off each other, producing psychoacoustic effects and secondary resonances that are more the site of attention than the individual musical materials that animate them.

The disputes in question bristle with such (minimal) tensions, creating powerful, dissonating forces of indistinction; indeed, these disputes are inherently impurifying: *dispute* is the disruption of the Latin *putare*, which has to do with the act of pruning a tree, but also more abstractly with purity and purification. (From *putare* we similarly get computation and counting; we need to trim away and distinguish elements to count them as singular purities.) Authorial disputes provide historiographic opportunities to stage the inherent impurities of authorship. Music history needs this. Perhaps more, *art music historiography* needs this, as authorship is an ideal that is too often taken for granted as a pure and uncontentious precondition to composition and performance. Singular, white, male, untroubled authorship is the fantasy that coheres art music. Musicology has a relatively weak critical discourse on authorship precisely because it is imagined as necessarily preceding its actions; accordingly, any effort to critique, break with, or denounce authorship's conventions is read as evidence of hypocrisy or ignorance on the part of that would-be antiauthor. Throughout the coming pages, it is left unspoken—in the way that things perpetually in mind so often are—that early minimalism is probably not an art music at all, but that its authors have consistently benefited from their training in elite art music institutions, and its dissemination (at least in the last two decades) as a moment in the history of "literate," white, Euro-American art musics. This present order of things is in direct conflict with its contemporaneous novelty, the fact that it was not initially a score-based practice.[35] Writing minimalism into the teleological history of art music *-isms* does extensive discursive work to sustain authorship, as it internalizes minimalism as an unsuccessful challenge to authority from *inside* authorship rather than imagining it as an effective, even if momentary, breach.

In many ways, this book traces the historiographic mechanisms by which the collaborative humming noise of early minimalism had its rough edges pruned away to reveal what could comfortably and retroactively be considered an art music called minimalism—this despite the fact that all of the novel contributions that made early minimalism striking in its time were framed in revolt against art music's institutional, authorial, and pedagogic norms. We can thus track its challenges to those norms—and the music-historical anxieties these raise—by how and where it has been pruned. Like all forms of white radicalism, early minimalism relies on the stability of its own referents even as it aspires to dismantle them; it appeals to a form of privilege that its protagonists knew would not fail them no matter how direct their attacks on its edifice. We need functional accounts of such forms of privileged revolt not because they provide models for political action, but because they might represent vigilant practices of carrying forward even minor successes as prehistories to contemporary efforts to work around authorship. Early minimalism grows out of a moment in which authorship was put in question; the history of minimalism, not only as reported by historians and critics but also by its major composers, has been a story of confiscating and dismissing the terms of the question as irrelevant, ignorant, naive. Contemporary projects are thereby dispossessed of their potential grounds, precedents, and reference points. How do we recognize even minor successes and build them into stories of sustained revolt against unequal institutional structures when our critical apparatus is designed always to call such efforts impossible, their agents hypocrites?

Dissensus stages polemical conflicts over homonyms. As coined by Rancière, dissensus places two ways of human being-together in the same humming, indeterminate space.[36] One is a well-ordered, harmonious relationship that insists on the proper allocation of parts and wholes, a clearly articulated connection between words and things, a scientific precision in the determination of causes and effects, a flawless counting of roles and places. Rancière calls this ordering—this "way things are"—*the police*. The second mode of being together assumes the equality of all things and proposes to trouble the conception of "harmony" that rationalizes the police allocations and demarcations. Rancière calls this *politics*, the force and logic of equality that enters a police situation and dissonates its relationship of part to part, cause to effect, and sense to sense. Where a police logic runs on order, equivalence, and seamless exchange, politics insists on disorder, equality, and redistributions. Politics is not only impure but *impurifying*; not only indistinct, but *indistinguishing*. (Early) minimalism, I argue, *dissonates authorship*.

These two modes of being together, placed under the same homonym, are central to Rancière's egalitarian conception of politics and historiography. We can think here of how *police* and *politics* are in fact two distributions or accounts of the *polis* as the political community. The goal for Rancière is to place different usages of the same term—as parallel (mis)understandings—on the same stage as a means of recognizing the fundamental, egalitarian footing provided by language in its various uses, appropriations, and poetic reconstitutions.[37] That is, language is an infinite resource, and one of the most effective and long-standing practices of revolt is to recast the language of the police as a means of redistributing its mechanisms of circulation.

In centering authorial disputes, I suggest that (early) minimalism impurifies authorship. Disputes over authorship are not only about who wrote what, but also about the (im)possibility of authorship, modes of claiming owner-ship over music (most often on magnetic tape), and the historiographic poet-ics that authors mobilize when the key referents—sounds, concepts, events, performances, conversations—are made indistinct through proximate, dif-ferential claims on their meaning, their relevance, or even their existence. Authorial disputes are inherently dissensual in that every term and figure becomes a buzzing, blurred disagreement over its proper share and allocation. This is how the disputes dissonate authorship. Each of the key conceptual and evidentiary determinants of a claim to authorship is split, made hom-onymic, and becomes a stage for the performance of authority now severed from its self-evident claim to historical necessity. I think here similarly of Dylan Robinson's writing on an "apposite" methodology, one premised on a dramaturgical form of writing that prioritizes relationality, proximity, and distance, even intimacy between writing, writer, and method.[38] We can step away from disputes as sites of arbitration via appeals to reified concepts, and instead watch the concepts being remade in conflicting narrative accounts drawing on the same homonymic terminology.

In this sense, I draw upon what Rancière calls the method of the scene. "The scene is not the illustration of an idea. It is a little optical machine that shows us thought busy weaving together perception, affects, names and ideas, constituting the sensible community that these links create, and the intellec-tual community [not just artists, but critics, writers, audiences] that makes such weaving thinkable."[39] The scene requires recognition of an egalitarian homo-geneity, not for the sake of maintaining it but for the sake of measuring the minimal distinctions between adjacent threads in the weave. I feel that these dyadic, homonymic, dissonant pairs—whether of authors or of homonyms—allow such reading. The scene allows us to recognize the apposite metaphor of dramaturgy, the way that characters, ideas, figures, names, and actions stand alongside one another in a contained space, even in instances when the his-torian or critic cannot "accurately" or "precisely" account for any reason for their apposition and pairing. The question becomes, How did the big-name minimalists, as historians of their own work, play themselves off against their collaborators to simultaneously distinguish their own careers and, at the same time, reassert the impossibility that work could be done otherwise? How do critics, audiences, and performers work together to simultaneously define and knit a univocal style and a critical context by holding together dissimilars and, quite often, holding at a distance the wrong similarities? How do I enter this weave without presupposing the capacity to engage at a different scale, external to and beyond their work?

The sole axiom of Rancière's thought is that all people are of equal intelligence—he writes that the work of thought is not about proving that substantive claim, but rather accepting it as an ethical orientation to the world and "seeing what can be done under that supposition."[40] He enacts this assumption of equality on all registers of his work, and I aspire to maintain that practice. For example, despite my decidedly "theoretical" leanings, I do not use the term "theory" in my reading of Rancière—or really of any author. That term has taken on a particular cast in academia, one that Rancière refuses and that I think is too easily put in its (policed) place in music scholarship.[41] "Theory" tends to imply a pure, abstract world located somewhere (or nowhere— perhaps that's the point) external to the internal, messy world of the disciplinary "object" of study. For this reason, I consider "theory" less an objective definition of a kind of writing or thinking than a formal or functional use to which particular texts are put. Theory, as I understand it, is thought extracted from its context, or perhaps thought given credit as universally applicable and transferable. It is to avoid such decontextualization that throughout the book I rehearse more of other authors' arguments than is perhaps strictly necessary. I am interested in working through how writers arrive at "theoretical" concepts, how they emerge from an object of study such as the Paris Commune, or workers' history, or disciplinary critique, or pedagogy, and not in extracting decontextualized key terms as resources toward my needs. In short, I am not interested in "applying" theories extracted from their practical context to bring them to bear on (early) minimalism; I want instead to call upon theoretical work that takes seriously the egalitarian (perhaps even utopian) narration of past events and place them in buzzing proximity to similar narratives from minimalism. It is an apposite staging of indistinguishing relationships.

Rancière's philosophy of intellectual egalitarianism, like a radical historiography, begins from rejecting binaries like theory/object, knowledge/ignorance, even cause/effect toward instead recognizing how disciplines construct such relations—for example, the narrative production of such intangibles as purity and impurity, or maybe how we render the line that divides im/purity. Under the name *poetics of knowledge*—or later and more popularly, as the "distribution of the sensible"—Rancière is keenly attentive to how (music) history relies on the tools of literature, poetry, and narrative to render historiography as a science.[42] Doing justice to the novelty of Rancière's thought as it might benefit music history requires thinking through and escaping the normative "uses" and "lenses" of theory as much as it requires outlining his concepts. His work is about how events of revolt, even on the smallest scale, are cast as ignorant through discourses of youth matured, ignorance remedied, revolt quelled, and indistinction distinguished. Such distinctions "do not designate any real difference; all they do is repeat the presupposition according to which, from a specific moment onwards, [a historical object] is no longer what it was, and, in no longer being what it was, has finally become what it is in itself, in clear-cut contrast to what it is not."[43] Such distinctions make things immobile, rather than allowing them to circulate.[44]

The historiographic articulations of "binaries of inequality" are evident in how minimalism has entered music histories. We see on the one hand minimalism treated as simply a reduction of materials (consider La Monte Young's definition of minimalism as music "composed with a minimum of means") and, on the other, its expansion into a historiographical metaphor, as when the amplified drones of the Theatre of Eternal Music are treated as a metaphysical, primordial essence and origin of minimalism—the imposition of a terra nullius from which minimalism could rebuild on empty terrain.[45] Consider comments made by Gunther Schuller in 1991:

> By definition minimalism is minimal. When we have all this maximal music that we've achieved over 700 years of development, to suddenly throw all of that out and reduce it to this primitive music is really sad. Of course that wouldn't have been a success, except that the *New York Times* and a few other would be tastemakers in the United States got behind that movement. They committed themselves, they invested in it and they sold it to a dumb, musically illiterate public.[46]

Writing on minimalism runs on the assumption, more and less distinctly articulated, that minimalism marks a kind of purification, a distillation, or a rendering down to the fewest possible elements. In holding minimalism in a binarized relationship to a maximalism (whether an imagined one or the historical antecedent of serialism), minimalism is made representative of ignorance or stupidity, austerity or absurdity. The critic Mick Farren noted as such in 1977. "One of the crosses the minimalist has to bear is that the lumpen public always tends to assume that his constant efforts to reduce everything to its basic components is a symptom of stupidity and lack of talent."[47] We should consider, then, how minimalism productively asks us to probe the knowledge/ignorance binary in relation not only to art music's definitional concern with il/literacy, but also to the historiographical narrative of 1960s revolt as (mere) generational malaise or youthful immaturity.

From Rancièrian historiography I develop a narrative mechanism for staging impurifications and indistinctions. Minimalism here is then not the reduction to a concentrated purity, or a regression to an earlier form, but a discourse and practice of impurifying. These impurifications result when we minimize distances between constellations of terms, positions, identities, and concepts formerly considered distantly related. As Ashon Crawley writes of Reich's *Music for 18 Musicians*, listening to minimalism makes him feel "as if I slipped into a crack the size of a neutrino . . . there is never a moment when it is decided that some *now* is the moment to increase . . . it just happens, it just builds, it constructs itself."[48] Minimalism is not an absolute list or collection that is minimized to its fewest possible elements, but rather a relational distance that is reduced to near proximity. Binaries founded on distances are reduced—*minimized*—to clashing, humming, buzzing, proximities, or what Davide Panagia, in his presentation of what he calls Rancière's sentimental style, calls "resonant adjacencies."[49] These come in many forms. Thinking only in terms of the identity "composer," they find themselves in much nearer proximity to the performances, audiences, and listeners in opposition to whom the role composer is too often defined. This is precisely how Philip Glass defined minimalism decades later: "We didn't think of ourselves as minimalists. We thought of ourselves as living in a world of music where composers and performers were one, and where the audience were right in front of us."[50] For Glass, minimalism was defined less by particular harmonic, formal, or rhythmic devices—by compositional style—than by a bodily posture, spatial location, and method of working.[51] This is common to most composers' definitions of the style. They were performing again, and they existed within proximate relation to an audience that was also their community of collaborators and friends, whether visual artists, musicians, or theater performers.[52] We can similarly think of how minimalism reduced the distance between rehearsal and performance, or between composing and recording, how the space of rehearsal—the lofts of Young and Zazeela or Glass, as many other artists operating "downtown"—became a space of performance, a studio space of work and labor into which the audience is invited.

Historiographically, in this book, we can consider the minimized distance between minimalism as a nihilistic and "primitive" reduction (as for Schuller) or as a constructive politics of authorship. Most often, minimalism was more at home recorded onto magnetic tape than manuscript paper; and these magnetic tapes were alternately commercial albums, archival documents, mnemonics for later transcription, rehearsal aides, the media of composition itself, or some combination of all of the above (and more). As I have argued elsewhere, while individual performer parts were often an aspect of early minimalist composition, it rarely originates in or takes its identity from fully scored compositional practices.[53] Later, I'll turn to the close proximity of "punk" and "minimalism" in a moment when both were often indiscriminately labeled "minimal." Indeed, I've already (mis)led the reader through such minimal/punk indistinctions; above, when Mick Farren wrote of a "lumpen public" convinced that minimalism was a symbol of musical ignorance, he wasn't talking about Reich or Glass, but rather the punk band the Ramones. Not only is minimalism a term of indistinction in that moment, but it was also used to locate lines of distribution across binaries of knowledge and ignorance, skill and amateurism, "punk" and "art music."[54] Such proximities and redistributions regularly resulted in dispute, historiographic intrigue, and practices of narrative confiscation. These proximities are not problems to be solved, but realities to be staged while resisting the imperative to reduce, clarify, or distinguish.

My claim is not that these adjacent terms become interchangeable. It is that minimalism became what it is through refusals of such clear disciplinary and institutional demarcations of roles. "Division between is imperceptible, but it happens," Crawley writes of Reich's phasing processes.[55] For Rancière and Kristin Ross, this was one of the novelties of May '68: a rigorous, dedicated practice of dislocation that refused discourses of the proper place of a particular activity—students were at the factories, philosophers were in the streets, workers were in the Sorbonne.[56] It's not that it becomes impossible to tell a student from a worker—though maybe at times it was. Rather, it became impossible to rely on a "proper" relation between (physical) place and (social) place. The former harmony through which a social position and a social destination were linked and could be assumed was dissonated. Being at the factory gates no longer guaranteed one was a worker, and one could no longer take for granted the relationship between place and knowledge that had long held sway. We take this prior order of things—the potential to presuppose the equivalency between place and place, sense and sense— for granted too often, and in ways that lead us to undervalue the severity of this change. Minimalism offers a productive way into thinking through this methodological problem in music histories.

Take the distinction between recording (to paper) and recording (to magnetic tape) as it plays out in how early minimalism abandoned the score as primary medium. Many musicians had of course worked without or around the score already, but I consider it central here that the best-known minimalists were white, male, Euro-American artists trained within the elite institutions of Western art ("literate") music pedagogy. As such, their move to tape was a *refusal* of notation and the score, growing very much out of the same antiauthority and anticonvention impulse that motivated the era's student strikes. It is not so much that we should praise the minimalist composers for this move in itself—the claim is clearly not that they discovered that music could be made without the aid of notation—but that, historically, the *refusal*, from within a decided context, is relevant to how that context was changed. This distinguishes the minimalists both from free jazz artists like Ornette Coleman (who had his own complex position to the writing/recording relationship) or John Cage (who certainly decentered the score, but nevertheless relied on it as a central aspect of his composerly practice). Alexander G. Weheliye writes that "because alphabetic script did not represent the primary mode of cultural transmission, the phonograph [in the late nineteenth century] did not cause the same sorts of anxieties about the legibility of music as it did in mainstream American culture."[57] For Weheliye, Black popular music plays precisely on this gap or groove—the homonymic groove between recording and recording—while white, Euro-American, institutional, and literate musics have been caught up in its "anxieties." Perhaps in parallel, music historiography has prioritized turning the fact of refusal into a necessary or inevitable negation, one stage in a broader dialectical dramaturgy in which abstract categories are made to survive—are even enriched—through momentary challenges.

Minimalist artists across composition and punk, sculpture and painting, theater and dance performed the breakdown of hierarchical arrangements through proximate dislocations of roles. These artists did not make these terms equivalent; they minimized gaps between binarized musical and political categories so as to produce humming, proximate relations of indistinction. All the better to then play on these buzzing proximities! Even so simple a relation as composer (or indeed composer-performer) and audience could no longer be taken for granted in the context of downtown avant-gardes of the 1960s; each becomes a contingent rather than an absolute role when most people in the audience will likely be performing down the street the next night. The musician Jill Kroesen expressed well how the minimal/punk moment came to New York in the late 1970s when she told me that she presented her "systems portraits"—staged, music-theatrical performances that were narrative, but with all characters as representatives of power dynamics and structural relationships rather than internal emotional states—as music rather than theater because, in that moment, "Music could be anything—it didn't have to be music."[58] I think in music scholarship we have too often undervalued the incredible role music played in this moment, perhaps in part because of our attachment to the performative disciplinary autocritique of insisting that music (and music history) follows other arts and disciplines rather than ever leading or being the model. Music is very, very often in the driver's seat, but it is part of our critical practice to assume that it reflects, sings, performs, or models preexisting social relations rather than fomenting them.

Historians of New York experimentalism are nevertheless perfectly aware of these blurrings. Indeed, indistinctions are quite often the focus of scholarship that sets out to reveal the imbrications of distinct styles, genres, and media. The problem is one of writing: most often such moments of intense crossing and indistinction are written as all manner of "postmodern" blending and hybridity. We should distinguish the work of the discourse of "postmodern" *blending* as opposed to the dissensual *blurring* I have highlighted. Where blending suggests distinct territories as combined in exceptional works or moments, *blurring* implies the preexistent imbrications and proximities of the realms that scholarship too often deputizes itself to distinguish. The postmodern discourse of blending stages a dramaturgical trajectory of distinct genres followed by exceptional blending that is taken as the particular domain of "the postmodern." A postmodern reading of Branca's work or Chatham's, for example, insists upon the "punk" elements of their work as opposed to the "minimal" elements as a means of marking the exceptionality of their authorial style(s).[59] (See Chapter 4.) The result is a writing-back-into-place of experiments in dislocation, to then mark exceptional subsequent instances of artists blending distinct territories. Such writing, I contend, is less about narrating the relevance or import of a particular event than about upholding the priority of historical work via the imperative to contextualize into a flat, gray mush. Historians claim their own position through carving scenes apart into their "proper" stylistic, generic, and class affiliations so as to then argue for the novelty of postmodern blendings. In this process, artists are made exceptional for their style, and historians are venerated for their critical or analytic insight, but each is rendered such against the backdrop of scenes, communities, neighborhoods, styles, and "supporting actors" who are cast in secondary roles. Just as genres and styles are kept in their place, so such writing puts the composer, the audience, the writer, or the performer right back where they supposedly belong. This reliance on blending stages the same skepticism as that toward authorial performance of antiauthorship in that scholars are unconvinced by any critique that is immanent to its own system, preferring instead to create transcendent escapes from norms that place a figure, a genre, a "theory" *outside* that normative domain. The work of critique then becomes to stage that escape. This practice of removal (or distancing, or distinction), I am arguing, undermines the specificity of the immanent hinge that this period of artistic and political radicalism played upon.

Throughout *The Names of Minimalism*, I play on homonymies as resonant adjacencies, conflicts over near repetitions, always holding close a Rancièrian insistence that most words can be heard in (at least!) two ways: one mode that rigidly defines its circulation and appropriate usage, and another that recognizes egalitarian distributions prioritizing access. History—as a discipline or a literature, rather than a collection of notable firsts—exists because of such homonymic collision, "because no primeval legislator put words in harmony with things."[60] Authorship is not only the necessary ground of any creative action in music, a musicological equivalent to liberal subjecthood; it is also the police distribution of parts and responsibilities in relation to which one might stage a musical (anti)authorship. Minimalism is perhaps the most multifarious homonym here, and I deal at length with its blurring trajectories in Chapter 4 during the period of its indistinct usage. But this is precisely the terrain of these *names* of minimalism: the history of minimalism, perhaps like all histories, is about names as indistinct identifiers that link authorship, historiographies, disputes, signatures, and collectivities. The root of the disputes of (early) minimalism can be as simple as where authors should put their name on a spool of magnetic tape, or as complex as whether "for Steve Reich," as famously written on the top of Philip Glass's score for *Two Pages* (see Chapter 3) was a titular dedication or simply the designation of performance forces. The historiographic staging of (early) minimalism, I want to insist, is more accurately about how one of these can possibly claim to be simpler or more complex than the other.

Against policed histories, I insist that authors do not preexist their work; they are subjectivized in it. Minimalism emerges from relational subjectivities in authorship—they became minimalists, and minimalism became minimalism, while they were hanging out together, and they were hanging out together because they considered the normative model of solitary composition to paper an unsatisfactory way to create work and a life. Early minimalism's disputes are more a result of insufficient disciplinary historiographies than any particular historical or political destiny. Authorship was already in question (we can point here equally to Cage and Coleman, among others, including La Monte Young in a generous moment, or Yoko Ono in Brigid Cohen's recent reading)[61] and the prominent minimalists sought new means to create work within a space where they knew their authorship would not be taken for granted. The question became: now what? Their activities were brought into a historical discourse ill prepared to make sense of it. And music historiography, I contend, has never sufficiently caught up, preferring instead to round off early minimalism's edges and jam it into yet another formalist "-ism"—albeit a deficient, ignorant, and naive-ism whose authors failed to recognize the necessity of their historical roles and conditions. My interest here, again, is not in repairing that discourse so that this work fits, but rather registering how to keep writing music histories beyond the recognition of the failures of a normative, nineteenth-century model that we all know is badly outdated but to which we remain tethered, at least in part because we dismiss as ideologically blinkered any artist who claims to have made a break with it.

I stand by the mode of authorship that recognizes authorship not as a precondition to producing work, or an inviolable reality that precedes any action. Rather, authorship is a material element of the work right alongside arranging notes, producing sounds, or booking gigs. Authorship is something performed in the course of the work; it is one name for the totality of what one *does* when authoring, rather than an inviolable status that precedes work. This totality is immanent to the structure rather than something that exceeds and represents it; as I will argue in the conclusion to this book, the model structure here is not the metaphorics of representation but *metonymy*—yet another figure and practice of naming. Authorship can stand in buzzing apposition to conventional power dynamics and property claims that are presumed to precede it. The simple fact is that some composers can write music that requires them to form bands as a means of providing their performers health insurance, while others can write music that requires an abusive power dynamic premised on devotion to the composer-as-guru. A modality of authorship is chosen just as much as the pitches and rhythms associated with it. Authorship is produced dialogically in conversations with interviewers, colleagues, audiences, partners, and institutions. Authors can aim their entire working career at destroying the model of authorship within which they were trained, or at undermining the institutional supports through which their career exists. I would not call these authors liars or hypocrites, but rather note that they are living within a system while trying to stage its faults—because who else can?

Who else can challenge authorship if not authors? Who do we name as disputants? What do we name a genre, and which names fall under it? In referencing the *names* of minimalism I want to think about not only the dissensual poetics of genre names, but also the important fact that *names* are the operative poetic determinants through which authorship and historiography are in dialogue. (Early) minimalism names the fact that we can only find an "aesthetic, style, or technique" called minimalism between its early radicalism and its later recantations.[62] Early minimalism took part, and in part succeeded, at rupturing the hegemonic place of art music authorship in its relation to white, masculine authority. In attempting to verify its arguments, I am insisting that we wind up somewhere else other than back in a revivified art music authorship. The authorial disputes captured under the name (early) minimalism—between the early practice and its dismissal as *early*—the now very long answer might run, are about an absent cause, repeatedly absented, as a means of ignoring a problem we don't want to deal with.

One

Policing Process

Music as a Gradual Process and Pendulum Music

───────

Two documents that Steve Reich wrote in the summer of 1968 have become focal points in staging what minimalism is. Whether in music history survey teaching or anthologized collections, the essay (or manifesto) "Music as a Gradual Process" and the text piece *Pendulum Music* can reliably be excerpted to represent minimalism both conceptually—in their articulation of a "sounding music and a compositional process that are one and the same thing"— and chronologically as products of late 1960s anti-institutionalism.[1] In their recurring and resonant adjacency, the two documents are often considered as mapping a theory/praxis, or perhaps argument/proof pairing. I want to argue that this pair, what I will call Reich's "1968 process documents," mark an event of politics in the Rancièrian sense. These documents manifest a dissensus in how they insist that the former space of perfect circulation of preconstituted parts and parties can become the space for the appearance of a new subject: the audience or listeners as on equal footing with the composer. The impurifying or dissonating tension in play here is between the (positive) reading of the political contribution of the process documents I want to argue for, and the ideas that are (negatively) ascribed to it under their police inscription within music histories. As is necessarily the case in any political confrontation, Reich staged this dissensus in relation to the concrete police situation at hand. That is, his argument was not an infinite, universal claim on the possibility of egalitarianism or the absolute removal of the composer's privilege; rather, he proposed a music of gradual process (decidedly not "minimalism"!) as a specific argument against the sites of reproduction of composerly privilege concretely present in mid-century art music composition. It is a local claim, and a compelling one that I consider an event, a polemical and promis-

28

ing one, for how it reframes composerly privilege as a factor of reproducing inegalitarian relationships.

In accepting the essay as a productive confrontation of mid-century authorial norms, I stand in stark contrast with musicological readings of the 1968 process documents. Their frothing reception is shockingly consistent, as I will show; within these negative receptions, I contend that we learn less about musical minimalism or Steve Reich's work than we do about musicological anxieties about the value of Reich's dissensual staging of a critique of authorial privilege. The musicological response makes palpable what Kristin Ross, drawing on Rancière, calls the police conception of (music) history: a breathless discursive labor oriented toward insisting upon an unsuccessful disruption, a consensual causality, a universal counting of parts, that ensures that nothing has happened. We encounter this police conception of (music) history at work when we read scholars dismantling the eventfulness of what we might register as events. Following on Rancière, the police concept of history musters evidence toward insisting, in response to a concrete political event, "Move along, there's nothing to see here!"[2] I want to argue that the process documents are the clearest and most prominent theoretical articulation of early minimalism (if not the first—see Chapter 2). The police conception of history is the mechanism by which the austere articulation of early minimalism found in the process documents is rendered "early."

I begin by outlining how "Music as a Gradual Process" reframes the relationship between composer and audience in the late 1960s, in specific rejection of the dominant, public concepts of compositional process at the time, serialism and chance. I then turn to *Pendulum Music* and the homogeneous insistence from music scholars that it represents a "pure" or "natural" demonstration of the ideas in "Music as a Gradual Process." I then show how these scholars use that relationship to insist upon the failure and impossibility of the process documents and, by extension, minimalism's political project. In the final pages, I turn to a close reading of the most extensive analysis of "Music as a Gradual Process," from Richard Taruskin, to show how his writing metaphorically relies upon the simultaneous student movements of the summer of 1968 to frame Reich's promise as *early* in that, breaking with the "proper space" of music-historical confrontation, Reich sought to liberate *people* rather than *sounds*. In all, then, I follow a simple trajectory: (1) from a compositional police distribution of the sensible premised on assumptions about the ignorance of the audience; (2) through a political rupture that insists an egalitarian relationship between composer and audience is possible (and proposes its method of realization); and (3) onto the musicological policing of that claim that reasserts the audience's ignorance by placing the composer and audience on equal footing in their *shared ignorance*.

"Music as a Gradual Process" Is a Contract with the Listener

Despite its frequent reproduction, "Music as a Gradual Process" is rarely subjected to extended reading. Its place in scholarship on minimalism is often as a metric for whether Reich held to his early ideas in his later work; it is a recurring feature of formalist analyses of minimalist compositions (particularly by Reich, but not exclusively) at conferences to hear a presenter formulate an argument along these lines: "In his famous manifesto, Reich insists that a compositional process and the sounding music can be one and the same; through a close reading of X, I will show that, in fact, Y." Such gestures rarely make it into print; nevertheless, in an essay that measures the various distances between post/minimalism(s), Robert Fink returns to Reich's manifesto to account for whether or not Reich, in *Music for 18 Musicians*, held to "minimalism's basic contract with the listener." Fink argues that because of the difficulty of hearing the eleven chords Reich cycles through, as well as some "arbitrary" movement through that cycle, he has in fact broken that contract. "Reich's disarming promise that he was not interested in hidden structures, that 'all cards were on the table,'" Fink suggests, has been broken. Fink's use of "Music as a Gradual Process" as a measure of Reich's fidelity is all the more striking in that he does not name or cite the "contract": "Music as a Gradual Process" holds such discursive weight as a result of its anthologization that even in an edited volume not squarely focused on minimalism, Fink considered it fair to assume readers would recognize the reference.[3]

If "Music as a Gradual Process" is a contract—let's leave aside the uncertainty as to whether it is an essay or a manifesto momentarily—what relationship does it guarantee? Synopses tend to focus on its proposal of a "compositional process and a sounding music that are one and the same," such that there are no "secrets of structure." Within the disciplinarily formalist and positivist orientations of music theory, Reich could not have put forward a juicier provocation than promising, in language redolent of 1960s radicalism, that there are no structural secrets to be found. Too often left out, though, is how this claim emerges from Reich's critique of the epistemological, pedagogic, and aesthetic inegalitarianisms dominant in his teachers' generation. Often chance and serialism are understood as binary opposites in relation to a concept like control. "John Cage has used processes and has certainly accepted their results, but the processes he used were compositional ones that could not be heard when the piece was performed." Much the same, "In serial music, the series itself is seldom audible."[4] Where one exercises rigorous control, the other aspires to abandon explicit subjective taste and composerly input. Reich reframes the entire terrain by holding them in relation not through their modalities of *control*, but to process and, more importantly, to *audibility* of process. Each relies on a precompositional process that leaves no audible remainder in the sounding music: we cannot hear either the twelve-tone matrix or the *I Ching*, to give two prominent examples. Accordingly, Reich introduces a new topography in which, rather than opposites in a binary premised on control, they share space under a rubric marked by *inaudibility of compositional process*.

Inaudible, we must ask, to whom? As I will show, music scholars have rushed to insist that they can, in fact, find and hear (in)audible structural processes going on. But let's not get ahead of ourselves. In redistributing the metric from control to process, Reich is indirectly approaching another relationship: that between the composer and the audience.[5] To Reich, before all else, serialism and chance stage and reproduce inequalities: mid-century composers, those who taught the minimalists, make their audience at once necessarily absent from the scene of composition (they can't speak for themselves) and, in any case, too ignorant to recognize the compositional process if they were present. The key statement of "Music as a Gradual Process" is not the contractual guarantee that there will be no more secrets, but rather the ethical promise, "We all listen to the process together." The fundamental provocation one might draw from the essay, I contend, is not "I bet I can find some structural secrets," but rather, "Who is *we* and what is the dynamic of our interaction?" Where does the audience or the listener sit in a composer's cosmology? What is the place of the listener or the audience in a musical style that gains its identity from precompositional processes to which the listener and audience constitutively have no access? And how would that place be changed by having access—not through program notes or didactic instruction, but through the sounding process?

At the risk of presenting a caricature of the situation, Milton Babbitt's "The Composer as Specialist" from a decade earlier is the best-known (and most extreme) articulation of the perspective on audiences or listeners from the generation by which Reich was trained:

> I dare suggest that the composer would do himself and his music an immediate and eventual service by total, resolute, and voluntary withdrawal from this public world [of concert life] to one of private performance and electronic media, with its very real possibility of complete *elimination of the public and social aspects of musical composition.* By so doing, the separation between the domains would be defined beyond

any possibility of confusion of categories, and the composer would be free to pursue a private life of professional achievement, as opposed to a public life of unprofessional compromise and exhibitionism.[6]

For Babbitt, in the context of the Cold War music department, composers are scientists. But unlike physicists, composers are hampered by the need for the approval of their audience, which consists of nonspecialists (unlike the journal-reading public of a physicist).[7] What composers do in their studio (their "lab") is beyond not only the intellectual capacities but the aesthetic concerns of any potential audience. Music that requires public performance is reformulated as exhibitionism, compromise, and a threat to the purity of ideas. The compositional processes are inscrutable and complex, and the resulting music should be judged less on an axis of good/bad or like/dislike, but rather correct/incorrect, or (to recall Althusserian scientism) even science/ideology. In calling upon the disciplinary standards of science, its conditions of veracity, the irrelevance of reader or listener's response, and its institutional support and funding, Babbitt dreams of the "complete elimination" of any interfering public. It is unlikely that Babbitt has ever been accused of such a discursive association, but he outlines an idiomatic Cold War utopianism. This utopianism is not one of optimism against cynicism or egalitarianism against control, but rather simply of a perfect space of zero-sum circulation, autocratic creation, and disinterested, informatic reception (as perhaps by a colleague who will analyze it in a music theory journal to reveal, in the notes on the page, the composer's genius at obfuscating beautiful mathematical structures).[8] It is Rancière's police.

Cage's limited commentary on the audience from a similarly popular text—1961's *Silence*—suggests less disdain than Babbitt's writing, but certainly reveals some similarities in cosmological positioning. The rhythmic structure of ballet is always clear, Cage writes: "Phrases begin and end in such a way that *anyone* in the audience knows when they begin and end, and breathes accordingly."[9] *Anyone*—italicized in Cage's original—denotes the traditional modernist positioning of the audience: the danger of their misunderstanding is baked into the listening experience. "*Anyone* in the audience knows" is shorthand for *even the most ignorant member of the audience knows*. Articulating the clarity of structure first requires audience ignorance as normative background. Elsewhere in *Silence*, we come across formulations of Cage's decisive contribution: reimagining the composer as, first of all, a listener. "What has happened is that I have become a listener and the music has become something to hear."[10] In this becoming-listener, however, Cage's effort is less one of empathy than of displacement: the ideal situation is one in which the composer is both composer *and* listener, thus making other listeners superfluous. Still, Cage is a far more nuanced—and far more influential—thinker than Babbitt. "A composer knows his work as a woodsman knows a patch he has traced and retraced," he writes, potentially setting up a mycological parallel to Babbitt's choice of the physicist, before he diverts: "while a listener is confronted by the same work as one is in the woods by a plant he has never seen before."[11]

In Babbitt and Cage, we have two stagings of the same assumption: the listener is at a disadvantage. Where Babbitt despises his audience for their ignorance, Cage pities them. Mid-century modernist composition is necessarily grounded in the assumption that the composer is more intelligent than the audience. Very much in line with the pedagogy-as-politics challenges of the May revolts, Reich sought to formulate a music that would not reproduce the conditions for such inequalities, and the clearest structural point from which to attack that reproduction was in the gap between sounding music and compositional process: the politics of structural secrecy. Under the critique of structural secrets, Reich articulated what serialism and chance share—they are no longer binary opposites but the same problem united by their orientation toward *inaudibility* and *secrecy*. Reich's task—a concrete one, in relation to a concrete structural critique—is to propose a music premised on audible, public process, "a compositional process and a sounding music that are one and the same thing." Yes, process and product should be equivalent, but the only valid measure of this equivalence—the only way we can understand the *equals* sign in this equation—is through clear *audibility*. In Reich's formulation, the process must be gradual, accumulative, and public, rather than precompositional, obfuscating, and private. The process must be these things to escape the drama of reproducing its own (imagined) listeners as ignoramuses.

In framing "Music as a Gradual Process" as a contract, Fink and others are insistent that minimalism *solve the problem of inequality*. Reich introduces an entirely novel conception, not only for his music but as a gesture in the musical avant-garde: he recognizes the listener's disadvantage as the simultaneously *a product of* and a *necessary condition for* the composer's privilege. Composers' privilege is generated by the hermetic methods of their compositional-process-as-musical style. That is, the "ignorance" of the audience is not an obvious fact, but rather a necessary condition to be constructed in advance of articulating the composer's intellectual superiority. It is the point of these musics. We should highlight here Rancière's conception of equality as not a goal to be reached through removal of inherent inequalities, nor the pure state of things before an impure corruption. It is simply a methodological (and I would add ethical) presupposition. Rancière would argue that the conception of inequality operative in mid-century composerly privilege *cannot be rectified or disproven* because a worldview premised on intellectual inequality will consistently reproduce intellectual inequality. The compositional practices Reich is criticizing produce a music in which their process leaves no trace, and then create a discourse that pinpoints the audience's disadvantage as a danger to this music. To turn to the structural language of pre-1968 Althusserianism, they create an effect defined by the absence of its cause. Rancière has criticized this as not only the central tautology of the Althusserian concept of ideology but also Bourdieuian sociology. Each creates a circle around "the people," "the audience," "the masses," or "the students" from which they cannot escape: "They are excluded because they don't know why they are excluded; and they don't know why they are excluded because they are excluded."[12] This is why Rancière insists that equality is not something to *prove* or to reference back to a fundamental, liberal conception of equality as an inherent possession that once existed and could be again under the right circumstances. Instead, equality is presupposed and constantly verified. A Rancièrian reading, I am suggesting, insists not that Reich's promise of equality was a rebuttal or proof against an inherent state of inequality, nor that a music of gradual process is the means by which to end inequality; rather, Reich's promise insists that music based on gradual process *stages the obvious fact of equality*. "The experience of equality" in May '68, Ross writes, was "neither . . . a goal nor a future agenda but . . . something occurring in the present and verified as such."[13] In hearing the process, we are offered such present space for verification. The gradual process is the proclamation of an event, or at least a space, in which the audience and the composer are equal in the act of listening to the process together.

Reich cedes the most important observation in the essay to his friend, the composer James Tenney, who visited Reich in New Mexico while he was writing up the essay. If the compositional process and the sounding composition are "one and the same," and we know they are identical because the process is plainly audible, Tenney says, "Then the composer isn't privy to anything." Reich placing these words in Tenney's mouth has gained no attention in the critical literature. In registering the shift, Tenney recognized the key aspect of Reich's interest without his having explicitly stated it as such. Like any good editor, Tenney pushed Reich to say the quiet part—the important part, the part too often forgotten—out loud. And by crediting

Tenney with the observation, Reich again presented his interest in opening the conceptual and compositional scenario into his broader community of friends, colleagues, performers, and listeners. I consider this a key question of historiography as dramaturgy: How differently would the argument have been if Reich wrote here, at the climactic moment of his essay, "I am not privy to anything"?

Reich was critical of the normative relationship that held between precompositional methods, sounding inaudibility, and the means by which "secrets of structure" became a perennial object of composers' discourse—even a disdainful weapon to use against their own listeners. Serialist and chance composers were making a system to generate their own privilege, Reich argued, and then chastising the listeners, at whose expense it was formulated, for not keeping pace. They made their listeners "early." In supplement to this state of affairs, Reich promised a new music in which the compositional process and the sounding music are one and the same, thus proposing a new, egalitarian listening community distinct from the privileges, secrets, and hierarchies often still imagined as definitive of "contemporary art music." This is the "theory" of "Music as a Gradual Process." In response to the structural reproduction of composerly privilege, the essay is about how to build a new "we" through critiquing the methods by which "we" are kept apart in specifically that concrete, local context. Reich imagines what we today call minimalist music—what for him was simply a music grounded in audible processes such that listeners were not left out of the process—as the best tool toward achieving it.

Pendulum Music Is an (Im)pure Process

The inclusion of the audience within a composer's theoretical inscription of their own work is, in short, a revelation in mid-century American art music. Reich not only considered what they may like or not like—he did not presume to listen for them—but considered the structural determinants and social relationships imagined as necessarily egalitarian rather than premised on a gap resultant from the audience's fundamental intellectual deficiency. I do not mean to make of Reich's manifesto (contract? essay?) a transcendent moment, but rather to insist upon an event of *politics* in Rancière's sense. Politics is always impure: it cannot set up a "system" or a "science" to follow because it will *always* be in response to the normative modes of thinking, speaking, and acting determined by a particular police sensibility. Politics always takes the form of dissonating a given egalitarian distribution of sensibility toward egalitarian contingency. But key to what makes an event political is the ease with which it can slip, if not properly narrated for its effects, right back into the dominant police order as merely a momentary eruption or a statistical outlier on the path to a historical destiny: "The tendency of a police logic is to refold itself around a political eruption," Chris Stover writes, "refiguring it in its own name and in the terms of a now-new dominant distribution in order to continue to reproduce the ideologically bound configurations that the police logic exists to enact."[14]

And indeed, scholars have been eager to question the possibility of a musical process whose audibility hails all parties as equal intelligences. In contrast to the severed community of Cagean chance—where Cage has supplementary mental access to the sheets of paper or graphs used to develop the piece—or the "complete elimination" of the audience for Babbitt, Reich proposes a music that harmonizes the musical community such that hierarchical divisions between composer, performer, and listener are removed—not eternally, but within the contingent listening environment that the 1968 process documents propose. That it took a sounding "music" that moved beyond what many considered legitimate music is not beyond the point, but perhaps the whole point. That is, *we all listen to the process together* is a political promise, not a compositional aesthetic.[15] He is telling us that the audible, gradual process *does this work*. It has already happened. It is not a program toward achieving that goal, but the construction of the stage on which it is happening. It is a music that proposes recognizing "input" or (cause) as identical to the "output" (or effect), and thus recommends listening as a relational space entered rather than a hermeneutic encryption to be decoded (or not). In Kerry O'Brien's words, the process documents provide "an instruction manual for listeners—how to listen, what to listen for, and what posture of attention to assume."[16]

Reich's promise has thus been a polemical one. Minimalism is policed in musicology—"early minimalism" is made *early*—through several interrelated methods of refusing the eventfulness of his critique. The first camp reveals a broad, gleeful cynicism about the (im)possibility of revolt: Reich made a promise, but it could never have been fulfilled. The second is accusatory: Reich promised a new community, and it failed to materialize. Indeed, with the benefit of hindsight, it may have been a strategic error for Reich to include didactic examples of gradual processes in his essay, as his examples have often provided the opening for scholarly confiscation. A text piece composed around the same time bears a particularly strong resemblance to one of Reich's examples of a gradual process: "pulling back a swing, releasing it, and observing it gradually come to rest." Attaching microphones to the end of the microphone-cable swings and suspending them over amplifiers results in *Pendulum Music*, also composed in the summer of 1968 while Reich was in New Mexico. The essay and the text score have often been held in close comparison, including by Reich: they initially appeared together in the Whitney Museum's *Anti/Illusion* exhibition and program in 1969 and were subsequently published as a pair in *Source* magazine in 1972.[17] Because it models a "pure" example of a gradual process—perhaps a didactic demonstration of his theory rather than a separate piece of music—*Pendulum Music* is often treated as a proof of the essay. The first task in such an argument, of course, is making it the case that *Pendulum Music* offers a "pure" model of anything.

Toward that end, little has been said about *Pendulum Music*—but very often. In the first monograph on minimalism, Wim Mertens set the trend by calling *Pendulum Music* "a clear illustration of Reich's well-known statement: 'Once the process has been set up it inexorably works itself out.'"[18] The trend introduced—the process set up—is staging the piece as a "pure" exemplar of "Music as a Gradual Process," while offering little or no further analytic engagement with the work. The nature of the relationship between the two process documents is treated as self-evident. Two decades letter, Keith Potter used the same passage as Mertens to argue that *Pendulum Music* is "the only work by Reich to adhere unambiguously" to the language of "unmanipulated" or "pure" process "in the overly mechanistic sense in which this is often understood."[19] In his book on minimalism, K. Robert Schwarz calls *Pendulum Music* "atypical of Reich's output" in that it engages a "rigorously structured musical process."[20] Alongside the parallel example of *Violin Phase*, Edward Strickland considers *Pendulum Music* a "pure process piece,"[21] while for Sumanth Gopinath it is, "arguably, the only piece of Reich's that works . . . as a *single* process."[22] In a widely read 1972 interview with Reich, Michael Nyman—still in the heat of the '68 moment—was eager to hold Reich to his political claims, noting that *Pendulum Music* is "the only piece of yours that one can talk of in terms of a *natural* process."[23] More recent journal articles have relied on the same narrative to stage minimalism within the critical discourse of hermeneutic unmasking. Referring to Reich's earlier tape piece *It's Gonna Rain*, Martin Scherzinger notes that Reich's processes are "not as *pure* as [his] hindsight assessment would have us believe," and Ross Cole quotes this passage from Scherzinger to bring it full circle: "The *naturalistic* paradigms of gradual process offered in ["Music as a Gradual Process"] . . . were only ever realized in *Pendulum Music*."[24]

As part of a broader flurry of writing on minimalism in the first years of this century—including Potter's *Four Musical Minimalists*, a brief spate of attention by Susan McClary, and Robert Fink's *Repeating Ourselves*[25]—

Scherzinger's article insists that a more critical ear be given to minimalism's global appropriations, as its borrowings from New York visual arts discourse (the parallel to LeWitt and the *Anti/Illusion* show) had overshadowed the influence of African musics on Reich. "Less a historical description of an artistic ethos than a conceptual apparatus through which history becomes possible," Scherzinger writes, "the myth of minimalism has practically eclipsed empirically-grounded historical accounts that lie outside its logical and conceptual reach."[26] Scherzinger's critiques were pivotal in rethinking score-based and formalist readings of minimalism, but the didactic and edifying tone of critical mastery is pervasive. Kerry O'Brien's concise response to his article reveals a generational shift in scholarly posture when she writes that Scherzinger risks "downplaying the real significance of composers' beliefs and strategies. Such beliefs are a crucial factor, because they catalyze what actually occurs." She continues, "Beliefs existed, too, and people certainly acted on them."[27]

Scherzinger's refusal of such beliefs and convictions results in a critique that—while extensive and compelling—thrives on the masterful squaring of instances in which discursive claims and practical actions do not align in perfect synchronicity. He considers it "striking" that the "uncommon magic" of the phasing process is not at odds with the "immediacy" of minimalism; this leads him to what he labels a paradox of Reich's work: "the co-habitation of structural clarity with inexorable ambiguity." The unmatched rhythmic complexity derived from simple processes in *Drumming*, and *Piano Phase* as "practically a study in patterned illusion," thus become problems for Scherzinger, in that they undercut Reich's goal of clearly audible processes.[28] The paradox that he points out is precisely the founding interest and contribution, the compelling and insistent tension, of Reich's work. And perhaps, by extension, of minimalism: that complexity need not be the result of cryptic processes. Instead it can be built up, accumulatively, perceptually, right in the audience's face—as is particularly the case in *Pendulum Music*'s galleristic and sculptural staging. To turn to a visual metaphor, isn't it specifically the mechanical simplicity of a kaleidoscope that makes the array of images both so complex and so compelling? The process and its gradual accumulation allow the clear perception of incredible "complexity." (We could perhaps call it "interest" to avoid the typical associations of complexity in Western art music discourse.) The simplicity of the process—even if it results in an intricate though unambiguously derived aural depth of interest—offers precisely the level playing field that makes imagining the simultaneous presence of listeners possible, even part of the design, rather than a burden or liability.

By relying on the metaphor of an "illusion"—certainly referencing the 1969 *Anti/Illusion* show—Scherzinger casts Reich simultaneously as like those he criticizes for their complexity via secrecy, and as something of a fraud or prankster. He was not alone in such a suggestion—like Fink above, Scherzinger cannot help himself from flagging a claim that "all cards are on the table" by revealing the staggering array of cards music scholarship can place in a composers' hands to make liars of them.

Describing Reich's 1968 process documents as "pure" or "natural" realizations of Reich's process ideal, on the one hand, and Scherzinger's paradox, on the other, provide two possible opening gambits in the same dramaturgical trajectory of policing minimalism by representing it as a failed political project. For Scherzinger, the (failed) relationship between Reich's simple processes and his complex results produces a paradox—one read not as a source of interest, but as evidence of a conceptual failure. Much the same, the (perfect) relationship between *Pendulum Music* and "Music as a Gradual Process" shows that there *can be* a pure process made audible in composition, but that Reich only produced one of them. In both cases, two halves are made to fit—whether poorly or harmoniously—to do the same work: denying the long-term efficacy of what everyone seems to agree was a political project. That is, minimalism is clearly acknowledged as a political project; the argumentative variability appears in how to prove it is necessarily a *failed* political project. My interest is in the manifold historiographical methods by which it can be transposed into the police conception of history.

Scholarship on minimalism is haunted by these methods of insisting, before the actual argument begins, that the politics of minimalism were failed. There is a consensual agreement within musicology that minimalism—as represented by Reich's essay—articulated a valid critique of the hermetic epistemology and intellectual supremacy of mid-century American art music. But before anything can be said about "minimalism," its authorial project must necessarily be defanged, effaced, confiscated, or otherwise explained away to arrive at the real situation: a necessary return of diatonicism after the complexity of serialism (a historiographic "pendulum swing"), or a "postmodern" use of repetition as desire production.[29] The political promise is considered failed, whether by a too-perfect realization of pure process that could never have been sustained, or by demonstrating a kaleidoscopic complexity that, rather than witnessing its potential, is seen as its antithesis (a "paradox" rather than, more generously, a productive tension). The status of *Pendulum Music* and "Music as a Gradual Process" as historiographical tropes, the reason for their limited and consensual, though recurring, appearance in histories of minimalism, is clear: they are evidence of minimalism's political project and, simultaneously, the measure of its impossibility. The history of minimalism begins from the requirement that Reich's promise of a community of listeners on equal footing with a composer "not privy to anything" be impossible.

The most extensive reading of "Music as a Gradual Process" deserves distinct attention for how it returns us to the relationship between the police conception of history and the production of the early-as-ignorance in defanging the political project of minimalism. In his expansive *Oxford History of Western Music*, Richard Taruskin used the agreed-upon pairing of the 1968 process documents to make a case for the impossibility of Reich's egalitarian promise. Taruskin's argument stands apart in that he chooses a third path for insisting upon minimalism's political failure—Reich's ignorance.[30]

In Chapter 3 I deal at length with how the major minimalist composers articulated their own interrelationship by substituting for their own earlier political radicalism and critique of authority a deeply hierarchical relationship founded on pedagogic priority and supremacy. I build there on Rancière's important book *The Ignorant Schoolmaster*. While I will wait to explore that text in more depth, I should draw attention to one term whose difficulty Kristin Ross highlights in a translator's note: *abrutir*. Ross chooses the word *stultify* to render in English Rancière's concept of how pedagogues teach students, first of all, that they cannot learn without the direction of a teacher. In its place, Rancière aspires to a method of teaching that "reveal[s] an intelligence to itself."[31] We will explore that more later. For now, the simple fact remains: for Rancière and Ross, an inegalitarian political dynamic must be staged relationally by appealing to the pedagogic imperative to stultify— meaning, more literally, to *render a brute*. This stultification was already in play above when I discussed Babbitt and Cage staged "the audience" to render an ignorant backdrop to their claims about listening and comprehension.

Taruskin joins in the inexorable process: *Pendulum Music* is "a limit case to test [Reich's] theory to a logical extreme" and "the conceptual paradigm . . . to which all of Reich's early works for conventional performing forces can be meaningfully related."[32] Once again, *Pendulum Music* is important for its paradigmatic purity, making it a valuable ruler against which to measure later work. Taruskin reads "Music as a Gradual Process" as shouted down from a political platform, and he disdains this in its writing style. He consistently calls it a "manifesto" (as do many other scholars), describes the brief, aphoristic writing style as like "planks in a political platform," and casts Reich as a "sixties agitator." This last description is particularly revealing, as it marks Taruskin's need not only to dismiss Reich's manifesto, but to place his manifesto outside of the domain of *music* proper. Reich, the sixties agitator, fails to join the long tradition of earlier avant-gardes because unlike "Schoenberg and Cage" he did not set out to "liberate sounds" but rather to "liberate people." We find in this element the origin of the chapter's incredulous subtitle: "A Harmonious Avant-Garde?"

This explicit discomfort with Reich's (early) politics aside, Taruskin's argument about the process documents is more nuanced.[33] He calls upon an important analysis of *Piano Phase* by Paul Epstein, who observed that Reich's tape-based process pieces have a second half that reproduces the first half in retrograde.[34] Like the lunar cycle, tape-based, mechanical processes (unlike the unmechanized process of *Pendulum Music*, which moves toward atrophy as it loses its physical momentum) go in and then out of phase, creating a palindrome. This is a necessary ("natural") fact of the mechanical process. Epstein relates these pieces to ternary forms, as if to say, despite outward appearances, the pieces are entirely in keeping with the ineluctable nature of Western art music: module, contrast, return. The police conception's weaponization of context often appears in this form: what you thought was different was really a modification of the same. Against Reich's foundational claim about why gradual process music models his egalitarian politics—we all listen to the process together, there are no secrets of structure—Taruskin and Epstein insist that there is in fact a structural secret in *Piano Phase* and other tape-based process pieces. Moreover, it's on the order of that ideal liberator of sounds, Schoenberg: the second half is in fact a retrograde of the first.

I already noted above, in relation to Scherzinger's proposed paradox, that I was skeptical of this basic analytic conceit. What Scherzinger calls a paradox—that the audible, gradual process produces audible complexity—Taruskin similarly considers a fault: that while Reich refused "secrets of structure," analysis unmasks forms that can be residually linked to high-modernist compositional trends.[35] "It turned out," Taruskin writes,

> that, in seeming *contradiction of Reich's manifesto*, there was after all a "secret of structure" in *Piano Phase* that listeners did not know. But, *as seems likely, the composer himself was unaware of (or did not envision) the retrograde*, which was irrelevant to his purpose in composing the piece, then his famous maxim—"I don't know any secrets of structure that you can't hear"—remains literally true.[36]

Paired with Taruskin's disdainful tone, we cannot overstate the argumentative method here. Taruskin is calling Reich an idiot, a brute: he reframes the key contribution of Reich's manifesto, its egalitarian proposal, its refusal of composerly privilege, by dragging it back into the modernist constellation of composer-performer-audience relations. This description compounds with Taruskin's framing of James Tenney's observation—"The composer isn't privy to anything"—as a "complaint." That is, Taruskin narrates the interaction as one in which Tenney was *complaining* that within Reich's proposed system the composer would no longer be privy to anything. Together, the two observations clearly reveal that Taruskin refuses, from the start, to believe the efficacy or sincerity of the political project outlined. Not only is the *audience* ignorant, but now the composer is too: *I* don't know any secrets of structure that *you* can't hear. That is: there are secrets of structure that *of course* you can't hear, but *neither can I*.[37] Audience and composer are made to share in their ignorance, which is weaponized to uphold the expert privilege and specialization of the scholar-historian: the Musicologist as Specialist has a very clear plan for mobilizing critique against minimalism. While Cage and Schoenberg remain heroic liberators of sound, Reich is put in his place by reframing the language of his egalitarian promise as a refusal of his intelligence that necessarily also, not by coincidence, calls upon the modernist dismissal of the audience's ignorance as a liability for composers.

Taruskin shows that the police conception regularly relies on a pedagogic logic of *abrutir*—making brutes or rendering stupid. The politics of minimalism is dismissed by rendering it, through the pedagogic relation, foolish or stupid; and it is rendered stupid precisely because it is a politics of antiauthorship, one that refuses mastery, privilege, and intellectual inegalitarianism measured through hermetic structural secrets. Taruskin implicitly ties this claim to the better-known manifesto writers and agitators concurrently active. The minimalists are cast as ignorant youth because of their simultaneous appearance with the student revolts of 1968, are represented as too ignorant, too *early* to have launched their critique.

The great irony of the pairing of the 1968 process documents, to me, is their pure mismatch, which appears as a nesting of the mismatch within *Pendulum Music* itself. There have been no published analyses of *Pendulum Music* by music scholars—likely because it never sounds the same twice. This is potentially true, of course, of any piece of music, and particularly one like *Piano Phase*. But more importantly, *Pendulum Music*, despite its title, might not be music: it is probably sculpture more than it is music. It cannot be—I would prefer *should not be*—transcribed into staff notation to analyze its complex rhythmic interplay. The really telling element, then, appears in the scholarly insistence on its *purity*: if the goal of "Music as a Gradual Process" is to construct a critical framework that insists upon the ability of listeners to follow what is happening, there is no more obfuscating piece by Reich when listened to—at least in the absence of the visual element—than *Pendulum Music*.[38] That is, the effort to proclaim the "purity" of *Pendulum Music* is inversely related to its absolute *impurity* as a musical manifestation of the point of the manifesto. It is a text score, for a piece of music composed of screeching feedback, "performed" by a quartet of closed circuits, "activated," at least in their original performance, primarily by nonmusicians. *Pendulum Music* is perhaps only "music" in name.

Moreover, I hear in the piece's *whoomps* a distinct process of impurifying and indistinguishing: what begin as discrete *whoomps* slowly converge and blend, progressively becoming indistinct until we finally arrive at a whirring, near-stable, droning feedback of indistinguishable, closed-circuit microphone-speakers feeding back. The piece is a process of discrete *whoomps* becoming indistinct. The performers are instructed to sit and listen together as the *whoomps* blur into a harsh noise drone. They are then tasked with bringing a stop to the noise, probably at a moment when the tension, annoyance, or pain has become palpable in the room.

The consensus in music scholarship has necessarily drawn upon a piece of music that is probably not music, to stage it as a *pure* musical depiction of a discursive problem when it is, more accurately, not only impure but *impurifying* of music's very conditions of possibility. Taruskin is right: Reich's concern is about liberating audiences. He has to work *outside music* to do so, and music scholarship has consistently begun from having to claw both *Pendulum Music* and the arguments of "Music as a Gradual Process" back into the domain of music scholarship and musical analysis to make their point: Reich can't do that!

Within a few years, he would repentantly agree with them. Scherzinger, Taruskin, and the other scholars quoted above are some of the most consistently compelling and thoughtful writers in music studies; their framing of these critiques is hard to fault on the grounds of historical evidence or analysis of the music in question. The fault is outside of these methods. My qualm is not analytic or historical but has to do with what Rita Felski has highlighted as the whole mood or tone or academic critique.[39] Indeed, it was not so much their critiques of Reich that initially raised flags for me—they are productive, accurate, thoughtful, well argued—but Reich's own self-criticism. In a 2006 interview with *Pitchfork* Reich split himself in two. There is the Young Reich who wrote the essay "Music as a Gradual Process," and there is a more mature, more self-aware Reich who distances himself from the writer of 1968, renouncing his earlier radicalism, thus ironically recognizing its potential and efficacy. His self-policing requires two elements: a generic disidentification and an *abrutir*:

> When I wrote "Music as a Gradual Process" in 1968, I was very accurately reflecting all the music that I had written before 1968. All good music theory is basically referring to music that was written before the theory was written. . . . But if it's a prescription for what you ought to do in the future, then you're writing a manifesto, and I think manifestos are inherently for stupid people who can't fly by the seat of their pants.[40]

"Music as a Gradual Process" is not a *manifesto* (future oriented), but *theory* (reflective, scientific); if it were a manifesto, he'd have been a stupid person. In 2006, Reich validates Taruskin's 2005 argument: he was dumb at the time to have claimed any music, let alone minimalism, could achieve the impossible task the essay promised.

Music historians, I hope it is clear, are uncomfortable with Reich's promise. I have argued for how I read in "Music as a Gradual Process" a promise of composer-audience egalitarianism founded in a local, polemical effort to minimize the composer's privilege. We are yet again in an instance of early minimalism's practice of minimizing gaps to the point of indistinction. I hear this same process made audible in *Pendulum Music* as its distinct *whoomps* blur into an indistinct drone. Once again the mechanism of policing this instance of early minimalism has been to call it early: there are, in fact, structural secrets; Reich's promise of an egalitarian community is naive and impossible; minimalism's proximity to the student movement, its desire to liberate people rather than sound, is embarrassing. Even Reich calls upon a contextual distinction between manifesto (which it is) and theory (which it isn't) to insist on an *abrutir*: he would have to have been dumb. Plenty of music scholars are ready to back him up.

Between the promise of an early minimalism—a form of composition that reduces distinctions to buzzing proximity, whether composer and audience or whoomp and drone—and its rendering *early* we again find (early) minimalism. Audiences, like students, must know that they are early—not only wrong or ignorant, but stuck in a circle that they can only escape by heteronomous intellectual guidance. With minimalism, *composers join them* as subjects to be stultified by music scholarship. And it once again occurs through insistence on the *purity* of foundational concepts—that is, by making the "purity" of a concept the first step in a teleological trajectory that implies its own impossibility. The untimeliness and the insistence on the too-early is built into politics and historiography when its concern is to sustain itself, at least when critique focuses on surfaces and depths, ignorance and knowledge, students and teachers, composers and audiences. What if we instead think on the order of dramaturgy, staging, surfaces, relations of nonrelation or constellations of dissimilar objects?

What if we think of adjacencies under homonymy, rather than the nestings, displacements, and equivalencies of metaphor? Taruskin creates a metaphorical parallel to the writing style—planks in a political platform—of Reich's "manifesto" to treat him like a "sixties agitator" set out to liberate people rather than sounds. This metaphor, the arrangement of his argument, *does extensive historiographical work.*[41] It allows him to talk down to Reich in the form of insisting upon his ignorance of his own work. Taruskin's argument stages a rendering-early that relies more on the reader's recognition of political-historical metanarratives than on musical analysis. "Sometimes," Susana Draper writes, "'68 itself is made into a label used to classify phenomena that are incomprehensible to traditional modes of political organization."[42] Perhaps rather than an ignorant politics, early minimalism proposes a politics incomprehensible within a disciplinary formation compelled to uphold both its liberal authorial politics and its hierarchical arrangement of roles. Minimalism's failed politics—when staged as a tragedy following on pure origins—is the failed politics of youthful revolt. Its presence in music history classrooms, represented by the 1968 process documents, has become a parable of the inefficacy of revolt. That it must be staged that way shows clear anxieties about the critique it launched and the efficacy of its afterlife. Recalling Ross on the dismantling of eventfulness, one of the fundamental tricks of historiography—not even a regressive form of critique within it—is to forget that the stage on which a new subject appears, on which a revolt is declared, had to be built in the first place.

Two

Writing Minimalism

The Theatre of Eternal Music and the Historiography of Drones

New York's 10-4 Gallery hosted a series of concerts in the summer of 1962. Reflecting on the performances decades later, Tony Conrad writes:

> While Young played saxophone, (somewhere between Bismillah Khan and Ornette Coleman), Angus MacLise improvised on bongos, Billy Linich (Billy Name [of Warhol's Factory]) strummed folk guitar, and Marian Zazeela sang drone. All in all, those were hysterical and over-wrought concerts; they went on for hours in overdrive, with frequent breaks for the musicians to refresh themselves offstage or in the john. The music was formless, expostulatory, meandering; vaguely modal, arrhythmic, and very unusual; I found it exquisite.[1]

Following Linich's departure, Conrad joined the group on violin in early 1963, and was subsequently followed later that year by the violist John Cale. The droning "iron triangle"[2] of Conrad, Cale, and Zazeela upheld the modal, wildly arrhythmic improvisations of Young and MacLise until April 1964, when MacLise left, and Young joined the drone with long, sustained pitches on his soprano saxophone. In the following months, Young left the saxophone behind to focus on singing, stabilizing the ensemble as two string players and two vocalists, all performing a sustained, long-duration drone in precise just intonation. The group then began using the name Theatre of Eternal Music, and alternately calling their performances "Dream Music" or other long, poetic titles drawn from MacLise's calendar-poem *Year*. By the fall of 1966 the group had gone through further changes in personnel, and their regular, often daily, rehearsals came to an end. This ensemble is foundational to the early history of the genre we retrospectively call minimalism in that it marks the first instance of drones as the sole content of Euro-American musical performance and composition.[3] This chapter examines the dispute over the authorial inscription of those drones. By what narrative mechanisms can drones become the material of authorship and, indeed, the content of music history? What forms of authorship and historiography do drones underwrite?

The group's dissolution in the fall of 1966 allowed each participant to move on to his or her own projects: Young and Zazeela undertook decades of study as disciples of the Kirana Gharana singer Pandit Pran Nath, developing a Hindustani-inspired vocal practice that prioritized precise, sustained intonation within installations of Zazeela's magenta lights; Cale cofounded the influential rock band the Velvet Underground and had a successful career as a solo musician and producer (of Nico, the Stooges, and others); Terry Riley, who joined the group after Cale's departure, worked on his intermedia performances around New York through 1969, when he moved back to California and had a long career as a composer and performer; and Conrad parlayed his simultaneous work in experimental film into a career as a professor in the trailblazing media studies program at the State University of New York at Buffalo. All members had apparently developed a working agreement on the authorial propriety of their music during its active period and maintained professional relationships beyond their collaborative performances. For example, at Documenta V in Kassel, Germany, in 1972, Conrad was hired to maintain the sine-wave oscillators at Young and Zazeela's *Dream House* installation, while also presenting his own solo video work. Conrad and Cale also briefly performed with a newly formed Theatre of Eternal Music in 1969 and in 1972 (the Documenta installation and at the Berlin Olympics) but quickly left, as they felt that, reformed by Young, the ensemble had become something different and was clearly under his authorial direction.[4] Meanwhile, the group's archive of tapes sat idly in Young and Zazeela's apartment; Conrad later noted that he was under the impression that the tapes "were our collective property, resident in their unique physical form at Young and Zazeela's loft, where we rehearsed, until such time as they might be copied for each of us."[5]

In the mid-1980s, the record label Gramavision expressed interest in releasing a series of records by Young. The chronology here is sketchy. It's likely that Young approached Conrad and Cale, even as early as 1972, with release forms that would recognize the tapes as representing *performances* by the Theatre of Eternal Music of *music* by La Monte Young.[6] Cale and Conrad were shocked and insisted that all members be given equal authorial credit in any potential release. While all members of the ensemble had seemingly agreed about the status of their work—or, perhaps, had all found ways to function within heterogeneous (mis)understandings of its authorial status— Young's request inaugurated an explicit conflict with Conrad, in particular, as the political, historical, and authorial terms of the drones were opened for dispute. As discussed in the Introduction, Conrad picketed a series of Young's concerts in Buffalo in 1990, holding up signs and handing out pamphlets reading "La Monte Young Does Not Understand 'His' Work."[7] Scholarly studies of minimalism began to appear, joined by a nascent experimental music press that made an enticing myth of an ensemble whose music no one had heard.[8] Despite (or perhaps because of) this inaudibility, the music's impact grew.[9] In an effort to finally make the music audible to contemporary listeners, Conrad worked with the Atlanta-based record label Table of the Elements. Owned by Jeff Hunt, the label released several albums by Conrad that claimed to recreate the sound and practice of the Theatre of Eternal Music's drones. Two of these albums, *Slapping Pythagoras* and the boxed set *Early Minimalism, Vol. 1*, featured long liner note essays critical of both Young's refusal to make the tapes available, and the Young-oriented image of author-centered, tonal, repetitive minimalism represented in popular and scholarly histories.[10] Around this same time, several low-fidelity recordings of the original ensemble were circulating through early online file-sharing communities like Napster; the distributors and creators of these releases are unknown, but in most cases, the music had been taken from radio broadcasts, in particular one on WKCR in New York celebrating Young's forty-ninth birthday in 1984.[11]

In 2000, with the consent of Cale and Conrad, Table of the Elements released *Day of Niagara*, a particularly poor-quality tape from April 1965, with all five performers—Cale, Conrad, MacLise, Young, and Zazeela—listed in alphabetical order on the cover.[12] This was the first commercial release of material from the tape archive. Young threatened legal action and published a twenty-seven-page open letter attacking the release, the history it proposed, and Conrad's arguments about collectivism in composition. The open letters continued: Conrad responded to Young, largely continuing his arguments from *Slapping Pythagoras* and *Early Minimalism*; and Arnold Dreyblatt, a Berlin-based American sound artist and composer, who copied the tape for his personal listening when he was Young's first tape archivist in the 1970s, released a letter apologizing to Young and Conrad and pleading with both sides to come to an agreement so that more of the material, of better quality, could be heard by the public.[13]

This chapter provides the first extended study of this ensemble—alternately known as the Theatre of Eternal Music (Young's and Zazeela's preferred nomenclature), or sometimes as the Dream Syndicate (Conrad's and Cale's)—that is not framed within a chapter or a book on either La Monte Young or Tony Conrad.[14] The "Dream Music" is my subject, and in particular, the arguments about historiography, authorship, composition, collaboration, collectivity, and inscription enlivened by those massively influential though largely unheard drones. I began with my own version of the narrative because the contentious nature of the dispute means that this chapter—like the entire book—often turns to heterophonic accounts of what happened when, who was responsible, and even what dates can be considered legitimate. Until quite recently, historians of this music worked in relation to a complete lack of written documentation, because the group privileged the political and historiographic gesture of "writing" their music exclusively to magnetic tape. This shift in site of inscription produced an archive of dozens of tape recordings held at Young and Zazeela's Church Street loft in New York City. The dispute centers on the tapes and is made possible by them: their authorial status, what they signify, the (im)possibility of their release, and the threat and value of their propriety. I have considered these tapes in both their musical content and their materiality as circulating bootlegs in another article that should be read as a dissensual twin to this chapter.[15] While the tapes propose that the music is best understood through listening as part of a material history of magnetic tape, there has been no absence of writing in response to the group's collaborative drones.

I want to consider the mechanisms by which Young and Conrad each narrated the ensemble's motivations, history, and authorial politics. I then turn to archival documents to consider the forms of inscriptive writing appropriate to the drones during the period of their performance. I argue that even as the group refused the necessity of the score as delegating document by centering magnetic tape, they highlighted the collective authorial possibilities of other means of inscriptive music writing including essays, manifestos, and Marian Zazeela's calligraphic posters. At all points in the six decades since the tapes were recorded, we see the participants struggling with how to ascribe authority and responsibility within a musical practice premised on early minimalist, collective practices of rehearsal and listening. Each of the performers was eager to work outside traditional composerly authorship, and their divergent understandings of how *authority* could be historiographically and literally (re)inscribed provoked often-bitter hostility and, perhaps just as importantly, some really interesting discourse on collaboration, collective organization, and writing history.

La Monte Young's Ensemble

In most literature on minimalism, Theatre of Eternal Music is the name of the mysterious ensemble that Young led between his well-documented early Fluxus works and his first commercial recording, the *Black LP* (1969). However, to declare 1962–1966 a homogenous period in which Young wrote music for his own ensemble requires extensive care in redirecting collaborative energies toward Young's sole authority. The scholarly history of the ensemble is rife with such distortions. Published in 1996 at the height of the dispute, K. Robert Schwarz's decision to entirely leave Conrad out of the ensemble in his overview of the group marks the height of such efforts: "To accompany his saxophone improvisations, Young assembled an ensemble; its *sole purpose* was to prolong static, endless harmonies while he played." He continues, "In its early incarnation of 1963, the ensemble consisted of Zazeela singing a vocal drone, Angus MacLise playing hand-drums, and a young Welshman named John Cale sustaining drones on viola."[16] John Cale was never in the Theatre of Eternal Music when Tony Conrad was not. While Schwarz is unique in entirely denying Conrad's presence, other historians simply downplay his contributions or misrepresent his argument by insisting upon the group as *Young's ensemble*. Wim Mertens agrees with Schwarz that "in *1967* [*sic*], Young "formed his own ensemble," called the Theatre of Eternal Music.[17] He continues, correcting the earlier dating typo: "In 1964 the personnel of The Theatre of Eternal Music changed and from 1964 till 1966, it included Young, who no longer played the saxophone but sang instead; Zazeela, voice; Conrad and Cale, strings and (sometimes) Terry Riley, voice."[18] Such basic factual errors in both early accounts point to confusion around the ensemble and, more than anything, to the dearth of material for these historians to work from. Together, these attest to the fact that the ensemble's historiographic import—the attractive narrative gesture of minimalism emerging from a drone—well preceded any musical audibility. Young's mythological claims about "his" group provided a firmer foundation for minimalism than the sound of the Theatre ever could have.

In his important text *Four Musical Minimalists*—published around the time of the release of *Day of Niagra*—Keith Potter set a new standard of critical and musicological attention to minimalism. He moreover finally drew attention to the dispute, though he did so by treating it as a clearly demarcated dispute over propriety between Young/composition and Conrad/improvisation. "The issue of whether the music in the many surviving recordings of the group constitutes compositions by Young or improvisations in which all the performers made important creative contributions . . . remains unsettled to this day." Potter continues,

> It may be asserted that Young provided the material; but others may also have had an input into this, especially at the earlier stages of such music's conceptualization. The group clearly provided the elaboration of it, each performer being ultimately responsible for his own part. But the interaction not only included Young as one of the protagonists but was also, on the available evidence, driven by someone who acknowledges that he is "very authoritarian" and—in an oddly characteristic moment of self-deprecation—"not fit to be collaborated with."[19]

The dispute finally enters historiography of minimalism in its moment of decisive legalistic challenge—but it's difficult not to read Potter's account as colored by Young's direct input as an interlocutor. As we will see below, Potter's account essentially follows Young's own in misrepresenting Conrad's claim as simply being that they were all improvising, rather than digging into the nuances of his argument.

Indeed, the talent, diverse creativity, and traceable input of the other members of the ensemble force us to question Young's depiction of himself to Potter as "not fit to be collaborated with." The most recurring and commonplace methods of policing Conrad's collectivist claim has been through prolepsis. This form of conditional present is most prominent in Edward Strickland's extremely valuable, multimedial history of the origins of minimalism in the arts. In his brief discussion of Conrad's role within Young's ensemble, Strickland describes Conrad as "a Minimalist film-maker trained as a mathematician,"[20] even though Conrad was not a filmmaker when he began performing with Young; his visual artworks rather grew out of this period of collaborative work with sound, and only came to public awareness in his 1965 film *The Flicker*. Strickland continues in this proleptical mode when he describes John Cale's entry into the group: "To this point, *Young's instrumentation* was entirely acoustic. The drone was augmented by the arrival of electric violist John Cale." Beyond the inaccurate presumption that the ensemble was originally an acoustic ensemble for which Young was writing music, we can further problematize the fact that the electric viola did not exist in 1963. Rather, amplification via contact microphones was a solution arrived at by the ensemble in relation to its specific textural needs.[21] Nevertheless, like calling Conrad a filmmaker, Strickland's assumption that Cale arrive with an electric viola in hand is based in a proleptical view of history in which individuals are always-already exactly who the dominant narrative expects them to be—side players of Young's ensemble—without taking into account the chronological and temporal development of the group in its material interactions. Such writing gives an incredible advantage to Young, the most famous person in the group when historians first began examining it. Or, returning to Potter's consideration, Young remains the protagonist around whom such disputes are staged. This mode of historical thinking and writing, entirely ahistorical and apolitical, negates the possibility of change. In such moments the musicological analysis and narrative of early minimalism has to elide its greatest novelties.

We get a clearer sense of how this proleptical mode of historiography is turned into a policing of the narrative when Strickland describes Cale's later career:

> [Cale] was later to become one of the founding members of the Velvet Underground . . . which pioneered proto-punk drone-rock under Young's influence. . . . Along with their harmonic stasis the Velvets borrowed their relentless volume from Young's drones. In this, Cale's arrival with his electrically amplified instrument had been crucial, as had Conrad's introduction of contact mikes, *which enabled Young to realize more adequately his construction*, in avant-garde adaptation of rock producer Phil Spector, of a "wall of sound."[22]

When read in terms of causality and historiographical conceptions of influence, this passage is incoherent. Eventual historical events are again made self-evidently and necessarily consequent upon earlier, entirely uncertain events, all of them colliding in an eternal present in which what we now know has always been the case. First, Strickland suggests that Young's influence on the Velvet Underground can be heard in the use of both harmonic stasis and relentless volume. He then states that in its relentless volume, "Cale's arrival . . . had been crucial" because of his (already mentioned as problematic) use of the electric viola. That is, Strickland grounds Young's influence on the Velvet Underground through features of the ensemble that he argues Cale brought to Young's attention. Such complex historiographical gymnastics evidence the music-historical concern to ensure that La Monte Young is the origin of everything related to the ensemble.

Angus MacLise's contributions to the group are dismissed in much the same way. MacLise was a percussionist and poet most often remembered today for his calendar-poem *YEAR*, in which he assigned unique names to all 365 days. Though he left before the ensemble took on its collective name, his poetic dates were used by the group and still regularly are by Young and Zazeela to name particular performed instantiations of their work. However, for Strickland, MacLise's departure for Kathmandu on 18 February 1964, is read as yet another sign of Young's compositional foresight: "With the drummer gone, the rhythmic element was essentially eliminated, and the music in a sense was permitted to retrogress toward the unaccented sustenance of [Young's] *Trio [for Strings*, of 1958]."[23] In his 2000 open letter, Young writes:

> Angus left New York on Tuesday, February 18, 1964 to begin a protracted journey to the East. Although *Early Tuesday Morning Blues* stands as a good example of what my fast sopranino saxophone playing was like without Angus, without the excitement of his remarkable drumming technique to play my saxophone rhythms against, *I discontinued the rhythmic element.* Carrying on the inspiration of my previous work with sustained tones, I began to hold longer sustained tones on saxophone.[24]

Both here and in the case of Cale above, Strickland narrates autonomous decisions by members of the ensemble as evidence of Young's foresight: Cale's use of electric viola and MacLise's departure both allowed Young to access a compositional plan that, it is suggested, both had been getting in the way of. Much the same, Conrad's contributions are treated as ornamental in that he is described as a filmmaker, merely interloping with musicians, without the technical background in music to have any impact.

I am not recounting Strickland's narration of the presence and role of other members just to be querulous myself; rather his account points to the problematic narrative renderings of all of Young's collaborators, as historians make them into supplementary characters orbiting him rather than equals. Indeed, writing on Young carves away collaborators' input, carefully positioning them as extramusical, to uphold the counterfactual image of a figure "not fit to be collaborated with"—this despite Young's constant, lifelong practice of particularly close collaboration. I have not even yet mentioned Marian Zazeela, with whom Young has been in quite literally constant collaboration, they both admit, since they first met in the early 1960s. Zazeela's crafting of a total light environment for early Theatre of Eternal Music performances pairs with the name and innovative staging to allow their work to appear as a total environment, a "happening" that the music occurs within, rather than simply a concert. We can further add Young's decades-long relationships with Terry Riley, Michael Harrison, Charles Curtis, Jung Hee Choi, and many, many others. It is not that Young is unfit for collaboration, in the sense of producing artworks in relation with others; it is that he is incapable of decentering his myopic sense of how his work works.

Histories up to 2000 articulate a progressive effort to turn the (inaudible) drones of the Theatre of Eternal Music into evidence of Young's singular compositional vision, with far too many historians uncritically reporting Young's oral testimony as fact. These scholars were not engaged in a nefarious plot against the other members of the ensemble. Rather, we must keep in mind two interrelated reasons for this narrative approach. First, these writers are all historians and critics of Western classical music. As such, their core assumption is that music originates with a singular composer; in the face of collective dynamics, their work is to reinstate proof of singular authority. But, second, and more practically, the lack of material on minimalism generally, and the Theatre of Eternal Music especially, during the 1980s and 1990s meant that Young and Zazeela became the primary references as oral historians. Their authority was all the more compelling thanks to the rich archive they claimed to speak on behalf of—one that few people have had access to.[25]

Against these historians' early efforts to keep change, contingency, and collectivism out of a history of (what they claim is) art music, it seems clear to me that the Theatre of Eternal Music was a band: individual members came and went, introducing new possibilities and impossibilities as they did so. And because Tony Conrad was not simply a line in a score delegated to "violin" and MacLise was not "hand drums," each member's entry and departure required shifts and concessions.[26] Arguably, if *Sunday Morning Blues* was a composition by La Monte Young that featured hand drums, he would have found a new hand drummer when MacLise left. Similarly, when John Cale left the ensemble at the end of 1965, there does not seem to have been an effort to find a new viola player; instead, Terry Riley was brought in as another composer-performer motivated by the same political and aesthetic impulses to supplement their work and bring it in a new direction (an impulse I would call [early] minimalist). We must imagine the remaining members, perhaps in a first rehearsal after MacLise's departure, sitting together on the floor, saying, "Now what?" and then finding a means to move forward. Conrad was explicit about this. He considered discussion and exchange a fundamental aspect of the collective's democratic organizational structure:

We sat around getting stoned all the time and had endless discussions of what microscopic shifts or changes we might introduce in what we were doing. *Everything* was discussed as a group activity, and it took a lot of time. It took a lot of time to go over *everything*, like which notes went with which notes, or like whether we should be amplified, and whether we should smoke some more weed.[27]

While musicologists have thus far tended to distill the argument into binaries of composition against improvisation, I contend that the Theatre of Eternal Music / Dream Syndicate did not perform music "by La Monte Young and Tony Conrad" or any other combination of people involved, nor was it open improvisation. Conrad has long insisted that the music signaled the "death" and "abjuration of the composer"[28]—a substantially more complex and nuanced political argument. The ensemble should be understood as practicing a form of collectivist and deliberative composition, in which all performers present, working on the "living sound itself" from "inside the sound" and directly to magnetic tape, are all given equal credit for its composition under the collective name, which is itself the result of that democratic process. Their methods, and even their sound at particular stages, is much nearer to developing trends in free jazz and rock music.[29] In their inability to take seriously collaboration in *composition* of work that we typically consider art music—rather than insisting that such group dynamic moves the music into the realm of *improvisation*—historians like Mertens, Strickland, and Schwarz were forced into extravagant readings to fill holes where there is no evidence of Young's priority as composer; the job of the music historian becomes to find the logical traces and formative moments for Young's contemporary status in his biography and earlier work.

Young's Time Travel

I would like to consider the logic of dating and naming operative in two of Young's prominent early works. In their disputes, each of the authors examined in this book becomes a historian putting forward narrative accounts that animate idiomatic conceptions of historiography. The interrelationship of authorship and historiography in the history of musical minimalism thus requires an account of Young's idiosyncratic practice of using names and dates as part of the conceptual architecture of his work. While this is a captivating element of Young's artistic practice, one that suits the evolutionary-static nature of his harmonic conception, we must also take into account its knotty function within documents brought forth as historical evidence.

Young's use of composition names—often several nested ones—to elide historical developments is clear in his "1962" piece *The Second Dream of the High-Tension Line Stepdown Transformer* from *The Four Dreams of China.* The piece plays an important role in Young's argument from his 2000 open letter for two closely intertwined reasons. First, it marks a heightened concern for tuning in his work, and second because it was the first piece of La Monte Young's in which Tony Conrad performed, during the YAM Festival on 19 May 1963. Young's discussion of this work eliminates the conceptual distance between his equal-tempered *Trio for Strings* (1958) and his later (post–Theatre of Eternal Music) work in thirty-one-limit just intonation. Young mentions four different tetrads of partials for the chordal drone that is the only material of *The Second Dream*: G-C-C-sharp-D (the [0127] set from the *Trio*), 12:16:17:18 ("which I specify in the current score,"[30] though the score is not publicly available to confirm), 24:32:35:36, and 42:56:62:63. Despite these latter tetrads, Kyle Gann notes in his meticulous analysis of tuning in Young's music that the *Four Dreams of China* "predate[s] Young's interest in just intonation."[31] Despite the conceptual difference between an equal-tempered tetrad from a twelve-tone piece and a thirty-one-limit tetrad held as the sole content of a drone composition, Young collapses this distance precisely to use it as evidence of his influence on Conrad. As a policing technique, this shares much with Kristin Ross's account of the police conception of history, particularly as acted out in something like Strickland's proleptical style. These practices hold us in an eternal present, so melted into its surrounding context that nothing ever happens.

Indeed, just intonation plays an important role in his dispute with Conrad. In the 2000 letter, Young cites a note from his archive on which Conrad's handwriting is visible labeling a "possible sequential order quantifying the combinations and demonstrating that Tony had seen my chart." He continues,

The handwritten chart includes written notations, also in my handwriting, qualitatively describing some of the chords, such as question marks, arrows, and the words "special," "far out," "doubtful," and most significantly "Dream," over the combination 63, 62, 56, 42. This "Dream'" is actually a version of my four-note "Dream Chord" from *The Second Dream of the High-Tension Line Stepdown Transformer* from *The Four Dreams of China* (1962), this time using 31 as the divisor of the

9:8 interval (63:56) instead of the 12-note equal tempered divisor used in the [19 May 1963] Segal's Farm performance.

Based on his use of the qualitative word "Dream" over Conrad's quantitative just intonation notation, Young turns this chord into a "version" of *The Second Dream* (1962), and then by extension to the *Trio for Strings* (1958). Earlier in his career, Young deferred to Conrad—perhaps even the same chart— when Richard Kostelanetz asked him how many pitches the Theatre uses: "I haven't taken a count; but *just glancing over at Tony Conrad's chart on the wall here* . . . we have used about twenty-seven frequencies to the octave, which is more than double the number used in the twelve-note system."[32] Because Young sees each tuning as a successive "version" of the same chord grounded in the *Trio* (1958), he can claim that they all originate in 1962 by attaching the name *The Second Dream of the High-Tension Line Stepdown Transformer*, rather than acknowledging the collaborative developments that occurred in the Theatre of Eternal Music period—including Conrad introducing him to the mathematics for working in just intonation. For Young, a serial collaborator who nevertheless imagines himself incapable of it, compositional authority is confirmed through a form of counting in which his own work is inherently more important than the work of his collaborators, which is reframed as supplementary, ancillary, or supportive.[33] Moreover, we see a different homonymy in play here, as the same composition name is used to elide development and change impelled at least in part by Young's collaborative engagements.

As an artistic gesture, Young's conceptual staging is fascinating; as history, it is troubling. That is, Young's development of umbrella titles for pieces— including labeling the entire output of the Theatre of Eternal Music *The Tortoise, His Dreams and Journeys*—provides compelling theoretical justification for his compositional language, but at what cost to historians? Are we forced merely into fact checking and disproving his mystical narratives? To paraphrase Henry Flynt, Young has granted himself the capacity to time-travel in his work. While the Theatre of Eternal Music's history is choked by a constitutive rejection of published documentation, Young's Fluxus and text works of 1960–1961 have a clear genesis in textuality and printing. Their heterogeneity and refusal of genre and medium make them a fruitful source for any argument about art in the 1960s. That musicologists have all prioritized #7, the only one to feature staff notation, is hardly surprising. Notably, music historians have not yet followed art historians like Branden Joseph and Liz Kotz in reading the *Compositions 1960* as fundamental moments in the socialization of 1960s arts. Joseph writes:

Compositions 1960 #3, #4, and *#6* formed an important, if consistently under acknowledged touchstone for the transformation from a "natural" to a "social" and potentially collective point of view, a social turn that would come to characterize the general ethos of both minimalism and Fluxus, as well as the more overtly communist projects of George Maciunas, Henry Flynt, and others, eventually including Cardew.[34]

Such close attention to the audience, within the frame of the composition, is evident in *#2*'s direction to "build a fire in front of the audience," or, in *#4,* to "announce to the audience that the lights will be turned off for the duration of the composition." Not all of the *Compositions* include such direct reference to the audience, but in the years immediately following Babbitt's essay and just prior to the publication of Cage's *Silence,* it is clear that Young's cosmology directly addresses the presence of an audience. Around this time Conrad too commented on the alienation felt by many audience members in relation to the avant-garde. The score for his 1961 composition *(Prelude and) Fugue for Strings* includes a diagram of the performance setup positioned against, in its lower segment, the "audience (if any)."[35]

Compositions 1960 #10 (for Bob Morris) became a particular touchstone for Young's continuing work as what Jeremy Grimshaw calls an "elemental teleology" to follow "through the compositional methods Young subsequently developed and the cosmological outlook to which he anchored them."[36] On 6 January 1961, Young conceived and wrote the complete *Compositions 1961.* Realizing that he had written, on average, twenty-nine pieces per year throughout his compositional career, Young decided to write his average yearly quota in one night: twenty-nine iterations, spaced thirteen days apart, beginning on 1 January and ending 31 December 1961, of the text of *Composition 1960 #10*—"draw a straight line and follow it."[37] In keeping with the norm of compositional practice, he dated each iteration:

Composition 1961 #1 (January 1, 1961)
Composition 1961 #2 (January 14, 1961)
Composition 1961 #3 (January 27, 1961)
Composition 1961 #4 (February 9, 1961)
. . .[38]

Commenting on the work, Young said, "What is also important historically is that I performed all of them in March, *long before many of them had ever been written according to their dates of composition.* I think that was interesting."[39] Henry Flynt agreed about the work's interest, particularly the "conceptual conundrum" of dating:

> I remember when he told me over the telephone how the works were to be listed in the program. As he dictated, he came to *Composition 1961 #8*, dating April 2, 1961! [The concert was to take place on 31 March.] He was going to perform 22 compositions before they were composed. In logical terms, he was going to follow a rule which he had planned, but which did not yet exist. From the point of view of the conventionalist explanation of the existence of abstractions, Young was introducing time travel at the level of whether given abstractions existed or not.[40]

The typography in the Harvard-Radcliffe Music Group program suggests that the pieces were not "titled" by date, but specifically that each number in the series, 1–29, was dated, in brackets, by Young (on 6 January). We must here ask whether the calendar dates should be read as conceptual material or as, simply put, *dates*. How do we distinguish—not only conceptually, but historically? Evidence of this chronological uncertainty produced interpretive and historical misunderstandings even as early as the 1980s. Wim Mertens wrote that in 1961, while Young was still focused on "the singular unique event," nevertheless *"at different points during that year he wrote the same composition 29 times*: Draw a straight line and follow it."[41] The anecdotal evidence from Kostelanetz's interview was either missed by Mertens or dismissed as historically irrelevant now that all twenty-nine dates were, in fact, in the past. Indeed, from Mertens's perspective, *Compositions 1961* was Young's first repetitive work in that, twenty-nine different times in the course of the year, he wrote the same piece;[42] for Flynt and others who are aware of the use of dating as material, that is its sole content—conceptual, textual, and nonmusical—and it thus stands as Young's final Fluxus work.

The *Compositions 1961* represents a case in which inaccurate dating is made material—even the sole content of a piece. This feels like a rather miserable argument to make; I deeply admire the conceptual gesture of Young's Fluxus work, but I think it is important to ask how historians should respond to such inscription. Like *The Second Dream*, *Compositions 1961* proposes historiographic problems both in how Young accounts for his works and in reference to his own archives, as well as in how the compositions fit into—and help reframe—the limits and capacities of authorship during the 1960s. In both works, Young uncouples the sounding event and its inscription on paper, making each a mobile, historical event whose name and date of origin are malleable to serve his narrative. His private archive provides the conceptual ground for such a practice, as it offered carefully framed and narrated material evidence to early historians of minimalism, even when they were only able to consider it as reported by Young and Zazeela. In the historiographic practices called upon to uphold Young's narrative—prolepsis, hierarchization of contributions, references to closed archives, counterfactual claims about the inability to collaborate, inaccurate dating, and intentionally elided titling practices—I think we witness, in Young's claims about the Theatre of Eternal Music, only a strong form of the distortions necessary to narrate sole authorship broadly. Young may be less an exception than a representative example of the narrative work of upholding private property in sound.

Tony Conrad's Egalitarian Poetics

I turn now to Conrad as a historian of the Theatre of Eternal Music / Dream Syndicate, focusing, as I did with Young, on his historiographical and political modes of self-presentation. Conrad's narrative shows the mark of having spent several decades as a filmmaker and professor in the media studies department at SUNY Buffalo, as he frequently draws on aesthetic and political theory, referencing scholars like Michel Foucault, Gayatri Spivak, Edward Said, and Chantal Mouffe in mobilizing his claims against Young. I will read Conrad in relation to Jacques Rancière's book *La Mésentente*. The book was first published in France in 1995, before it was translated by Julie Rose for English publication in 1999. It thus appeared simultaneously with Conrad's arguments; while I do not want to claim that Conrad was inspired by Rancière, I also would not rule it out.[43] Reading the two together reveals resonances between the structure, tone, and content of their arguments. I do not bring Rancière in here as "proof" that Conrad's arguments have a foundation in "theory." But because Conrad's claims have gained little traction among music historians and composers during his lifetime, my hope is that Rancière's established arguments for an egalitarian art, politics, and history will provide productive language to support Conrad's performative method. I will move away from "Young's ensemble," the Theatre of Eternal Music, and further investigate Conrad's argument that the Dream Syndicate created identical music, and featured the exact same individuals, but was in fact differently organized as a collaborative, deliberative, democratic ensemble that heralded collective composition in art music.

In creating a context for Conrad's egalitarian declaration, I would like to turn to Jacques Rancière's important text *La Mésentente*, and in particular to his idea of the *wrong* (*tort*) in democratic politics. What is the nature of this disagreement in Rancière's writing?

> We should take disagreement to mean a determined kind of speech situation: one in which one of the interlocutors at once understands and does not understand what the other is saying. Disagreement is not the conflict between one who says white and another who says black. It is the conflict between one who says white and another who also says white but does not understand the same thing by it or does not understand that the other is saying the same thing in the name of whiteness.[44]

We must note immediately a slippage between French and English already highlighted by Samuel Chambers and Davide Panagia: *la mésentente* more accurately means misunderstanding, and puns on its homonymic relationship with a missed listening. Panagia notes a parallel to familial "bad blood" precisely in the sense that a *mésentente* is not something that can be resolved through more communication or further clarification; it is precisely a speaking at cross-purposes without recognizing the site of homonymic fault in that misunderstanding. (More importantly, Rancière rejects that model of deliberative democracy because it takes the goal of politics as achieving consensus, which he equates with the police.) Disagreements result when conflicting parties are talking about different devotions to the *same* thing—or perhaps more, disputes about drastically different knowledges or experiences of the "same" thing, *in name*, without recognizing the fact of that difference. There is no resolution here even on the order of an "agree to disagree"; the disagreement *is politics* in the sense that it is about the negotiation through imperfect language and indistinct experiences of what is the nevertheless a common sensorium.

Within this common world carved up through practices of naming and being named, Rancière insists on two fundamental modes of human being together: *politics* and the *police*. The police "puts bodies in their place and their role according to their 'properties,' according to their name or their lack of a name."[45] The police insists on the private nature of relationships in terms of the contractual and legal delineation of parties and responsibilities. As part of a sweeping, polemical gesture, Rancière defines most activities typically associated with (party) politics—the aggregation of consent, the organization of powers, the distribution of roles, and the systems for legitimizing all of these—under the logic of the police, "an order of the visible and the sayable that sees that a particular activity is visible and another is not, that this speech is understood as discourse and another as noise."[46] It is the well-established "way things are" called upon by the representatives of order—move along, there's nothing to see here!—when faced with a challenge to the regimented mode of sensibility that is meant to be the *only* mode of sensibility.

If elections, opinion polls, the management of power, the attainment of consent, the distribution of resources, and processes of power and legitimation are all *the police*, what is left for Rancière to label "politics"?

> I now propose to reserve the term politics for an extremely determined activity antagonistic to policing: whatever breaks with the tangible configuration whereby parties and parts or lack of them are defined by a presupposition that, by definition, *has no place in that configuration*—that of the part who has no part."[47]

This second mode of being together "disrupts [the police] harmony through the mere fact of achieving the contingency of equality . . . of any speaking beings whatsoever."[48] Politics emerges from the assumption that the present configuration, the police distribution, has a gap, a void, or an exclusion that is being repeatedly reasserted as "the way thing are." Often politics involves making those private, contractual relationships a matter of public record by staging this void as not something that was *forgotten* in a count, but was rather excluded to create the impression of order and harmony. Staging this exclusion means maintaining vigilance to its reinscription—not a new tally of parts, but a new conception of space, relationship, and sharing in light of the very *possibility* of exclusion from the police count. Politics enacts a proof that the police cannot in fact count everything. Such disordering is well captured in one of Rancière's most famous statements: "A worker who had never learned how to write and yet tried to compose verses to suit the taste of his times was perhaps more of a danger to the prevailing ideological order than a worker who performed revolutionary songs."[49] That is, the police distribution of sensibility, at least after a given point (perhaps following the revolts of 1830 or 1848 in France) had an understanding of "the worker" as one who appears in the streets and sings revolutionary songs. Much more threatening is the literate worker, the one who refuses to rest at night but rather fraternizes with the children of the wealthier classes, exchanging poetry.[50] In Rancière, the political danger is not in established, "pure" radicals; politics erupts from those whose disidentification with existing identities makes them impossible to place, to predict, to account for.

This possibility of exclusion, the fact of there being an operationality outside of the harmonious, contractual, police definition of roles and responsibilities, is claimed through appeal to a *wrong*. Rancière draws this term from the classical notion of the *tort*, as in tort law, an account of "the obligations and duties of citizens and the penalties incurred for not executing" basic social concerns of how people should treat each other, the rules society imposes on citizens in their treatment of each other, and so on. Within the Rancièrian framework, *tort* becomes homonymic for the indistinct relationship of rights and wrongs, authorship as (dis)possessive, or, more specific to the case at hand, the synonymous tension between the Theatre of Eternal Music and the Dream Syndicate as identical sounds under different claims of property in sound through authorship. That is, *authorship* is the wrong, and it is the source of homonymy as the two forms of being together are distinctly understood in relation to claims of property-in-sound. Whereas the Dream Syndicate insists that authorship can be collaborative and collective, indeed must be in such a case as theirs, the Theatre of Eternal Music marks an instance of a police articulation in which there are authors and there are collaborators, all clearly defined to their own, proper locale. By contrast, Young's sole property in the sound, through authorship, can be understood as the mechanism through which the droning, buzzing, humming, collaborative noise of their deliberative, droning early minimalism became a well-placed, harmonious drone as the coherent, metaphysical, inaudible origin of musical minimalism.

There are certainly other methods of narrating the structural dynamics in play here—we have already considered the normative narrations through how music historians have understood Young's role, and how Rancière might extrapolate on Conrad's dissonant claim. Most important here is that a Rancièrian perspective notes not that the dispute between Conrad and Young is the grounding of politics, but rather that their dispute only occurs on a stage that they built in the very fact of having shared something: their work together as an ensemble, its investment in the tapes as records of a history, and the absence of a disciplinary norm (a police sensorium) within which to account for that mode of phonography. We should now consider how each narrates his own autobiographical foundation for their work. They both acknowledge that the work did not come out of a vacuum—but how do they do narrate its origins?

First, we should attend to their individual mytho-biographies as rationales for the drone. Young's has been well rehearsed and will not be repeated at length, other than to note that Young articulates his interest in drones in stories of his youth in Bern, Idaho, listening to the stepdown transformers and the wind through the walls of his family cabin.[51] By contrast, Conrad's essays from *Early Minimalism* discuss his childhood violin lessons with Roland Knudsen, "an excellent young symphony violinist." While Conrad "hated vibrato,"—which he marks as the expressive core of his instrument's heroic nineteenth-century performance practice—Knudsen's introduction of seventeenth-century music that included double stops changed things drastically: "I discovered what it was like to hear two notes sounding together." Kundsen urged Conrad to play slowly, with precise intonation, and to listen carefully; he later brought a book on acoustics to the lessons, thus enlivening Conrad's lifelong association between music and mathematics.[52] Among the new pieces Conrad encountered during his violin training were the *Mystery Sonatas* of Heinrich Ignaz Franz Biber. Writing about Biber's music, Conrad's narrative turns ecstatic: "For the first time, my violin sounded truly wonderful. It rang, and sang, and spoke in a rich soulful voice." Biber's music was the first Conrad had encountered that he perceived "as having been constructed according to timbre, not melody."[53] Together Biber and Knudsen facilitate an alternate narrative of Conrad's travels in the avant-garde, founding his childhood practice in seventeenth-century violin technique he learned through thinking of duration, intonation, and listening.[54] Knudsen's lessons provide a foundational model for the activities undertaken in Theatre of Eternal Music rehearsals: "long conversations about the harmonic series, scales and tunings, intonation, long durations, [and] careful listening."[55]

Second, Conrad narrates from later in his life, in the years of the Theatre's rehearsals, a set of "three pathways that made sense to the performers" as a means of moving past the Cageian critique of authorship. The first is the complete dismantling of the whole edifice of high culture, an option investigated by Benjamin Piekut in relation to Conrad's "anti-art activism" with Henry Flynt.[56] Conrad undertook hours of listening, with Flynt and John Cale, to musics they did not like or understand: rock and roll, African American, and hillbilly musics, and other forms of "new ethnic music," to use Flynt's term. Centered primarily around their loft at 56 Ludlow Street, the three understood Cage to be demanding that listeners find a path toward music they disliked or found boring. This active listening practice allowed Conrad to hear in Biber a seventeenth-century "hillbilly" music. The second option was to "dispense with the score, and thereby with the *authoritarian trappings of composition*, but . . . retain cultural production in music as an activity." Here Conrad opens himself to what Christopher Watkin calls the "tired old performative contradiction" critique, which has led many composers, critics, and scholars to consider Conrad a prankster at best and a hypocrite at worst.[57] Here we come to a critical split enlivened by the contemporaneous discourse of the death of the author: *cultural production* is marked as distinct from *authorship*. The goal, for Conrad as for so many others, is to root out obvious sites of heteronomous authority and delegation while maintaining the (often collective) work of cultural production. The death of the author is not the end of production, but rather a severing of the necessary link between authorship and the authoritarian:

> When we played together it was always stressed that we existed as a collaboration. Our work together was exercised "inside" the acoustic environment of the music, and was always supported by our extended discourse pertinent to each and every small element of the totality. . . . Much of the time, we sat inside the sound and helped it to coalesce and grow around us. . . . In keeping with the technology of the early 1960s, the score was replaced by the tape recorder. This, then, was *a total displacement of the composer's role, from the progenitor of the sound to groundskeeper at its gravesite.*[58]

Magnetic tape is able to capture sound for posterity, without the delegating intermediary act of authorial inscription of notes on paper; many of the minimalists and other composers of their generation recognized this potential, while carefully holding it in a space distinct from contemporary expansions of commercial popular musics. Cultural production remains a possibility, but the role of the composer as writer of a delegating document is rejected. The collective shapes the sound in rehearsal—developing a performance practice that is also a compositional language—without delegations from a writer who makes marks on paper rather than smearing textures across a living sound and who, most importantly, might use the fact of that delegating document or its structural secrets to claim privilege.[59]

Conrad's third post-Cagean option completes this trajectory: "Move away from composing to listening, again working 'on' the sound from 'inside' the sound." He continues,

> Whenever any of us altered our performing premises in the slightest way, our ensuing discussion brought every justification or objection by any member of the group to the surface. . . . There was a baseline which stabilized the group—our (then) shared conviction that

the collaborative composer/performer identity was the way to proceed (historically), and that the mechanism which could make this congruence fruitful would be attention to, and preoccupation with, the sustained *sound itself.*[60]

In short, listening is made conceptually prior to composition, and it demands greater emphasis. The new composer-performer becomes, first of all, a listener searching for the mode of production in which his or her privileged role is removed in favor of the music staging a common sensorium. In this Cagean overview, or this response to Cage's challenge, Conrad outlines the contexts through which he arrived at the material practice of early minimalism, certainly refracted—in being written decades later—through the Reichian language of a listener not "privy to anything."[61] What Conrad understood as methods of getting beyond the Cagean provocation are all fundamental to what I am calling early minimalism: break with elite culture, abandon the score, focus on listening.

Rather than claiming authorial propriety, in his writing Conrad highlights his contributions to the ensemble as a listening-based performance practice that negates the possibility of—or the need for—singular authorship. That is, Conrad narrates his travel with the drones, both in rehearsals and in home conversations, as always about opening authorship to its outside and new potentials rather than closing it down around himself. He nevertheless draws attention to his own contributions as a means of marking how the venture became collective. Conrad knew when he joined Zazeela as a second performer on the drone in 1963 "that my presence would introduce entirely new standards of attentiveness to pitch and stability."[62] He continues:

At the point of my arrival in the group, the sound itself . . . was incontrovertibly good, but [it] had no particular sustained structural integrity or richness. At first, as co-drone (on violin) with Zazeela (on voice), I played an open fifth. . . . After a month or two, however, I suggested that I might also sometimes play another note. What should it be?—And so began our extended discourse on the advisability of each of the various scale degrees.[63]

With his arrival, the sound of the group becomes singular—*the* sound—with deliberative compositional practice made possible by the drone's elimination of melodic and rhythmic content ("discussion brought every justification or objection by any member of the group to the surface"; "and so began our extended discourse on the advisability of each of the various scale degrees"). The ensemble is constituted in this deliberation, Conrad argues; it becomes a collective capable of inscribing sound to tape, rather than an ensemble reciting the notated delegation of an Author, precisely in having a shared terrain of deliberation. The subject is constituted in the event, in building the stage for its appearance (rather than preexisting it, as in Strickland).

Conrad construes these modalities of listening and performing as the foundation of the sound for which the ensemble is known:

> I played two notes together at all times, so that I heard difference tones vividly in my left ear. . . . Any change in the pitch of either of the two notes I played would be reflected in a movement of the pitch of the difference tone. I spent all of my playing time working on the inner subtleties of the combination tones, the harmonics, the fundamentals, and their beats—as microscopic changes in bow pressure, finger placement and pressure, etc., would cause shifts in the sound.[64]

If Conrad wanted to stake a claim against Young, on Young's terms, to argue who was the true, single author of the music, this quotation could be its foundation. If this were the case, we would have a "rational" liberal debate between two homogeneous claims for the same role of Composer, to the same share and on the same terms: La Monte Young is the composer because X versus Tony Conrad is the composer because Y. But, as Branden Joseph notes, the disagreement is one of kind and not content:[65] while Young argues about his priority as author, Conrad is discussing the conditions of possibility of that institution within the music they were creating, its function as a constitutive *wrong* within the interpersonal dynamics of performance and listening as set discursively animated in Western art music historiography. "At their core, the hundred or so recordings of Dream Music emblematically deny 'composition' in its authoritarian function as a modern activity."[66] This form of listening, grounded in both his prehistorical, biographical stories of studying with Knudsen and his reading of Cage (not to mention his background in mathematics), becomes the defining feature of the group's performance practice. "We lived inside the sound, for years. As our precision increased, almost infinitesimal pitch changes would become glaring smears across the surface of the sound."[67] For Conrad, at all points the ensemble was a collective, and its status as a collective was grounded in the potential offered to them by turning to listening rather than writing, manifested by using magnetic tape, rather than a delegating written score, as documentation. This both enabled their deliberative processes in rehearsal and short-circuited the typical division of labor in art music grounded in the score as documentary evidence of sole propriety in the resulting sound. Conrad's line of argument suggests not that they performed drones as an austere minimization of compositional means or a modernist authorial gesture. Rather, they performed drones as an ideal terrain for collective deliberation and listening.

"Not Fit to Be Collaborated With"

And indeed this is what Table of the Elements records attempted to articulate on the cover of the CD release *Day of Niagara* in 2000. The album cover was intended to be representative of the poor quality of the tape, but Conrad and Cale were insistent that it had to include the names of all five performers listed alphabetically. Young was furious; he immediately made a copyright claim on his master copy of the tape, the only registered US copyright on any of his archival recordings. And he called upon the police discourse of music history to remind that authorship is, in fact, a closed system.

In the last section of his 2000 open letter, Young provides three categories to uphold his claim of sole authorship of the music performed by the Theatre of Eternal Music / Dream Syndicate: public opinion, the opinion of "informed individuals," and Young's own opinion. For the first, Young points out that "many articles in dictionaries of music, histories of music, music journals, newspapers and magazines" credit *The Tortoise, His Dreams and Journeys* to La Monte Young. In this context, the normative history of minimalism is called upon to assist in maintaining order, with Young able to point to the reproduction of his own historiographical taxonomies and idiomatic dating practices in prominent texts. Second, he quotes colleagues: the composer Dennis Johnson states that he has never seen La Monte "do anything where everybody is 'doing their own thing,'" again suggesting, like Potter, that the only other option than Young being the composer is an improvisatory free-for-all. The poet Diane Wakoski claims that "no one who has spent any time around La Monte could ever perceive him as a collaborator." Terry Riley notes that Cale and Conrad were "certainly . . . inspiring collaborators for La Monte," but in spite of the "elements that were contributed by Tony Conrad (such as the math for getting around in Just Intonation) and Angus MacLise (incorporating his names of the days as part of the title . . .), and most prominently the stunning visual art of Marian Zazeela," the "framework for the composition" was Young's. Zazeela defends her partner, noting that she designed flyers, staging, and lighting, and that even though "the lighting developed into a major projection work of my design, for which I trained various projectionists to perform during concerts . . . none of the projectionists I worked with . . . ever considered themselves the 'lighting co-designer.'"[68] Third, Young defers to authorial relations in other musical traditions, arguing for the "extraordinary understanding, bond and trust that had long existed between composer and performer":

> The bonds that existed between European classical composers and their performers in a time when improvisation was very much in vogue, the bonds that exist between composers and performers of Raga, the bonds that exist between composers and performers of jazz compositions, that Conrad and Cale, either naïvely, or intentionally, betrayed, taking advantage, unbecoming to their stature and acclaim, of an established tradition existing between composers and performers back into time.[69]

This revered "bond" is fundamental to Young's conception of authorship. Later in his career he constructed relationships with his students and collaborators as one of guru and disciple to undercut any retrospective equality claim.[70]

Strickland's construction of relationships and identities around or in relation to Young becomes clear here. Like Riley, Young points out that Conrad and Cale made many contributions to the ensemble, in the "realms of performing, theory, acoustics, mathematics and philosophy," and that Conrad's own archive of tapes includes the names of all performers as having been the "Composers" of the works. "This shows that Tony Conrad has a very particular sociological approach to the problem in which he concludes that anyone playing in a work that is improvised comes under his very broad definition of co-composer."[71] Young treats any case of collaboration onto tape—any music that is not written down in advance and then performed based on that command—as "improvisation." To Young's mind, then, any case of improvisation—if one person present has an idea of the direction it might take in advance—is actually not improvisation, but that far-seeing individual's composition. Such a conception is of course ripe for misunderstanding. Young writes that when he approached Conrad and Cale to sign off on his tapes and say that they were performers on music in which Young was sole composer, they refused and "threatened to block releases of my fast sopranino saxophone playing with Angus accompanying, on which they (merely) held drones."[72] Young places a value judgment on the (mere) performance of drones by attaching it to the guru-student "bond" in Indian classical music, suggesting that Conrad is ignorant of these hierarchies rather than that he is rejecting them. Music-historical norms of both improvisation and authorship come together to create a world in which anything done in and around Young is Young's idea. Pointing out that Conrad's tape archive lists all performers on a tape as composers (again, not really, he just lists everyone on the tape with no role attached), Young continues: "For example, Tony lists the tambura player as a co-composer. The tambura can only play a drone. It is a very beautiful instrument but it would require great creativity to get a composition out of a tambura that was any different from the music that all tamburas have played throughout time."[73] While Young is the composer most immediately associated with the drone (as mentioned above by Mertens and Shank), in the final paragraphs of his twenty-seven-page essay, he relies on the profoundly hierarchical relationship of the droning tambura player to his or her master in Hindustani music as final proof of the invalidity of Conrad's argument.

Drawing on scholarship, copyright law, the testimonial of friends and colleagues, and the traditions of both Western art music and music of other cultures, Young argues that there is a specific place for performers to stay as delineated by their "bond" with the composer. He simultaneously argues that Conrad and Cale calling this "bond" one of servitude and unfair hierarchical assumptions is "unbecoming of their stature."[74] The wrong here, the homonymic term, is authorship. Authorship is both the right Young calls upon to commit the wrong, and the tool that Conrad can use to pry open that mentality and highlight its fault. Authorship's historiographic inscription relies on a reiterative and dialogic ecosystem of everyone deferring to the necessity of authorship: just as music historians purify the dissensual, collaborative origins of (early) minimalism to draw out La Monte Young as evidence of authorship's survivance beyond its supposed "death," Young calls upon the same music-historical scholarship to defend himself against Conrad's challenge to Young's sole authority. Authority, as both the reason for and the goal of Young's sole claim to property in the Theatre's collaborative sound, has no grounding beyond this recursive play of composers and historians appealing to each other under the assumption that authorship is simply what there is, and it is what there is because everyone assumes it precedes the creation of music.

Conrad's *Early Minimalism* project included not only the record release, the music, and the revisionist essays, but also picketing, pamphlets, and media interviews. As discussed in the introduction, he picketed Young's 1990 Buffalo performances not because Young would not listen to him, but to make his "noisy" discourse a matter of public record:

> La Monte Young's social elitism makes it impossible for him to take my picketing for anything other than interpersonal bickering, but for me that has nothing to do with the message. . . . Picketing—picketing for or against something, and handing out literature—these are conspicuously formal actions. They have to be understood as indirect communication. Yes, I am "in communication" with La Monte Young, of course, when I picket and he is there to perform his public action— but by clearly shaping my own action as "picketing" even though there is only me there, I am making my action [interpretable] only as a public or political action, not as a private communication.[75]

Again, his argument comes from Young's policing—and Conrad is fully aware of this. As he told the New York Times in 2000, "If I had all of these tape copies sitting on my shelf right now, you'd probably not have the advantage of all this rich discourse."[76] Politics emerges from the police and requires it; it appears within a heterogeneous space in which the logic of order is confronted by the force of equality to open a space of dissensus.

Conrad's noisy discourse is heterogeneous to the system that Young recognizes and that sanctions his practice of authorship. At every moment that Young argues for the precedence of his cultural actions, Conrad introduces gaps premised on a different articulation of the scene through the recognition of collective, democratic labor and production. What has hopefully become clear is the rather asocial and sometimes ridiculous role authorship can take, particularly in mid-century avant-garde art music, when it relies simply on the heroic transcription of collective labor, understood in relation to a frontier mentality of new terrains opened. Continuing the spatial metaphor here is productive: where Young insists on expanding his fence further outward to claim more property under the existing logics of ownership in property, Conrad argues for the removal of the fence and subsequent disinvestment in the possibility of sole ownership in property. The buzzing drones of the Theatre of Eternal Music are used homonymically to argue both cases.

The drones can do this homonymic work—but how are they written as history? The important facet to me is how the name "Theatre of Eternal Music" has been written down. Young *could have* written music under his own name, or even performed it and insisted upon his own priority. The inscription of a collective nomination insists that it is *not* a single human, under a proper authorial name, doing the work alone.[77] The name attests to group activity, which we can safely assume to be heterogeneous. What makes the Theatre of Eternal Music unique, as opposed to the music of La Monte Young, is that the Theatre is a collaborative venture, inclusive of mathematical work in just intonation, a visual dimension in lighting and calligraphy, technical expertise with electronics and heavy amplification, poetic titles drawn from an idiomatic calendar, extensive deliberative discourse, and, perhaps most importantly, public presentation under a collective nomination. Music history's operative concept of authorship wants us to register each of these as less important than a proprietary claim about the positivist organization of pitches. Philosophy, acoustics, theory, lighting, mathematics, poetic titling, amplification, teaching, tuning, listening—the operative order of historical reason insists—are not acts of authorship in music, because they were not performed by people already (or even retrospectively) labeled Composer, the person whose place it is to *write* music (and this even when the music is not written down, but only piggybacks on the historical connection between musical genre and material inscription). They are merely resources to be extracted and organized by a composer who knows better. Authorship in Western art music—even in the mid-twentieth century—functions at least in part through the *wrong* of its ability to deny others the equal validity of their self-determined contributions to a musical relationality.

By contrast, La Monte Young's vision of authorship is grounded in misdating, as in the *Compositions 1961*, or retrospective naming to set up precedent, as in the *Pre-Tortoise Dream Music* or *The Second Dream*, or the subsumption of the labor of others by creating hierarchies of input and tying each person to a role through historical "bonds." How has this been upheld as a positive vision of authorial politics? More importantly, what is it about art music historiography that demands a representative author be drawn out from the would-be collective? Is it still "art music" when that work of excision is required? Practices like dismissing supporting figures, investing in hierarchical relationships between particular contributions, and discursive assumptions around the authorial nature of performers' "bonds" emerge from a white supremacist devotion to the priority and privilege of the singular author. That is, art music historiography has found means of carving away "external" encounters that might draw away from the narrative of white composers begetting others in a continuous and singular causal lineage. History does not critically reflect or prove such devotions; rather, historiography is the stage for such claims, the language through which such appeals become not only viable but sanctified. Historiography carves out authorship, and authorship appeals to history for support. Even if we credit Young as the sole "composer" of the music (I do not), what distinguishes the Theatre of Eternal Music from La Monte Young is the possibility of claiming a *we* that is more than the sum of its parts as each is deliberatively refracted through the others.

Writing the Dream Music

I contend that the Theatre of Eternal Music functioned in its short time as a deliberative, collective community of equal "composer"-performers. This chapter has critiqued the existing history of this music that reads "Theatre of Eternal Music" as the name of "Young's ensemble" from 1962 to 1966. I chose instead to acknowledge how authorship can be differentially understood as a *wrong* across Conrad's synonymous nomination under the Dream Syndicate or the homonymic tension of the Theatre of Eternal Music redistributed in its proprieties.

I now turn to several archival traces to argue that the Theatre of Eternal Music was an adventure in collective composition that existed for less than two years, from December 1964 through the fall of 1966, and consisted of John Cale and Tony Conrad, strings; La Monte Young and Marian Zazeela, voices; and, in 1966, Terry Riley, voice. In taking on the collective name the Theatre of Eternal Music, these musicians manifested in their performances a compositional *we* for the first time in Western art music. Though, once again, in noting such, I want to argue strongly for the notion that minimalism probably should not be considered an "art music" for precisely such reasons. The construction of such a paradoxical space of indistinction is key to (early) minimalism's politics: the means by which the Theatre stakes its claim of radicalism and refusal (collective composition) at once dislocates them from one of the definitive criteria of "Western art music" while necessarily calling upon that generic association to retain the novelty of their immanent, polemical enunciation. Rancière's thought is important not only because it gives us the conceptual tools to recognize such moments, but also because it provides a history of such moments of revolt in dislocation through homonymic activity and redistributions of space. A liberal political theory would insist that the music of the Theatre could not simultaneously exist as a radical challenge *within* art music and *external to* art music as a result of its radical challenge. It is precisely this metonymic, recursive structure of the *wrong* that fuels many histories of radicalism as read by Rancière, and also the terrain on which the police call—nothing to see here!—comes into play as a call to order.[78] Indeed, the constitution of insides and outsides in response to the tactical staging of an inside that is outside (and vice versa) is a recurring site of insurgent revolt against hegemonic institutional structures. For example, while I will insist upon the historical relevance of the Theatre of Eternal Music for the rest of this chapter, Conrad's and Cale's identification with the name "Dream Syndicate" should not be forgotten: like the anarcho-syndicalist workers who occupied their factories to run them in the absence of their bosses, Conrad and Cale made the Dream Syndicate an ensemble identical to and inside of the Theatre of Eternal Music. They thus maintained their identification with and pride in their work but refused the logic of order and authority that allowed their production to be subsumed under the name of a delegating, managing authority. Such a definition draws attention to the metonymic workings of Rancièrian politics, which insists not on either work or its refusal, but the reconstitution of work as a source of disidentification rather than alienation.

The group's public self-presentation is visible in concert announcements and program notes, especially the invitations to small concerts written in Marian Zazeela's calligraphy.[79] Notably, then, in refusing the "authoritarian trappings" of the score, they nevertheless did not abandon textual inscription. In his 2000 open letter, Young claims conceptual responsibility for a diamond-shaped presentation of members' names, as a means of "giving the musicians billing as performers with no mention of a composer, in order to give me time to think over *a problem that I had never dreamed of.*"[80] The problem in question was the insurrectionary claim by Conrad and Cale of the music's collective provenance. Young claims this occurred around the time he began singing rather than playing saxophone—what Cale would call the time the rest of the group "drove [Young] off the saxophone."[81]

The diamond is present in typed print, with Young's name bolded and larger, in the announcement for the series of concerts at the Pocket Theatre on 20–22 November (Figure 2). A few weeks later, a 10 December 1964 preview in the *Village Voice* for the performances at the same venue on 12–13 December still feature Young's name in bold font in contrast to the other three performers (Figure 3). Their names now encircle the collective name "Theatre of Eternal Music," several months earlier than Edward Strickland's claim that, "according to Young, the first documented use of the name dates from February 1965."[82] The next available use of the name is the 4 March 1965 performance at the East End Theatre, the program booklet of which includes on its cover only the words "The Theatre of Eternal Music." The first inside page repeats the collective name, laying out below it, in a typed diamond, the four constitutive names, all of equal size and density (Figure 4).[83] (This same

Figure 2. Theatre of Eternal Music concert announcement in the *Village Voice*, 19 November 1964

Figure 3. Theatre of Eternal Music concert announcement in the *Village Voice*, 10 December 1964).

typed layout is used for an undated program note from a performance of *The Ballad of the Tortoise or Pierced Earrings*, a work that Jeremy Grimshaw's chronology lists as having been performed sometime between *The Obsidian Ocelot*, the piece transcribed for Young's score for the *day of the antler*, and 7 early in 1966).[84] The rest of the East End Theatre program's contents are considered below.

The group's most striking self-presentation frequently leaves aside the collective name in favor of Zazeela's inscription of all four members' names

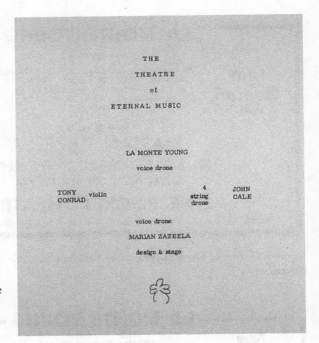

Figure 4. Internal page of East End Theatre Program, American Poets Theatre

in an increasingly ornate diamond formation that attests the group's evolving collective organization. Among Zazeela's most compelling calligraphy works are the small, folded cards on heavy white paper sent out to people like Peter Yates and Steve Reich (among many others, presumably) inviting them to small, private concerts.[85] Posters for the 30–31 October, 20–22 November, and 12–13 December series at the Pocket Theatre present all four names, in equal font size, encircling the title of the performance (Figure 5).

Another, to be held at the apartment of Museum of Modern Art curator Henry Geldzahler on 7 March 1965, just days after the East End Theatre performance, presents all names equally, eschewing much of the ornamentation from the Pocket Theatre card (Figure 6). Here, in place of a specific performance title, the names surround the broader genre name, "Dream Music," which the group had used for the first time in the program to the 1964 Pocket Theatre performances (discussed below). Despite using the more generic title, a work list that Young sent to Yates in late 1965 suggests that the group was performing *The Obsidian Ocelot, the Sawmill, and the Blue Sawtooth High-Tension Line Stepdown Transformer*, the same work that they performed at the East End Theatre and later that year at the Theatre Upstairs at the

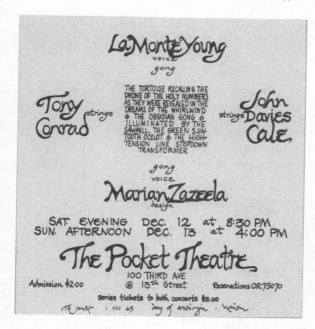

Figure 5. Detail of invitation to Theatre of Eternal Music performances, 12–13 December 1964. Calligraphy by Marian Zazeela.

Playhouse on 16 October 1965 (and which Young transcribed for a Guggenheim fellowship grant in late 1965, and was subsequently published in Potter's *Four Musical Minimalists*).

A pair of invitations from 1966 show the developing artistry of Zazeela's calligraphic presentation.[86] The first, at the invitation of Larry Poons and Geldzahler, is for a concert series at Poons's loft, "The Four Heavens," on 24–27 February 1966 (Figure 7). The title of the performances is simply *7*, with all four names encircling the single number. The names have changed though: Terry Riley now fills space on the right side of the diamond left open by Cale's departure after the Filmmakers' Cinematheque concerts of December 1965.

A final invitation marks the height of Zazeela's calligraphic representation of their collective organization: an invitation, "On the Occasion of the Opening of Midsummer '66," to Christoff De Menil's festival at her home in Amagansett, Long Island, for two evenings of performances of a newer work, *The Celebration of the Tortoise* (Figure 8).[87] In a bootleg recorded that weekend, Riley's voice—much lower than either Young's or Zazeela's—creates the impression of root movement as the three voices intertwine and move around Conrad's solitary strings. Riley sent a letter to Steve Reich on 2 August

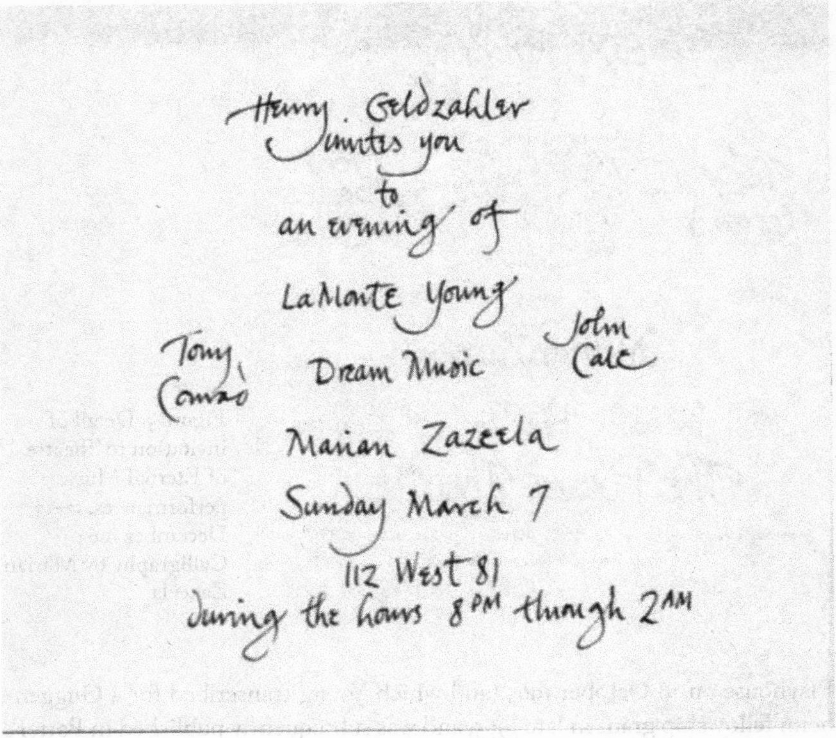

Henry Geldzahler
invites you
to
an evening of
La Monte Young
Tony Conrad
Dream Music
John Cale
Marian Zazeela
Sunday March 7
112 West 81
during the hours 8 PM through 2 AM

Figure 6. Detail of invitation to Theatre of Eternal Music performance at Henry Geldzahler's loft, 7 March 1965. Calligraphy by Marian Zazeela.

1966—dated "the day of the great return" in MacLise's calendar—where he says they had just returned from a week in Long Island performing concerts for people whose extreme wealth seems distasteful to Riley. The letter is sparsely typed in metered lines across a whole page in a playful, post-Beat or psychedelic style: "huge artistic and financial expense produced another jeweled tortoise and best playing weve done together that is tony lamonte marion terry together playing best."[88] Riley suggests at this point, following one of their last known performances, that it was their best ever, and is clearly of the impression that this was a collective creative effort rather than a performance of Young's music.

Two transcriptions of the Dream Music help fill in the archival gap between the early 1965 invitations and those of 1966. First is La Monte Young's score for *the day of the antler*, which he claims was written out in

Figure 7. Detail of invitation to Theatre of Eternal Music performances at "The Four Heavens" (loft artist Larry Poons), 24–27 February 1966. Calligraphy by Marian Zazeela.

Zazeela's calligraphy in November 1965. The "score" should more properly be considered a transcription for two reasons. First, it was written down after the fact, from an 15 August 1965 tape recording of Cale, Conrad, Young, and Zazeela. In contrast to the Cagean "chain reaction of paper," provoked by his belated transcription and publication of *Variations II* and other works, Young did not publish the work.[89] Indeed, in keeping with his practices, he kept it entirely locked away and private, aside from submission for a Guggenheim grant, until allowing Potter to publish it at the height of the dispute between Young and Conrad (and on the eve of the release by Table of the Elements of *Day of Niagara*).

Moreover, the "score" was never used as a set of performance directions for a work by La Monte Young. We are once again drawn into the recursive historiographical problematics of Young's authorship. Within the pages of a musicological text like Potter's, the presentation of the score makes a stronger claim for authorship than Young himself may have intended when he

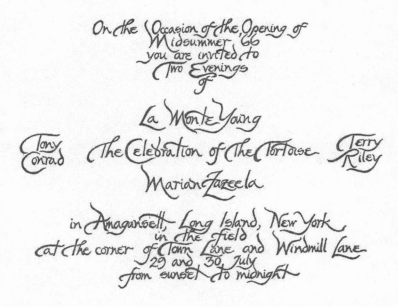

Figure 8. Detail of invitation to Theatre of Eternal Music performance in Amagansett, Long Island, 29–30 July 1966. Calligraphy by Marian Zazeela.

had Zazeela write it out for submission for a Guggenheim grant in 1966. When one reads a score, even an unconventional one like *the day of the antler*, the name at the top is read as author of the sounds because the written document is presumed to have authorized and directed performance. In never having fulfilled this role, the score, as foundation of Potter's defense of Young's authorship, enables a conceptual leap that is exposed as such in light of more recent available evidence.[90] Allowing Potter to publish the "score" is entirely at odds with Young's typical secrecy; giving permission for its publication during the period of intense critique, and only months before Table of the Elements released *Day of Niagara*, was likely strategic: Young could now point to his writing in a peer-reviewed, scholarly publication, rather than in a filing cabinet in his apartment, as evidence of his sole propriety of the music. Such a claim would have been well received in court.

Young's score takes the form of a chart, a "system of frequencies," outlining the just intonation pitches performed on 15 August 1965 as part of *The*

INSIDE THE DREAM SYNDICATE

Tony Conrad

"*The Obsidian Ocelot, the Sawmill, and the Blue Sawtooth High-Tension Line Stepdown Transformer Refracting the Legend of the Dream of the Tortoise Traversing the 189/98 Los Ancest- tral Lake Region Illuminating Quotients from the Black Tiger Tapestries of the Drone of the Holy Numbers*"	Meyer-Epp the binary te: a new focus (turn a latter earlier Japan as easily like terially partic perceive sou because of el
La Monte Young	chain the foc
Tony Conrad *John Cale* *Marian Zazeela*	been a big i:

Figure 9. Detail of *Film Culture* 41 (1966): 5. Printed header for Tony Conrad's essay "Inside the Dream Syndicate."

Obsidian Ocelot, The Sawmill, and the Blue High-Tension Line Stepdown Trans- former. The page's gridded array designates which pitches were played by each member of the ensemble, written out equivalently in cycles per second, lowest binary form of partials, factors of the partial within the three octaves 512/64, nearest equal tempered pitch, and so forth.[91] "Theatre of Eternal Music" does not appear anywhere on the page, and the other members of the group are represented as (merely) "articulating instrument(s) or Voice(s)" in one col- umn, inscribing a delegation of pitch content that very likely never took place—at least not coming monodirectionally from Young to the performers. Notably, the individual's names are present, revealing that even Young at the time knew that to designate the score for "violin, viola, and two voices" would have undercut the collective labor of their project. Young imagines his posi- tion, as Potter notes, as "more equal" in being listed as both an articulating voice and the top-billed figure casting his sovereign, authorial glance down upon the entire score—a composer-performer among performers. As Pot- ter writes, "The group clearly provided the elaboration of it, each performer being ultimately responsible for his own part. But the interaction not only included Young as one of the protagonists but was also, on the available evi- dence, driven by someone who acknowledges that he is 'very authoritarian.'"[92] Unlike all other contemporaneous concert announcements, program notes, and invitations, the diamond formation of proper names is entirely absent, suggesting that Young considered it a concession unnecessary in this context.

Both the ecstatic tone of Riley's letter and the diamond-shaped presentation of names are present in another transcription of the Dream Music from around the same time as Young's score. In 1965, Conrad's film *The Flicker* gained enough notoriety that the journal *Film Culture* dedicated three items to it in its first issue of 1966: an interview with Conrad, Conrad's November 1965 letter about the structure of the film, and an essay he wrote about his analogous work in music.[93] Conrad's essay, "Inside the Dream Syndicate," begins with the same title as Young's score, suggesting that the essay is, in some sense, a transcription, if we take that to mean broadly the inscription of marks on paper in response to music (Figure 9).

Conrad's techno-utopian essay is dated June 1965, and thus was written prior to the August 1965 *day of the antler* tape, though only shortly after the *day of niagra* tape, later released by Table of the Elements, from April 1965. Throughout, Conrad writes in the first-person plural.[94] He explicates the theoretical foundations of the ensemble, their performance practice, influences, political goals, and interaction with technology—features that I have outlined above in relation to his writing in *Early Minimalism*. Predating Reich's better-known "Music as a Gradual Process" by three years, "Inside the Dream Syndicate" can be seen as the first manifesto of early minimalism: "Our music is . . . droningly montonal [*sic*], not even being built on a scale at all, but out of a single chord or cluster of more or less tonically related partials"; the "seven[th harmonic] sounds to us as clear as vulgar 5[th; major/minor thirds] once did; the ear does magically retrain." "We sometimes modulate to 7, 9, or 63, but rarely."[95] Turning to the group's political goals, he writes: "The genius of conglomerate [i.e., collaborative or collective] action raises the overall harmonic operative level beyond what is rationally controllable [by a single author] without great care."[96] The possibility of their conglomerate action is based in a technological utopianism developed from their interaction with the noises of the city, which "are not ever pitchless":

> [The music opens up a] collaborative awareness of the machines. Alternating current is pouring into this building; we only alter, modify, store, and use it as our energies direct. We treat it with respect of machines for the source of all power, and it gives us the 6th partial of our Tonic, 10 [cycles per second]. It is in the air. Outside the domain of 60 cycle current, our music will fall less resonantly on the city ear, the most tonal of all cultures.[97]

This new form of listening in which performers harmonize, in pure tuning, with the power grid leads to the timbral indistinction that Peter Yates described in his *Arts and Architecture* review of an October 1964 performance: "The resulting accumulation of never more than four tones in correct acoustical relationship produced a play of overtones and difference tones which, via loudspeaker, seemed almost orchestral."[98] Conrad sees this as a musical realization of their collectivist political goals:

> After the years pass, we fail to have consciousness of the changes: the voices sound like something else, the violin is the echo of the saxophone, the viola is by day frightening rock 'n roll orchestra, by night the sawmill. . . . Ours is the first generation with tape, with proper amplification to break down the dictatorial sonority barriers erected by the master instruments of the cultures.[99]

The Dream Music is a political action, grounded in collectivity and listening, enabled by both modern technology and the deliberative process of composing drones. And the group composes-performs drones precisely because they challenge the norms of musical authorship, offering a pitched and rhythmic minimization such that group deliberation over resources is possible while individual effort plays out through attentive listening to timbre, texture, intonation, while avoiding the rhythmic beating of clashing overtones. Amplification bypasses individual performers' sound differences, and tape the necessity of the authorizing gesture of the score.

These two examples from 1965—Young's *day of the antler* "score," and Conrad's "Inside the Dream Syndicate" manifesto—are both "transcriptions" in that they present their creators inscribing marks on paper in retroactive response to the new music they were making in rehearsal and onto tape; they are both documents of a new sound, in relation to which choices had to be made as to what means of inscription were appropriate. The distinction here of the genre of writing is extremely important, as it was when we considered the contrasting receptions possible when "Music as a Gradual Process" is differently framed as a manifesto, an essay, or "theory" (see Chapter 1). While I criticized Young for his sole billing on his score, I do not think the critique is necessary in terms of Conrad's byline in his manifesto. The conventions of reading a score suggest that the author on top of the page is the author of the *sounds* transcribed; the same generic convention is not assumed for an essay, and perhaps even less so for a manifesto. Conrad, as a member of the group, is writing about the sound; nothing about his essay suggests his sole authorship of the sounds about which he is writing. For Conrad, writing provides a chance for an ecstatic manifesto drawing on the group's performance methods and constituting the Theatre of Eternal Music rhetorically within the pronoun "we"; for Young, the music is an opportunity to cast a collective effort within an authoritarian medium from which several members thought they had found an escape.

Lastly, I would like to consider another set of documents of this music—documents that would have actually been read by audiences in the same space and time as performances of the Dream Music, providing context for what they were hearing. Jeremy Grimshaw notes that Young's "Dream Music" essay first appeared in an "unknown" concert program in 1964.[100] The essay was subsequently reprinted in literature on Young, and scholars have cited the essay from any of three sources: Young's 1969 *Selected Writings* published by the Heiner Friedrich Gallery; the 2004 online "second edition" of the writings by ubuweb.com; or issue 9 of *Aspen* magazine, "The Psychedelic Issue," edited by Angus and Hetty MacLise.[101] The essay draws extensively on Young's tortoise imagery, discussing the animal's conceptual influence on the music's longevity. He also theorizes his compositional practice, noting "the Disappearance of Melody" in that this music's sole melodic content is implied "by the overtone structure of the fundamental" of one sound, leaving any notion of melodic movement to the listener's preconditioning. He argues for the development of "Dream Houses" that will create a living tradition, become literal organisms because of their internal standing waveform interactions, their longevity, and their precise intonation that ensures that all intervals are constantly the same.

Though Young notes in his 2000 letter that the essay was first published as part of the program note for the East End Theatre performances, he certainly cuts short its context. Indeed, the essay was embedded in the middle of the essay presented at the first concerts billed collectively as the Theatre of Eternal Music, those in December 1964 at the Pocket Theatre, and in March 1965 at the East End Theatre. As Grimshaw notes, the program was unknown or lost, but scans of the full East End Theatre program were recently posted online as part of an archive of materials from the American Poets Theatre, and Young's correspondence with Peter Yates includes a letter dated "16 I 65" (16 January 1965) in which he attached the program notes for the December Pocket Theatre concert series.[102] The East End Theatre program, as originally printed for all of these concerts, introduces Young's much-quoted essay with this introduction:

Welcome to this presentation of Dream Music. *We are pleased* to be continuing our performance of "The Tortoise, His Dreams and Journeys."

In "The Obsidian Ocelot, The Sawmill, and The Blue Sawtooth High-Tension Line Stepdown Transformer Refracting The Legend of The Dream of The Tortoise Traversing The 189/98 Lost Ancestral Lake Region Illuminating Quotients from The Black Tiger Tapestries of The Drone of The Holy Numbers," *we have chosen* to demonstrate only a select group of pitches which are found in the structure of the overtone series of bowed strings and vocal cords.

"We" is clearly the Theatre of Eternal Music of the cover page, credited—as in Conrad's essay, but unlike Young's score—in a diamond shape on the inside page of the program, with no composer or author suggested. Young writes about this in his 2000 open letter: "after the first group concerts in which I did not play saxophone, but rather sang"—spring or early summer of 1964, when they had not yet taken on the name Theatre of Eternal Music— Conrad and Cale began to raise the issue of all four members' collective input into the works they performed. Young was caught off guard, but in an effort to avoid "hurt[ing] their feelings," and because he "did appreciate their collaborative contributions on the levels of performance, philosophy, theory, physics and mathematics," the "problem was *temporarily* ameliorated by establishing a method of billing the artists on posters and in advertisements" in the diamond-shaped layout shown on the title page of the East End Theatre program, and in Zazeela's poster/programs.[103] Young writes, "This did not deal with the problem of who was the composer, but rather avoided coming to an agreement on the issue by simply listing the individuals as performing artists and giving me top billing, Tony and John equal billing to each other, Marian symmetrical billing to me, and each of us equal distance from the title of the work being performed."[104] Young never dreamed that any performer would claim that they had helped develop the piece, rather than simply performing it and accepting that as their "place," as the historical bonds (and hierarchies) in relation to the composer had long been established. For Conrad and Cale, "bond" is surely the wrong term, marred as it is by particular social conventions and formations.

Adding to Young's problematic reproduction of the content of the "Dream Music" essay, it does not end at the point where Young stops it in his own publications. I would like to underline several passages following the point where Young's own publications suggest the essay ended, at "the tapestry of Eternal Music."

First, the "we" continues throughout: at no point is any member made to speak for the whole group. In keeping with one of the primary rhetorical functions of collectives throughout history—whether a new republic ("We the people"), a workers' union, a political party, an arts collective, and so on, all of which often turn to the manifesto as a genre—the essay relies on the first-person plural to acknowledge that, in banding together under a collective name and cause, though still revealing the constituent parts, no single member can or should speak as sole representative.[105] As Marianne DeKoeven writes, this "communal 'we,'" in the context of the 1960s counterculture, arts manifestos, and student protest, "was always an aggregate of consenting, actively participating individuals."[106] This is the clear and intentional rhetorical positioning in the essay, as it is in Conrad's *Film Culture* essay. Second, the "we" engages in very careful positioning of influence and performance practice:

> We recall [from past performances of *The Tortoise*] . . . that in order to produce convincing textures exemplary of more complex rational frequency ratios than are used in almost any other music and at the same time to maintain the forcefulness of just intonation as found occasionally in Oriental, Country and Western, or pre-Baroque music and often in sounds of electrical equipment and machinery, the performers avoid vibrato or other rhythmic changes.

The influences mentioned here draw upon on all members of the ensemble: the "Oriental" music of Ali Akhbar Khan, whose first American LP (1959) had a substantial impact on Zazeela, Young, and Conrad;[107] the country-and-western music on which Young was raised in rural Idaho, and to which Conrad and Cale had been obsessively listening with Henry Flynt; and, most strikingly, the pre-Baroque music of, presumably, Heinrich Biber—a genealogical trace that has never been mentioned in any literature on Young and Zazeela, but is central to Conrad's autobiography. These influences were taken up in a performance practices that refused vibrato (as in the pre-Baroque "fiddling" of Biber) and rhythmic changes, which subsequently "led the group to amplify each sound source, so as to make the presence of partials and combination tones accessible to the listener."[108]

The document retains this close focus on the listener, and is something that we can find in both Young and Conrad—as well as in Reich and Glass later—in stark contrast to the other American art music of the time, which had a decisive and frequently noted lack of concern for audience listening practices. Even more concrete confirmation of the presence of more voices than simply Young's in this program note comes from Young to Peter Yates, where he explicitly claims that the program notes were created in much the same way as the music: through collective collaboration and improvisation. Young tells Yates that he wrote the sections that constitute the "Dream Music" essay, while Conrad wrote paragraphs 4 through 7.[109]

Young's comment neither entirely seals the case on "who wrote what," nor suffices critically to merely label him as a hypocrite and move on. Indeed, we need only look at the sole letter that Conrad sent to Yates, in November 1965, at Young's suggestion, in which he explains what the string players were doing when Yates heard them in performance in October 1965. Conrad writes of how proud he is of the music he has "been involved in for the last several years in collaboration with La Monte Young, Marian Zazeela, and John Cale." He continues by calling Young the "leader of the group." Conrad still held to this label in our conversation in September 2015, noting that Young was a person of great influence in the New York art scene, with money, connections, gear, and a loft to make the whole thing possible.[110] He nevertheless rejects the conceptual leap that would turn this set of contingent social facts—and much less the act of having transcribed one of the tapes—into legal or theoretical sole property in the sounds produced in their rehearsals and performances. In refusing authorship as grounded in the score, the Theatre removed the possessive grounds of authorship. To return to Conrad's Buffalo picket, the concern was not a misunderstanding of the music, but of the relations of production and property as passively imagined under the normative conception of authorship. Authorship, in short, could no longer be assumed—it had to be constructed, and the modes through which that happened were less through collaborative production in sound than through their written, historiographic account. Where Young has insisted that his authority self-evidently preexisted the members' daily arrival in their rehearsal space, Conrad has argued for the presupposition of egalitarian relation following the removal of delegating documents.

The Theatre of Eternal Music provides a clear account of such processes of collectivism policed. When a group claims to write and take responsibility for their music together, they are already butting up against the foundations of a distinct generic concept, a new way of hearing and thinking. Art music conventions are predicated on the belief that a collective is not capable of the same large-scale formal or conceptual coherence as an individual author writing down music in advance. This is the logic that nominates La Monte Young as the sole author of the music played by the Theatre of Eternal Music: his priority comes from the fact that the group's "dream" of its being deliberative is taken as clear evidence of Young's being in charge even while letting those around him think they are "doing their own thing." The music-historical production of a distinct literate practice called "art music" requires this singular authorship be extracted from the collective form just as much as Young does. According to Young, Wakoski, Riley, Johnson, Zazeela, Strickland, Potter, Schwarz, and others, collaborators like Conrad and Cale should have been aware that they were not and could not have been collaborators "doing their own thing" as a result of who they are and who Young is—they are performers of secondary status, and Young is the "founder" of minimalism, as evidenced retrospectively by a twelve-tone string trio written in 1958 and tied to their collective efforts several years later. Histories that handle authorship in this way create it as a discursive tool through which to dismiss or devalue, through deference to "the way things are," the work of some in relation to that of others. It is not only a retrospective analysis, but an inscription that carries forward a powerful model of how authorship will continue to be (mis)understood.

Three

The Lessons of Minimalism

The Big Four and the Pedagogic Myth

At some point between February 1969, when he wrote it, and April of the same year, when it was performed at the New School, Philip Glass shortened the name of his piece *Two Pages for Steve Reich* to simply *Two Pages*. Or at least Steve Reich has frequently made this claim. In his interview with the composer William Duckworth, for example, Reich maintained that the erasure of his name from the title caused "some grief" between him and Glass, and serves as a clear signal of Glass's unwillingness to recognize his friend's influence and pedagogic impact.[1] La Monte Young echoed this claim when he told Duckworth that Glass is convinced he came out of a "vacuum" compositionally.[2] At the time of the interviews, published in 1995, authorship, influence, and citation were major concerns among the minimalists—and both Young and Reich felt that Glass had built his career on refusing to recognize their impact on his own work.

Duckworth's interviews were not the only instance in which these issues were broached. Questions about the collaborative and fractured relationships among the "big four" minimalists are recurring features of their interviews not only with Duckworth, but also with Edward Strickland (1991) and K. Robert Schwarz (1996) from around the same time. In contrast, earlier interviews with Walter Zimmerman, Cole Gagne and Tracey Caras, Ev Grimes, or Michael Nyman never included questions about a minimalist lineage, or the relationship among these four composers.[3] Their interlocutors were certainly aware that these individuals had worked together, and that composers influence, teach, and help one another. But by the mid-1990s, it had become definitive of "minimalism" that Glass downplay Reich's influence, and interviewers seemed to run on the assumption that Riley or

Reich would spend part of each interview discussing the relative weight and importance of their exchange around the time of the premiere of *In C*. (And there was certainly no conversation about the roles of Tony Conrad, John Cale, or Laurie Spiegel in creating the style.) Wim Mertens, in the only book on "minimalism" written prior to these interviews (though the book's original Flemish title only mentioned "American repetitive music"), makes note of Young and Riley's collaboration, without ever dividing the space of collaboration into teacher and student.[4] Similarly, Riley and Reich go unmentioned in Mertens's chapters about each of them; Reich only comes up in a footnote in the chapter on Glass, when Mertens claims, directly against the ordering of the normative narrative, that "it is possible that *Glass influenced Reich*" in the use of sudden modulations.[5] There was simply no narrative ideal of minimalist collaboration and its inevitable failure that would encourage interviewers to probe its prehistory, who had been responsible for which developments, and whether or not appropriate credit was given. Nevertheless, in Strickland's *Minimalism: Origins* he was able to write, "It would be unfair and misleading to suggest a Minimalist 'genealogy' from Young to Riley to Reich to Glass, but," he continues, "one might suggest *a line of transmission of influence* in that chronological order, perhaps the inverse order of their current notoriety."[6]

In the previous chapter, I argued for the importance of collaboration and mutual exchange of ideas in making possible the Theatre of Eternal Music, and criticized La Monte Young's campaign of refusal. In this chapter I extend this argument into the less direct network of collaboration shared through the later 1960s among the three most famous minimalist composers—Terry Riley, Steve Reich, and Philip Glass. At its largest scale, this book is about the methods by which existing historiography of minimalism has refused and, in Kristin Ross's language, "confiscated" any political potential articulated in the early years of the style. In the case of the "big bang of minimalism"[7] in the Theatre of Eternal Music, this led me to stage what Rancière would call a moment of dissensus by returning to archival documents to put forward the claim that the group always *was* a compositional collective; that is, that there never was a "pure" authorial origin to minimalism in Young's primordial drones. Here, by contrast, my goal is to consider the discursive means by which the standardized "metaphysical narrative of minimalism" has been formed. Most importantly, I want to examine the underlying ideas of authorship, collaboration, influence, and pedagogy with which historians and critics have held together Riley, Reich, and Glass as "the minimalists."

How have historians simultaneously written up their early collaborations as fundamental to the style's countercultural origins while simultaneously tearing them apart as actual collaborators and friends working toward shared politico-aesthetic goals?

What I want to show is that the metaphysical account was largely narrated by the big four composers themselves, as is often plainly visible in their responses in a handful of interviews from the 1990s. Whereas much scholarship takes the view that critique should be based on an inversion of thought, or an assumption of composers' naivete and alienation from their own working methods, my mode of critique here goes in another direction by insisting that these composers are theorists and historians of their own practices. The public and historical priority of these four composers is certainly a matter of historical contingency—I could just as easily have been critiquing the discursive priority of a group that included people like Conrad, Charlemagne Palestine, Laurie Spiegel, Meredith Monk, Jon Gibson, and many others, in addition to or in place of the big four—but there are nevertheless grounds to argue that the big four minimalists, from at least the time that they all were living and working in New York, had already constituted a "scene." And if it was a scene, it was a particularly strong one: they were developing their ideas collaboratively, performing together in venues focused on similar work, and using these opportunities to compose to tape rather than paper, with collaboration and communication often spread across the two coasts.[8] The big four themselves paradoxically highlighted the very close interaction of their collaborative period by introducing, at each stage, an inegalitarian "pedagogic relation" of knowledge to nonknowledge. Maintaining the metaphysical narrative requires the insertion of an inegalitarian conception of pedagogy as a means of tying together the big four under the singular label "minimalism" while tearing them apart as equals or potential collaborators. Within the broader context of the critique of minimalist historiography outlined in the Introduction, there was a turn to filling the authoritative void created by the minimalist critique of compositional authority with a proleptically imposed and hierarchical idea of pedagogic authority. The suggestion that Young begat Riley begat Reich begat Glass is a pedagogical trajectory that ties them all together as a community in the 1960s, while simultaneously, in interviews and histories from the 1990s, tearing them apart as equals—and upholding the eminent dignity and individuality of compositional authorship as parceled out into discrete chunks of exchangeable "influence."

Abrutir: Stultification and Confiscation

That a particular narrative formation or historiographical politics has pedagogical foundations does not simply mean that it implies a program for teaching. Possible relationships between knowledge and ignorance, student and teacher, leaders and crowds were major themes of concern within '68-era thought. Indeed, it is in relation to thought about education, pedagogy, and authority that Rancière's relationship to his teacher Althusser is most often discussed. I would like to outline some of the major themes in Rancière's thought on pedagogy and intellectual equality. Doing so requires a brief diversion into what he was arguing *against* as represented in Althusser's work.

In "Student Problems" (1963), Louis Althusser argued against the demands of the Sorbonne student strike ongoing at the time by articulating to his readers the importance of the "pedagogic relation":[9] the fundamentally unequal relationship between knowledge and nonknowledge as embodied in the teacher and student. This inequality produces the need for the school, an institution charged with closing that gap. Rancière criticized this position at length in *Althusser's Lesson* (1974); later, in *The Ignorant Schoolmaster* (1981), he transforms the pedagogic relation into the "pedagogic myth": an image of the world split in two by those in positions of mastery—pedagogic, political, or otherwise—determined to uphold their own positions of authority by scorning the intelligence of others.[10] Rancière labels the mode of affirming one's own intelligence by presenting others as ignorant the *abrutir*. Rancière reflected more recently on the broad applicability of the *abrutir*, thus providing a clear sense of the driving ethical maxim in his work:

> I've imposed on myself a practical rule to work every day, to go to the library, learn something, write, and so on. For me, that's an egalitarian maxim. To caricature it a bit, the inegalitarian maxim says that it's a bit of a bore to have to go out, that it'd be better to stay at home and look at the papers or watch telly to see just how stupid people are, and tell yourself: I must be really intelligent since everyone else is so stupid. The choice of maxim is also this: *are you intelligent because everyone else is stupid, or are you intelligent because they are intelligent?* That's a Kant-style maxim: am I betting that the capacity to think I'm granting myself is everyone's capacity to think, or is my thinking to be distinguished by the fact that everyone else is a moron?[11]

This is perhaps the only maxim that comes up in Rancière's reflections on his own work: I read, I learn, and I tell myself—every day, constantly—that my intelligence is one shared with everyone else, and not something to be understood in *contrast to* the actions of others. This is a more universal articulation of the problem, positioned outside the distinct species of student-teacher relationships that were core to "Student Problems," *Althusser's Lesson,* and *The Ignorant Schoolmaster.* Here, the problem simply comes down to how we recognize our own innate intelligence: am I intelligent because everyone is (in our own, distinct, remarkable ways), or am I intelligent because everyone else is a moron?

Articulating the pedagogic foundations of a historiographical practice does not need to be specifically about education, then. Nevertheless, Rancière's thinking developed out of his own experiences during May '68 as well as a less epochal historical-scholastic event. *The Ignorant Schoolmaster* of his title is Joseph Jacotot (1770–1840), an exiled French academic who taught students at the University of Louvain in 1818 despite not speaking Flemish. (Jacotot worked in a more forgiving academic job market than the one my generation has inherited.) As a result of this inability, he developed a pedagogic philosophy—he called it Universal Teaching—premised on the belief that all people are of equal intelligence and, accordingly, that anybody can teach anything to anyone. The challenge of teaching, then, is not to portion out kernels of knowledge, but to find the means by which "to reveal an intelligence to itself."[12]

A keen piece of archival work and a compelling philosophy of politics and pedagogy, *The Ignorant Schoolmaster* has drawn attention to Rancière's writing style for how he ventriloquizes Jacotot's words, creating zones of indistinction between who is speaking, from which historical period, and toward which disciplinary and discursive ends. In her translator's introduction, Kristin Ross outlines a further dimension to the book in how it proposed an allegorical intervention into the 1980s debate over French president François Mitterand's pedagogic reforms. Drawing upon the work of Pierre Bourdieu on the reproduction of distinction and inequality in the education system, the French educational reforms focused on the racist and infantilizing suggestion that "the children of the working class—and especially immigrants— should be provided with a less 'abstract' or 'cultural' curriculum."[13] Rancière insisted that any pedagogical system that presupposes the relative ignorance or intelligence of anyone based on their social background is guaranteed to reproduce the same stratifications. The text is thus an intervention, from the 1980s, into the developments that had taken place for many of the concepts (equality, education, authority) and figures central to the 1968 moment, all through the guise of a recovery from the Romantic archive of Jacotot, a figure that Rancière describes as an Enlightenment anachronism in his own time.

The Jacotot-Rancière philosophy of intellectual egalitarianism criticizes pedagogues who operate from the assumption that the "essential act of the master [is] to *explicate*: to disengage the simple elements of learning, and to reconcile their simplicity in principle with the factual simplicity that characterizes young and ignorant minds."[14] Explication is rendered as "the myth of pedagogy, the parable of a world divided into knowing minds and ignorant ones, ripe minds and immature ones, the capable and the incapable, the intelligent and the stupid."[15] This logic of explication regresses infinitely, with the constant need of more pedagogues to explicate more concepts and to bring to life the muteness of texts that, before all else, teach students of their inability to make sense (to engage in sense-making) without the oversight of the great explicator. The pedagogic myth, grounded in explication as method, teaches a child "that he doesn't understand unless he is explained to."[16] Jacotot calls this mode of teaching—the typical mode of teaching, well known in most childhood learning with the notable exception of the mother tongue—*enforced stultification*. We can recognize Althusser's pedagogic relation in play here. Despite how regressive such a philosophy of teaching sounds in the twenty-first century, we must not forget that much revision in pedagogic theory, for decades now, battles against what Paulo Freire calls the banking model of education, in which students are imagined as empty vessels to be filled with valuable knowledge.

Stultification is an imperfect rendering; Ross includes a footnoted caveat that "in the absence of a precise English equivalent for the French term *abrutir* (to render stupid, to treat like a brute)," she translates the term as "stultify."[17] This chapter revolves precisely around this *abrutir*—that is, a critical staging of particular pedagogies as a *rendering brutish*. We already witnessed the immodest lesson Richard Taruskin provided to Steve Reich, the "sixties agitator" in Chapter 1. Pedagogy thus names the rendering brutish assumed of the enforced stultifications of typical explication while also naming the possibility of an egalitarian teaching. As always, the name includes both politics and police: an inherent tension between an egalitarian assumption and a historically specific call to order. We are therefore obliged to remind ourselves that our intelligence is reflected and echoed in all other acts of the human intellect, rather than as standing in relief against them.

Vigilance to stultification in historiography requires keeping a keen eye for writing that articulates a before and an after demarcated by a form of revelation or discovery. (It can also appear more literally as in Taruskin's and Reich's criticisms of "Music as a Gradual Process": manifestos are by stupid people.) I recognize the metaphysical narrative of minimalism as having a foundation in Rancière's pedagogic *myth*: that the world is divided into those who know and those who do not, those of superior intelligence and inferior intelligence, those of capacity and those of incapacity. Rancière's egalitarian project insists that this is not the case, and thus that those who insist upon it are constantly reasserting and upholding its fiction through the *abrutir*. The practices of stultification examined below among the minimalists most often take the form of one or another figure enacting an *abrutir* by suggesting that another composer with whom they worked was a brute before their mutual encounter, after which the latter failed to properly credit the teacher with the revelation. It would of course be uniquely brutish to actually call someone, particularly a friend and collaborator, a "brute" with any seriousness, but it is the rhetorical structure of this claim that is important: the suggestion that one's colleague or collaborator was *merely* writing in such a way before— temporal demarcation—I showed this benighted individual the light by becoming a guide across an intellectual divide. The interviews with the minimalists discussed below frequently operate in the language of education and pedagogy, teachers and students; the *abrutir* nevertheless arrives on a more abstract scale that, at times, requires working through. The staging of befores and afters marks an event in the sense of a conversion that operates under an authorial proper name revelatory of a concept in relation to which discourse is oriented. The *abrutir* of stultification is another practice of rendering early.

Interviewing the Big Four

In interviews with Edward Strickland (1991), William Duckworth (1995), and K. Robert Schwarz (1996), the relationships between Terry Riley, Steve Reich, and Philip Glass are portrayed along very consistent lines. Beginning briefly in California in the early 1960s before all arriving in New York in 1965, the big four organized and authorized their relationship three decades after the fact into a cohesive narrative well known to fans of minimalist music. With the support of their interviewers, the four composers produced a minimalist commons founded on failed collaborations articulated through theories of pedagogic priority.

From his earliest work, as Wim Mertens has noted, Terry Riley's practice centered on performance and collaboration.[18] After his "inseparable" friend La Monte Young's move to New York following their graduation from University of California at Berkeley in 1960, Terry Riley headed to Paris in February 1962 and spent several years performing ragtime on military bases, and in bars, floor shows, and circuses. This situation was quite distinct from most composers recently graduated from prestigious universities at the time, though he shifted his attention back to composition when Ken Dewey asked Riley to score *The Gift*:

> Ken rented an old chateau in the Valdomois, south of Paris. All the actors and everybody lived in it while the show was being put together. . . . We rehearsed in the barn. . . . I'd come to the chateau at night and bring back the tapes I'd been working on. We'd listen to them, and the actors would try to get a sense of how to relate to the music. Occasionally Chet [Baker] and the band would come out to the chateau and we'd have a full rehearsal with everybody. Ken would watch the whole thing and would try to get the actors to interact more with the musicians, and try to get the musicians to be more involved with the action.[19]

Communal and collaborative development of work, as well as directors who view their role as encouraging interaction, is definitive of artistic production in this period. Paired with the "very straight guy in a white coat" from French National Radio who created Riley's now famous "time-lag accumulator,"[20] Robert Carl suggests that writing *Music for "The Gift"* provided "the last piece in the puzzle" in assembling a set of compositional precedents—and working methods—for *In C*.[21]

When the army clubs that Riley had been performing at abroad were closed as a sign of respect following the Kennedy assassination, Riley returned to the United States. He tells Strickland, "*Music for "the Gift"* made me want to try a live piece that would have the same effect"—not only the tape effects but also the communal and collaborative method.[22] He began working with small modules looped by performers, but the ideas were not working out. Around this time, his friend Bill Spencer invited Riley to join him at a performance of the San Francisco Mime Troupe, featuring music by Steve Reich's free improvisation group. "It was Steve and a few other people. I can't remember, but maybe Jon Gibson was there. They were performing music that Steve had done for the Mime Troupe."[23] Riley continues the story, noting that he was not impressed by the music: "I went to the first half and left." Reich, presumably aware of who Riley was, noticed the slight. Riley says:

> The next day at my studio in a garage up on Bernal Heights, where Steve also lived, though I didn't know it, there was a bang on the door, and it was Steve Reich. He was so *furious*, right? So I told him

to come in. We sat down and got to know each other. I showed him
In C, which I was working on, and he helped me a lot. He was really
enthusiastic for the project. He wanted to *do* it.[24]

Reich and Riley's relationship around *In C* is discussed at length below; for
now I am interested only in setting up the terms of their introduction.

"In despair of Vietnam," Riley sold Reich his tape equipment and headed
to Mexico in June 1965. Reich moved to New York in September, as he was
"no longer easy with the cultural situation in California . . . including the
emergence of a heavier drug scene."[25] Riley followed, arriving in New York
in October, having driven with his wife and daughter to Veracruz in their
Volkswagen bus with the intention of shipping it to Tangiers. When they
could not get a boat—at least not the cheap one a hippie friend had told
them of—they drove back up to New York to get a boat from there, "but [he]
started hanging out with La Monte again and renewing old acquaintances,"
as he told William Duckworth.[26] Riley immediately began rehearsing with
the Theatre of Eternal Music, soon to replace John Cale after his final performance with the group in December 1965 at the Filmmakers' Cinematheque.[27]
During the years that Riley stayed in New York (1965–69), he and Reich
saw one another but did not work together professionally: "Several associates confirm that at the time [Riley] was annoyed that Reich was gaining
recognition *by exploiting ideas he had originated*." Reich confirms this: "There
was definitely strain. Terry felt that I was ripping him off, *just the way I felt
later that Phil was ripping me off.* We saw each other, but it was not comfortable."[28] Keith Potter has similarly considered their close interaction, noting
that beyond their collaboration on *In C*, the two had frequently exchanged
tape compositions, including Riley's *She Moves She*, which Reich recalls having heard. "Riley's insecurity over his friend's adoption of modular repetition
using speech material on tape was compounded when," according to Riley,
"people would say, 'Oh, you're doing the kind of stuff Reich does!' And that
hurts, you know."[29]

Despite the absence of professional collaboration, a letter from Riley to
Reich dated "day of the great return"—2 August 1966 in Angus MacLise's
calendar-poem *YEAR*—informs Reich that he was headed back to New York
from the Theatre of Eternal Music's *Celebration of the Tortoise* concert. Riley
responds to a suggestion or offer (it's unclear as no carbon of Reich's letter is
present) from Reich for Riley to put on a performance of *In C* at the Film-
ore in San Francisco. Despite being the only letter from Riley in the Reich
archive, it clearly shows a friendly relationship between the two at that time.

This stands in contrast to ongoing insistence that the two were on bad terms; Strickland notes that when Reich moved back to New York after a long road trip,[30] he "did not seek to collaborate further with Riley." The end of his formal performance and collaboration with Riley reoriented Reich's affiliations, marking a shift from a Californian to New York aesthetic. Reich tells Strickland, "I came back to New York in the fall of '65. At the time I felt very much out of place. Downtown it was basically works by or in imitation of John Cage, Morton Feldman, Christian Wolff, and Earle Brown. Uptown it was pieces in imitation of Stockhausen, Boulez, and Berio. I felt equidistant from both."[31] Reich continues, "I began to realize that I was somewhat in isolation. I knew what Riley was doing, and I knew what La Monte was doing [they were working together at the time]. They were the people I knew who were doing something like this, but we didn't get on personally at that time. When Phil [Glass] came along, I befriended him and gave him the ensemble to use because it was nice to have somebody to talk to."[32]

In the 1990s interviews, the genre concept "minimalism" has been cohesively standardized alongside an instrumentalization of the roles of each of the big four composers who constitute it. It was simultaneously more stable than it had been in the prior two decades, and had not yet gained the critical attention it has received since. As with many prior "-isms," the label relies simultaneously on stylistic or aesthetic affinities and actual personal relationships—indeed, to the point that the biographical encounters come to color the musical understandings. Riley becomes a conduit between Young and Reich in his movement from Berkeley to San Francisco (to Paris to Mexico) to New York much as Reich becomes a connection between Riley and Glass. While these biographical affinities are certainly factual, they take on an overdetermined importance in understanding their musical engagements and the *conceptual* exchange that operated between them. This is perhaps clearest in considering how each responded when prompted to explain the origin and transmission of minimalism.

Asked by Duckworth to define his idea of a "minimalist hierarchy," Riley highlights Young's influence, calling the *Trio for Strings* "the landmark minimalist piece." "La Monte introduced . . . this concept of not having to press ahead to create interest"; Riley continues, "Without that there could have been no *In C*, because *In C* is a static piece in that same tradition." Riley then continues on from his relationship with Young:

> Even though [*In C*] uses fields with repetitious patterns, it *couldn't have existed* without this other concept [Young's stasis] being born first. So then, Steve Reich played in the first performance of *In C*. Before that,

he was studying with Berio and his music, I think, reflected more of an interest in European music. So obviously, after *In C* he *changed his style*, and starting using repetition and developing his own style of phases and pulses.[33]

He makes even stronger claims in his interview with K. Robert Schwarz. Young had "very evolved thoughts about music, and I thought it was better than what I was getting from the teachers I came to [Berkeley to] study with."[34] Riley's conception of history as grounded in influence and teleology centers on the pedagogic function: the idea of *concepts* in place of techniques, and that concepts beget other concepts; that Reich's studies had been in one (more conservative, European) direction, but that the trajectory was altered by his involvement with Riley. In continuing his concept of minimalism onward to Glass, Riley only intensifies the pedagogic language: "Then after that, Phil Glass played with Steve, and of course *Steve was his teacher*." Riley's commentary on the dispute between Reich and Glass makes clear that this was a going concern at the time, and extremely visible; indeed, I would argue that at this point, in the early to mid-1990s, *the fact of dispute* was the connective logic of the minimalist hierarchy.[35]

Popular press handling of these and similar disputes often recalls for me the trope in action films or detective fiction of the archenemies who *used to be partners* prior to a, generally unmarked, falling out. The basic narrative impulse is cliché, frustrating: the fact of having been close, even partners, colleagues, friends, in a "time before" is a simple means of hinting at prehistorical conflict, creating the impression of complexity outside of a story without doing the actual work of character development within it. The mere revelation of the having-been becomes the narrative hinge and psychological kernel that can grant the impression of complexity to an otherwise underdeveloped story. Riley tells Duckworth: "Now, I don't know why [Reich and Glass] have this problem with each other, but that's my honest impression of what happened." He continues, however, offering his unique perspective on these disputes entirely within the language of pedagogy and citational power:

You know, there's room in the world for everybody's ideas. *But you have to give credit where credit's due.* You always have to acknowledge your *teachers*. Otherwise you won't go anywhere in the world. It's part of the respect of a tradition. It's great to be a student; a student is one of the highest forms. Once you're a teacher, then you're in a very hard role. It's very difficult; it's laden with great responsibilities.[36]

These accounts consistently center *dispute* as the organizing logic of minimalism rather than the *fact of having been in collaboration*. We are returned to the Rancièrian dramaturgy: do the parties precede the dispute, or are they formed in it? The difference between the two, it must be noted, is not one of facticity or "revisionism" in historiography, but merely of narrative emphasis, and indeed of valuation. Is there a story of functional collaboration and authorial critique to be found in the early development of minimalism? Or is minimalism simply the musical parable of the naivete of composers who, swept up in the general zeitgeist of 1960s utopianism, foolishly convinced themselves that things could be otherwise?

Reich relies on the same story as Riley, though oriented to his own interests, when he brings up, unprovoked, "the history of this kind of music" to Strickland:

> It does not begin with Terry Riley, it does not begin with me, and it *certainly* doesn't begin with Glass. It begins with La Monte Young, who was at the University of California in Berkeley with Terry in the late '50s. . . . La Monte was dragging gongs along the floor, doing neo-Cage things, and was otherwise getting interested in long tones—and we're talking *real* long tones. He wrote the *Trio for Strings*, a pivotal piece, based mostly on perfect intervals sustained for long periods of time on three strings. This had a profound effect on Riley, who as I understand it was still writing serial-type stuff.[37]

For Reich, it's important—as it was for Riley in relation to Reich—to point out that, before he met Young, Riley "was still writing serial-type stuff." Despite whatever differences they may have encountered, the minimalists articulated their historiography along almost identical lines, based on 1980s and 1990s methods of defanging earlier revolt. That is, earlier radicalism is displaced by an encounter that fundamentally alters the trajectory of what is to come. It is an oversimplified relationship that, looking on it with our own proleptical hindsight, takes its part within a broader practice of apology for and distancing from earlier revolt.

Reich described his reintroduction to Glass at the Park Place Gallery in 1967 along these same lines. "After the second night my old friend from Juilliard, Phil Glass, came up and said he was back from studying with Nadia Boulanger and working with Ravi Shankar and had a string quartet he wanted me to see, which was certainly not anything like what he's doing now but which was getting *away from dissonant intervals*."[38] Describing the monodirectional influence that Reich sees as constituting their relationship, he tells Strickland:

> From then until the beginning of '68, he and I played some things that I would basically *give him criticism on* and my reactions to. He knew Arthur Murphy from Juilliard. I said, 'Listen, whatever you write, we'll get together and play it with Arthur.' I introduced him to Jon Gibson and James Tenney, who became his group. All of this is in programs and can be verified historically. In early 1968 he wrote *One Plus One*, which was for rapping on a tabletop in groups of twos and threes. That indeed *was his original insight*, and he was very much off on his own from then on.[39]

Reich connects *One Plus One* immediately to another work: "The next piece he wrote was called *Two Pages for Steve Reich* . . . which subsequently became *Two Pages*." Typical of his pointed way of speaking, Reich concludes, "So there's your historical sketch." The story is almost identical—though he makes the comparison to his own education—to the one he told Ev Grimes in December 1987:

> So I would say that between March of 1967 and the beginning of 1968 basically *I did for [Glass] what Riley did for me which was to clarify ideas and set them in motion.* . . . In early '68 he did a piece called *1 Plus 1* which was groups of twos and three beats added together or subtracted from one another which was the basic insight of his and he was off and then he wrote a piece which was dedicated to me called *Two Pages for Steve Reich* which I have copies of and which subsequently became known as *Two Pages*.[40]

Reich clearly has a set narrative in mind, that is barely altered, and follows a very clear trajectory: Glass introduced himself, asked me to look at his work, I coached him, he made his major breakthrough, dedicated a piece to me, and then removed the dedication. He not only failed to "give credit where credit's due," as one must in Riley's image of the student-teacher relationship, he, worse of all, gave that credit explicitly before revoking it.

Within this instrumentalized conception of the style, Young regularly operates outside the scenes of dispute, positioned beyond the petty squabbles of quotidian life in favor of an eternal, foundational, avuncular perspective. Nevertheless, he is not above petty squabbling, and agrees about Reich's influence on Glass's compositions. In his conversation with Strickland, Young claims that—in the one early concert that had featured music by all of the big four to that point—"Phil brought a piece that was just a single line." Zazeela interjects, "A single meandering violin line, sort of unfocused," before Young takes over again: "Clearly [from] before he had worked with Steve Reich." The story is nearly identical—interjections and all—in their conversation with Duckworth:

> YOUNG: Well the story I tell is that there's only one concert that I know of where all four of us appeared together. This was a concert that was put on by a group at Yale called Pulsa.[41] They were doing a lot of work with light and . . .
>
> ZAZEELA: A lot of art and technology stuff.
>
> YOUNG: This concert was in 19 . . .
>
> ZAZEELA: I think '67 or '68 . . .
>
> YOUNG: . . . and it was all tapes. I played a tape of *Map of 49's Dream*— very sophisticated La Monte Young. Terry probably played some of the two-tape-recorder stuff that he was doing with a saxophone— very clearly Terry Riley. And Steve Reich was sounding like Steve Reich. But Phil Glass played a piece that just sounded like a single line. It was either a violin or a saxophone . . .
>
> ZAZEELA: It was a violin.
>
> YOUNG: . . . And it just went on. It was incredibly dull. There was none of what you would call *minimalism* going on at all.

Young likewise follows the line of pedagogic transmission; asked by Duckworth if he was "pleased with being considered the 'Father of Minimalism,'" Young responds:

> I think that's true. I think it would have never started without me. Terry Riley was the person who began the kind of repetitive phase-shifting music that is known as minimalism, and there's no question in my mind or Terry's *but that I was a primary influence on him*. . . . And [Terry] influenced Steve Reich, who played in *In C*, and who came to Terry afterwards and said he wanted to write like that. Actually, Terry discouraged him. He said, "No, you should find your own way." But Steve really wanted to write that way, and he did. And although it's different from Terry, it's clearly out of Terry. Then, according to Steve, Phil and Steve had a group together, and Phil began to play the way he does after *he was in that group with Steve*.

(There has been little narrative relation between Young and Glass. Strickland writes that Glass was never impressed by Young's "more conventional [i.e., audible] compositions," though he greatly admired Young as a conceptual artist, and writes that Glass attended Young and Zazeela's February 1968 voice and sine-wave performance at the Barbizon Plaza in New York, but left after half an hour. Strickland continues, "Young, like Reich, objects to Glass's refusal to acknowledge the influence of his Minimalist forebears and summarizes Glass's contributions to classical music as 'record sales.'"[42] Young's comment is meant as a dismissal or degradation of Glass's compositional originality; nevertheless, I hear in it an important historical observation: with Glass, with the *minimalists*, "classical music" finally became not only something that lives, ontologically, on commercial LP, but that sold exceptionally well for it.)

Several themes recur across these interviews. First of all, by the 1990s, these composers had consistent (I would go so far as to say rehearsed or at least prepared) autobiographical narratives, based on asserting an inegalitarian "pedagogic relation" between themselves and the other members of a style that gained its universal cohesion as "minimalism" during these interviews. Further, they were all acutely aware that they were being grouped together into a continuum, and thus that the only way to stake the claim of their unique contribution was by positioning it in relation to the others; this had the perhaps unintended result of positing an eternal minimalist formalism into which a series of firsts and conceptual innovations were then outlined. As a result, these interviews helped frame the context of the big four. That is, beyond the claims that Joseph has made for the metaphysical cohesion of the group put forward in chapter organization by scholars like Schwarz and Potter, in these interviews we find Strickland and Duckworth developing this grouping, framing their questions around the fact that the four worked together early in their careers and were not only aware of but had been directly involved in developing each other's styles, thus cumulatively producing what we call "minimalism." It is not enough for Young, Riley, Reich, and Glass to stake their own claims to the value of their work; rather, each must position his own work as being in reaction to, a development, elaboration, or clarification of, and so on. This is particularly evident in Strickland's conversation with Riley, where many of his questions come through a clear interest in using him to gain access to Young—including nonquestions like "La Monte had the same background of dance bands," and "You met [Young] as grad students at Berkeley in 59." He offers Riley the chance to acknowledge the relationship while dismissing their grouping: "It was an important meeting in the development of what's called Minimalism. I guess my next question is 'Are you tired of the term?'" These continue:

DUCKWORTH: What was it like to meet La Monte? What was he like
   back then?
DUCKWORTH: What was it like to hear the *Trio for Strings*?
DUCKWORTH: How did confronting La Monte's music affect your own
   compositions? Did you ever follow him into long tones?[43]

One that seems to be a question directly for Riley and perhaps challenges
the viability of defining Young's early work (indeed anything before *In C*
and *It's Gonna Rain*) as "minimalist" turns back into a question about Young:
"Even though La Monte originated the Minimalist style, he was still writing atonally. The most important things that you added were repetition and
the re-embracing of tonality. He wasn't composing tonally at all, was he?"[44]
No question better testifies to the strength of the minimalism narrative
in the mid-1990s. It's as if Young's earliest actions were already minimalist, or inherently proto-minimalist, even when they had nothing to do with
minimalism.[45]

   In contrast, what do we make of the fact that Strickland does not ask
Glass any questions about the minimalist lineage? It seems likely that Strickland views Glass as the end of the line, a dead end in dispute with his prede-
cessor, and perhaps considered it rude to probe that area with someone whose
career was understood as a repository of past influence, rather than a master
in his own right. Similarly, Ev Grimes, in a 1989 interview called "Education,"
focuses entirely on Glass's university education—he learned "not much" at
Juilliard—and his studies with Nadia Boulanger.[46] On the other hand, that
Glass never attempted to create an *abrutir* over any younger colleague by
suggesting his own position of mastery perhaps helped, in its own way, to
end the hierarchy with him. Keeping in mind Glass as a cutoff point in the
minimalist / big four hierarchy clearly articulates the terms of that grouping: it is not stylistic affinities that draws them together, but the fact of their
having been in collaboration. The heterogeneity apparent in their styles has
caused decades of headaches for those eager to analyze the music and place
it in clearly demarcated boxes. For all of the stylistic or conceptual parallels
among them, it is certainly likely that the particular historiographical light
that has fallen on them has much to do with their particular social scene and
community in mid-1960s New York, at a period when they were collaborat-
ing. We have been accounting for that period since.

   Much as I focused on Conrad's and Young's differing historiographical
methods and priorities in the previous chapter, examining how each of the
big four minimalists tracks their transmitted influence from Young down

reveals clear priorities among them. At this point, in the era of the canonization of minimalism as an art music, these composers felt that their legacy clearly relied on their grouping with the other three, but were simultaneously insistent upon their priority and novelty within that grouping. Most importantly, the nature of their time together had to be registered not in terms of the egalitarian, non-zero-sum, and communal language of collaboration and sharing, but in terms of the equivalencies and exchange logics of credits and debts, teachers and students.

I would like now to turn to a set of case studies drawing upon prominent, well-known early minimalist compositions by Riley, Reich, and Glass in which collaboration played a major role. My interest in these four pieces is simply to consider whether the typical pedagogic lineage implied by the metaphysical narrative—Young begat Riley begat Reich begat Glass—holds up to scrutiny.

In C

Terry Riley's *In C* resulted from a comparatively egalitarian and mutually beneficial exchange of influence between Riley and Steve Reich. It thus offers a strong point of comparison before entering into some more contentious interactions. The piece has garnered extensive commentary in the musicological literature, which I draw on at length here to narrate the collaborative relationship between Riley and Reich and how it has been staged by scholars.

That *In C* was closely tied into the hippie counterculture of the era—both in its development and its reception—has been long discussed. Keith Potter's commentary on the piece is an anomaly in focusing on formalism as a means of dismissing its communal orientation: "The notion, all too frequent, of *In C* as a kind of glorious, hippie free-for-all—the more the merrier, appreciated all the better if you're on certain substances—has tended to encourage performers to 'do their own thing,' to use the terminology of the period, and not to attempt to relate much to what other musicians were doing."[47] In contrast, in his oral history of the development and premiere of the piece, Robert Carl speculates that Riley showed Reich the score for *In C* when the two met at Riley's studio ("he was *furious*," discussed above), at a point when the score would have been complete, though "hot off the press."[48] The rehearsal process "remains vague," Carl writes, as a result of the fluctuating nature of both the piece and the potential roster of performers. However, when Riley's old colleagues at the San Francisco Tape Music Center offered him a one-man concert, he quickly planned the premiere of an "experimental chamber ensemble"[49] that now reads as a who's who of contemporary Bay Area experimentalisms. Potter writes that *In C*, like *The Gift*, was put together with "a high degree of collective input" from the many composers in the room, and lists the composer-performers involved in the premiere:

> Werner Jepsen (Wurlitzer electric piano), Sonny Lewis (the tenor saxophonist who had played with Riley in Europe), James Lowe (electric piano), who in turn was introduced by Lewis, Pauline Oliveros (accordion), Ramon Sender (who played a Chamberlain organ relayed from an upstairs studio), Stan Shaff (trumpet), Morton Subotnick (clarinet), Mel Weitsman (recorder), and Phil Windsor (trumpet), plus the composer himself on electric piano. With Reich, who also played electric piano, came two other performers: Jon Gibson (soprano saxophone) and Jeannie Brechan (electric piano), Reich's girlfriend at the time. In addition, an artist called Anthony Martin, also onstage, projected "a rhythmic/melodic light composition" of various shapes and colours simultaneously with the music.[50]

This large group of friends and friends-of-friends were all well acclimated to the anti-institutional, antiauthority, communalist ethos of the time. "My memory of the early rehearsals was, at least the first couple, [there] were just a few of us." Riley says, "And then we had one which was almost everybody, including a couple of hippies who came in off the street, who tried to blow over it, and Steve threw them out because he was totally intolerant of anything like that. . . . I would have probably let them do it [*laughs*]."[51] Riley's memory of the events is very much in keeping with his lifelong commitment to a generous and open performance practice, counterbalanced by presenting Reich as more of a traditionalist or even schoolmaster. (Indeed, Richard Landry later said of working with Reich, "Performing with Steve was like being around a teacher who, if you made a mistake, would rap on your knuckles with a ruler.")[52] Riley was interested in creating a noninstitutional space in which not only the performers but also the audience could contribute to the nature of the event; this was exemplified at the premiere at the San Francisco Tape Music Center when Riley suggested, "Why don't we just leave the chairs by the door, and let people sit wherever they want and see how they organize themselves in the room." He adds, explicitly referencing the connection to his earlier work, "I started playing *Music for the Gift* as they were walking in, so it wasn't like walking into a concert."[53] It is these simple disruptions of concert norms—no proscenium stage or seating, audience members choosing where (and how) to sit, music playing on arrival, an ensemble consisting of composers rather than professional performers—that disidentified what would later become "minimalism" from the norms of concert music. It is in the very constitution of this distance—cultural and political, organizational and institutional, rather than purely formalist or aesthetic—that the style initially marked its difference. But this distance is marked through practices of indistinction—composer(s) and performer(s), classical concert and rock show, lighting projection and ensemble member.

In C left a mark on Reich not only aesthetically but also in its mode of group interaction, concert organization, and performing forces. The piece, he claims, is chamber music at its best in that "there's a lot of listening to other people."[54] Still, that Reich offers such positive commentary is often part of bringing it up specifically to tie himself to the piece's formative development; asked by Duckworth if he had any "composer friends" in 1964, Reich responds: "I became friendly with Terry Riley in 1964 and helped him prepare the first performance of *In C*. I gave him a lot of my players to play in the first performance; I played in it, and I also suggested to him in the course of rehearsals that he put a pulse in to keep everybody together."[55] It takes him two sentences, in response to "Who did you know?" to make a substantial claim about his own imprint on Riley's work. Despite prioritizing his own influential role in making the piece possible—not to mention Riley's comments about his keeping out itinerant hippies—Reich continues, "While that was important, perhaps, I certainly learned a tremendous amount from putting the piece together, and I think it had a very strong influence on me."[56] Reich's framing of the piece is always about bidirectional influence—Riley on him, him on Riley—but across the board, the discussion prioritizes practices of listening, of group interaction, of the relational and respectful involvement that made these events collective or communal. These marked their difference from the norms of art music performance. That is, when Riley or Reich (or Potter or Carl) talks about *In C, what* they talk about, first of all, is organization, politics, and listening. But the *way* they talk about those issues, through discussion of influence, exchange, and group dynamics among many young experimentalists in San Francisco, is directed toward different effects of the same, consensual cause.

The relationship of influence between Riley and Reich is surely one of collaboration and mutual influence, rather than the monodirectional, confiscating image of pedagogic authority discussed at the beginning of this chapter. Reich says much the same in a 2014 interview with Seth Colter Walls leading up to his Brooklyn Academy of Music performances with Glass:

"The important thing with *In C* was, I certainly learned a lot about how to organize repeating patterns from playing in the piece. And Terry in turn got the pulse from me, which has now become part of the piece. So it was a very healthy exchange."[57] In light of this, we can perhaps frame the collaboration that produced *In C* as—hardly surprisingly—a much more communal, egalitarian, and, indeed, "hippie" type of interaction than subsequent projects of collaborative influence discussed below. Perhaps more than any other work, *In C* has remained exemplary of "early" minimalism musically.

It's Gonna Rain, or Meet Brother Walter in Union Square after Listening to Terry Riley

Reich uses much the same language to discuss the positive influence *In C* had on him as he would later use to criticize Glass for effacing the dedication of *Two Pages for Steve Reich*. In this light, it is extremely revealing to consider Reich's first cataloged work: *It's Gonna Rain*, which was originally followed by the supplemental clause *or Meet Brother Walter in Union Square after Listening to Terry Riley*.[58] In contrast to the relatively stable role of collaboration and influence in *In C*, and in stark contrast to the historiographical confiscation mobilized by Reich regarding *Two Pages*, *It's Gonna Rain* requires a little more attention, though from a decidedly theoretical perspective. My interest here is in considering, first, Riley's influence leading to his proper name being included in the title, and moreover, the role of *listening* not only to the Black voice of Brother Walter in 1964 or to Terry Riley's music, but specifically to listening to Brother Walter *after* listening to Terry Riley; that is, listening to Brother Walter speak while still under the influence of Riley's music.

Through working alongside Riley, Reich moved from twelve-tone and collage-based compositional practices to a more "organized and consistent kind of pattern-making."[59] As much as Reich has been willing to recognize Riley's influence, he has never publicly commented on lesser-known pieces like *She Moves She* (from *The Gift*) or *You're Nogood* built from tape phasing of (often Black) voices that sound almost exactly like Reich's earliest catalogued work. Reich seemed to have wanted to make a clear, citational fact of this indebtedness to Riley in the title of *It's Gonna Rain*, which, even as late as January 1968, was still carrying its full title on concert programs. Indeed, this was the title of the piece for many of Reich's most important early performances: on 27–29 May 1966 at the Park Place Gallery; at the Farleigh Dickson University Art Gallery on 5 January 1967; and again, in January 1968, at the Philip Exeter Academy.[60] In his program notes at Farleigh Dickson University, Reich writes, "Brother Walter was a young negro Pentecostal preacher who appeared occasionally on Sundays at Union Square in San Francisco. Terry Riley is a young American composer and was the first to use repeated figures in his music." The title was used through much of the time that Riley was living in New York.[61]

In contrast, further from the East Coast, on 12 July 1968 the piece was simply listed as *It's Gonna Rain* at the University of New Mexico, where Reich was teaching for the summer. Riley goes unmentioned in the program notes, and Brother Walter has been made anonymous: "The voice on the tape belongs to a negro preacher the composer recorded in Union Square in San Francisco." At a series of concerts in February 1969 at the North Shore Country Day School Arts Festival (in Illinois), no mention was made of the sound source, focusing entirely on the technological means of producing the piece: "Eventually, the two voices divide into four and (at the end of *Come Out* and *It's Gonna Rain*) into eight." We can gain some sense of the travel of the piece—as well as Riley's own rising influence following the 1968 release of *In C* by Columbia—in the program for a concert on 30 October 1970 at the University of York in England. There Richard Orton led what was likely the first concert of Reich's music to be performed without the composer present. Orton writes in the program that "during the summer of 1970 [Reich] briefly passed through London on his way to study African drumming, and in a very friendly way gave me the scores which will be performed this evening." These included *Pendulum Music*, *Phase Patterns*, and *Four Organs*, as well as presentations, from the LPs, of *Come Out* and *It's Gonna Rain*. While the Columbia LP from which Orton presumably reproduced the music used the abbreviated title *It's Gonna Rain*, the program included the full title—the last such reference to Walter and Riley in any program in Reich's archives at the Paul Sacher Stiftung.

The erasure of Brother Walter has been a recurring topic of commentary in the literature on minimalism. Lloyd Whitesell critiques Reich's use of a Black voice as one further example of how "white culture seeks vitality and even definition through the foregrounding of non-white cultural characteristics."[62] In *It's Gonna Rain* and *Come Out*, he continues, "The entire sound material for both pieces consists of recorded black voices" such that "each piece's frame is filled with a black vocal presence." The problem for Whitesell is that Reich frames the Black voice such that whiteness is entirely absent, or is present exclusively in the form of an unmarked ideal of objectivity—a framing intended to disappear into the (hegemonic) background.[63] In the end, "Whiteness is the unspoken field of play."[64] Sumanth Gopinath's exceptional reading draws on Asian and African influences on American culture of the time, transcription and formal analysis, and reflections on the place of religion, mass culture, and contemporary political events such as the civil rights movement and the Cuban Missile Crisis.[65] Martin Scherzinger similarly highlights Reich's discursive positioning of Walter's voice between speech and song as emblematic of the African American voice for white ears, such that "Walter's agency," Scherzinger writes, "is assimilated into what one might call a 'historical-transcendental' musical tradition." He continues: "The ideological effect is to incorporate the Other into tradition—first causing a rupture with tradition and then overcoming it—which ultimately serves the interests of a progressive music history, characterized by a quasi-deductive logical line of formal innovations."[66] In Siarhei Biareishky's psychoanalytic reading, Reich's (very white) compositional process produces a "split subject" that makes the Black voice "completely incomprehensible."[67] Reich does so, Biareishky contends, as a means of creating a nonracist white subjectivity that nevertheless maintains its privilege—that is, by drawing on and representing the Black voice without allowing it to shift normative practice and conception. All four scholars argue, more and less directly, that this is a necessary moment, regularly reproduced, of reconstituting of the (white) musical avant-garde.[68]

These readings combine to make *It's Gonna Rain*—and the problematic of Walter's vocal presence—perhaps the most discussed issue in scholarship on minimalism. Rather than arguing with this line of argument, my interest is in a much more modest and perhaps more material consideration: thinking about the constitution of listening in minimalism as attested to in the gap between the original title and its subsequent effacement.

The original title invites us to reflect not only on Reich as a listener to both Terry Riley and Brother Walter, but to sequential and hierarchical listening—to Brother Walter *after* listening to Terry Riley. In his conversation with Duckworth, Reich is asked about how he got the initial idea for *It's Gonna Rain*. Beyond his earlier discussion of his interest in "real sounds" in opposition to musique concrète, which he considered "boring, partly because the composers had tried to mask the real sounds," he tells the interviewer: "It was when I was fooling around with tape loops of the preacher's voice, and *still under the influence of In C*."[69] What seems important to me, and has gone unacknowledged perhaps as a result of its mundane obviousness, was that something about the context of San Francisco, the Tape Music Center, his collaboration with Riley, his dissatisfaction with his work with his improv ensemble, and so on, led Reich, on the advice of a filmmaker friend to, as

Gopinath writes, "undertake using a portable Uher tape recorder and a shot-gun microphone in front of the St. Francis Hotel in late 1964."[70] As Reich told Strickland a few years earlier, *It's Gonna Rain* only happened because Reich had been put into a particular frame of mind by the way that *In C* drew upon "tape loops, African music, John Coltrane—and tied them all together." Reich says, "Undoubtedly this was the trigger for *It's Gonna Rain*." He originally intended to approach the source material as a collage (which does happen at the start of Part II), but when he began rehearsing *In C* his filmmaker friend said to him, "Come on, you've gotta come down to Union Square and hear this preacher."[71] These knotted impulses—tape loops, Riley, Coltrane, African music, civil rights—put the composer into a frame of mind in which, under the sway of a "young American composer" working with tape loops, going into Union Square and recording the voice of a "young black preacher" made sense and seemed important.

None of this should be read as apologetics for Reich's machinelike destruction of Blackness that Whitesell considers the role of the white avant-garde, or the "becoming animal" to which Reich submits Walter on Scherzinger's reading. But keeping in mind its original title, robust with a citational economy of listening modalities, I think that *It's Gonna Rain* was not initially about white erasure of Blackness, or the technological manipulation of a marginalized Other. Rather, early on, as tied to its longer title, the piece more transparently focused on listening as a compositional act, and composing as beginning in a particularly contingent and structured distribution of listening as sensory engagement with heteronomous sources—a form of listening made possible by portable tape recording. It is a composing about a listening that assembles from earlier listenings. The title was citational, referential; an account of a particular listening, to Brother Walter within a specific frame of mind, rather than to an anonymous Black body that has been turned into an archetype of the songful nature of African American speech. This formalization-through-anonymization only occurred in the summer of 1968, before which Walter had been not "a Black voice" but a particular reference to listening in a time, place, and context.

I think here of the Blackness that Ashon Crawley hears in Reich's music. For Crawley, Reich's interest in Pentecostal breath and in African musical heritages is something worth taking seriously:

I get it now. *Music for 18 Musicians* is a sermon, a preached word. My Black pentecostal heritage would say it's a rhema word, on time, appropriate to the moment, contextual, full of feeling. I get the sermonic feel for the piece, for the song, by the way it moves, by the way it grows then decreases in intensity, how it sorta tarries in seeming stillness only to explode into a sorta praise, a sorta shout after a whoop, explodes into a dance and then a sorta quietude, a nothing music that's there but almost sparse, almost bare.[72]

Scholarship on minimalism has been so eager to assume its engagements as purely appropriative and racist rather than, as Crawley writes, an instance in which the "Africanist presence of western thought itself" is acknowledged. It's not that Crawley's reading as one Black scholar undermines the claims of appropriation made so frequently in relation to Reich's music, but that his commentary draws attention to the very whiteness of the discourse and the music to date. As several friends—musicological or not—have commented to me throughout this book's gestation, it's hard to imagine how a music could be so "rhythmic" and groove so little. But Crawley's own words point precisely to a *sermonic* reading of Reich's work even in the music he wrote a decade after he encountered Brother Walter, in relation to *Music for 18 Musicians*. In such a context, I find Reich's citation to Brother Walter important to underline. What is the (minimal) presence of Blackness in minimalism? How is it named, and where? How has the (often very white) musicological discourse held those two in relation?

Of course, the key point here is that Reich removed the citation—perhaps throwing Walter out with Riley's bathwater. Reich here models, perhaps more than anything else, the early ethnographic practice of dismissing the individual subjectivity of voices captured when producing field notes. Read on its own terms, the piece may have been one of the few spots where the primacy of Black musicality and Black voices was explicitly recognized within the broader history of minimalism's elisions and appropriations. And if such a thing was possible, if the citation could have been explicit, it runs entirely on the piece's name. With the removal of the combined dedication and citation (to an influence, Riley, and to a source, Walter), the piece changes drastically. Why the effacement? Why the erasure—a more literal one than the theoretical erasure of Blackness with which Whitesell charges Reich? Can the name of a piece really alter it so profoundly?

Once again, pedagogy is key. Riley tells Duckworth, "Steve Reich played in the first performance of *In C*. Before that, he was studying with Berio and his music, I think, reflected more of an interest in European music. So obviously, after *In C* he changed his style, and he started using repetition and developing his style of phases and pulses." A few years earlier, when Strickland asked whether Steve Reich invented the process of phasing, or only the term, Riley responded:

> RILEY: Well, I don't think so, because I'd already done that . . . he had this piece he'd recorded in Union Square called *Brother Walter*. In Union Square he'd recorded—
>
> STRICKLAND: *It's Gonna Rain.*
>
> RILEY: *It's Gonna Rain*, right. He was driving a cab then. He played me fragments, and then he started making a piece out of it. The first thing he tried before he heard what I was doing was sort of a collage piece. It's funny that if you listen to Brother Walter and hear [*sings*] It's gonna *rain!* It's gonna *Rain!* It's like the first two notes of *In C*. It's C and E. I don't know if it's C and E but it's major third. Not only that, but I'd made pieces with words and tape loops before that. And when you play two tape loops on the same machine they don't play at the same speed. *What Steve did, because he's very methodical and clean in his work, was to make the phasing work very gradually and to make a process out of it.* I made the tapes go backwards, forwards . . . it was fun, very funky. So I think his contribution was to clean all these things up and make kind of a method out of it, but what's important here *is my invention of the form built solely out of repeating modules.* When two identical modules are playing simultaneously by either tape machines or live performers, imperfections in speed or pitch result in "phasing." *I introduced the process into music composition; Steve correctly labeled it.*[73]

Riley introduced an innovation—he was *first*, in keeping with the modernist impulse toward innovation and newness. But Reich *named it*—and as such, inscribed it in a knotted relationship to his own proper name. The constellated relationships to the practice of phasing (if not the name) closely mirrors the idiosyncratic personalities of the two composers: "While Reich built his early aesthetic on the rigour with which his compositions are constructed," Potter writes, "Riley was uninterested in applying such structural severities in his material."[74]

The long interview passage from Riley requires further unpacking. First of all, Riley does not recall the full original title, including reference to his name, but simply highlights that the piece was voiced by, and, he thought, named for, Brother Walter. While Reich brings up *Two Pages for Steve Reich* the second anyone mentions Glass, Riley's associations with *It's Gonna Rain* go directly to the material-semiotic entanglements of Brother Walter's voice. Further, while *It's Gonna Rain, or Meet Brother Walter in Union Square after Listening to Terry Riley* is "about" a material practice of listening and recording, and while *It's Gonna Rain* has become "about" the Cuban Missile Crisis and apocalyptic faith—or white erasure of Black vocality, in its more scholarly veins—Riley's imagined *Brother Walter* is "about" the man whose voice is the sonic content. The same Black vocality that more recent scholars read as erased at the price of constructing an objective and invisible white frame is, for Riley, the piece. The name of the piece, whether temporary, imagined, or real, provides a different account as to what is named.

Second, Riley draws comparisons to his own work by highlighting the presence of major thirds and, more importantly, stakes a territorial claim over having begun working with tape loops years prior to Reich. Recognizing a potential terrain of indistinction between his lesser-known early tape pieces and Reich's canonic work—compare *She Moves She* to *It's Gonna Rain*, for example—Riley introduces a new distinction: where Reich's may be the proper name associated with the concept named phasing, Riley devised the technique. Strickland notes of this difference in application, "Reich was to systematize the phenomenon, whereas Riley in characteristic fashion had been playing the tape-loops in reverse, changing their speed randomly, and so on."[75] Reich's role was only in conceptual clarification: "Riley always allowed his patterns to accumulate into a psychedelic wash of sound," while "Reich generally stressed the audibility of his 'gradually shifting phase relations.'" The major difference, Potter notes, is Riley's intuitive method versus Reich's rigor.[76] In a word, Reich singled out a particular element of a larger practice and gave it a name. Such are the stakes of claiming property in a common conceptual innovation.

As minimalism was not a "collective revolt," surely Riley's compositional practice with magnetic tape loops cannot be considered one either. What is important is the staging of a conflict between two composers over the development of a specific practice and its redeployment in a slightly different context—and, perhaps more, the practices of nomination and the way that other proper names get attached to names-as-concepts. Were Riley and Reich both writing out scores, at home in silence at their desks, there would be very little chance of a dispute over who did something first. First, authorially, because the development would not be as immediately, sonically noticeable; and second, historiographically, because they could point to dated documents and their isolated working realms in defense of their claims of unrelated developments. But because the two had been working together, developing ideas in close proximity—perhaps talking *about* their ideas as much as presenting them—there is much more space for overlap and misunderstanding, and for dissimilar approaches to the same compositional problem. There is fertile terrain for (mis)understanding. When composers are out in the streets with their portable recorders, the possibility for historio-graphical indistinction is greatly exacerbated, creating the strong possibility of dispute. In being dislocated from their proper sphere of production, they introduce unaccounted-for possibilities, differently understood and differently counted in historiography. In the cases under consideration throughout, material practices constituted in collaboration led to sounds on tape whose paternity can be contested—not in their sound, but in their *concept*. Reich did not see a problem in clarifying the idea of looping tape into the rigorous *concept* of phasing. Conceptual and authorial paternities are a mess in such histories—let's still leave out the Radio France technician who built Riley the time-lag accumulator—but they are the terrain of dispute in historiography.

Much of the modernist rupture of the period—even when tied to efforts to escape the institutional pressures of traditional modernist practice—comes down to the assumption that giving something a name makes it *one's own*. It is planting a flag on "new" terrain—which consequently implies always problematic assumptions of terra nullius, or the possibility that any terrain is "empty," open, or available to be claimed by Eurocentric notions of white, masculine authority. Nomination stakes a claim of authorship, thus tying two names together: Reich's name is tied to the name phasing as a result of his earliest (official, cataloged) works. While Riley surely worked with phasing at various points in his career (*She Moves She* especially), Reich *owns* phasing as a compositional practice—not because he created it, but because he recognized it, separated it out, distilled it to a "pure" process, and gave it a name. We can track the dispute between the two to documents, making clear claims about which is more viable or well grounded, but we must not forget the historiographic act of (re)inscribing these names, and the role that scholars have taken in these debates both directly and in framing their appropriate terms. Within these dramaturgies, how is Brother Walter introduced on stage? Is he the protagonist of the piece, à la Riley? A source or informant, as in Reich's recollection? The perennially elided resource for white modernism, as in the dominant critical readings?

Two Pages [for Steve Reich?]

Let's finally return to where I began this chapter. Reich frequently draws attention to Glass's 1969 piece *Two Pages* as evidence of his unrecognized influence on his (very slightly) younger colleague. Within the legacy of the big four minimalists, the piece stands as the major exemplar of the problem whereby collaborative exchange does not result in proper accreditation. Here's Reich, in his interview with William Duckworth:

> And *One Plus One* was to Phil what *It's Gonna Rain* was to me. It was his first original musical insight—the additive process. After that, he wrote a piece which he dedicated to me, but later took the dedication away. It was called *Two Pages for Steve Reich*, but is now *Two Pages*, subtitled *Music in Unison*. Basically, what happened between Phil and me was very much *the kind of thing that had happened to me with Riley*, which is that *a lot of things are floating around in your mind and somebody comes along who really sets things straight*. The difference is that, for whatever reasons, *he has been unwilling to admit that*. And that has been the source of some grief between us, for sure. I don't quite understand, with all the success that he's had, why that remains something that he's very uptight about. But those things happened; they are documented in programs, reviews, and scores. It's not conjecture.[77]

Despite where he begins—a parallel between Riley's influence on *It's Gonna Rain* and Reich's own influence on *One Plus One* as the moment *before* a compositional and technical breakthrough—Reich of course does not point out that that very same piece by Reich originally included a dedication to the person to whom he is giving credit. The irony may be lost on Reich when he (frequently) makes the comparison in interviews. What's more, as noted above, *It's Gonna Rain* was performed under its original title for several years.

In stark contrast, a program from a joint Reich and Glass concert on 18 April 1969 at the New School—only two months after the score of *Two Pages* dated "2/69"—only uses the shortened title, with Reich performing on clavinet in the performance. That is, while Reich frequently brings attention to the effacement of his name from *Two Pages*, the abbreviation seems to have happened almost immediately; neither he nor Riley has ever mentioned in interviews the inclusion of Riley's name in *It's Gonna Rain* for at least *two years* after its completion. Keith Potter offers the clearest dismissal of the dedication issue: "Reich says that Glass originally headed the score *Two Pages for Steve Reich*, but, when the recording came out in 1974, dropped the homage to his erstwhile friend." (This of course misses the fact that the April 1969 performance already did not have the dedication.) He continues, "Glass says that Reich liked *Two Pages* so much in rehearsal that he appended the words 'for Steve Reich' to a score and presented it to him, never intending this as anything more than the spontaneous gift of a copy."[78] What should we make, then, of Reich frequently (and unprovoked) bringing up the (well-rehearsed) story of Glass having removed the dedication on *Two Pages*? What does Reich stand to gain from constantly adding this feature to his autobiographical narrative, particularly when he is the only person who supposedly has evidence of the title?

Glass is unique among the big four. While interviewers regularly ask Young, Riley, and Reich about their interrelationships, Strickland and Duckworth notably leave that line of questioning aside entirely for Glass. When he is raised in interviews of Reich and Young, it is often as a critique of his ahistorical belief in the development of his work—in Young's words, the idea that he came out of a "vacuum" in that he refuses to recognize the input of Reich. Glass similarly rejects the influence of Riley, at least on his early work: Strickland quotes Reich in February 1992 saying, "I undoubtedly played the tape [of *In C*] for Philip" and Glass in September of that same year saying, "No, I never heard the tape, Steve showed me the score after I wrote *Two Pages* and asked where I'd gotten the idea for writing in modules. I first heard Terry at the Electric Circus" in April 1969, which would suggest that Glass did not even take notice when Columbia released the LP of *In C* in late 1968, or that he was unaware of Riley despite having gone to see Young as early as February 1968.[79] Further, Glass can be considered, at least in these limited contexts, something of a classicist within the group: he studied with Nadia Boulanger, whose pedagogy returns students to counterpoint and voice leading, leading to a situation in which Glass, unlike the others, seems never to have at any point entirely turned his back on the score, and never worked with tape as a compositional medium. Glass's refusal of having heard *In C* is confusing and almost certainly untrue, raising the question (like the one above about Reich bringing up *Two Pages*) as to what Glass would possibly have to gain by denying its impact on his early compositional output. What is this form of autobiographical positioning intended to achieve?

Glass, I think, is more thoughtful about the period than is let on by Young and Reich. While Reich considers it a "smokescreen" to avoid acknowledging his debts, Glass stands apart from the other minimalists for having rejected the label "minimalist" not on the grounds of inappropriateness (as well be discussed at length in the next chapter) but "as journalistic shorthand which misrepresents the collective nature of the 'very intense generational search' that was transpiring." Strickland continues, "The generational search, as opposed to the search of a few individuals, in reductive musical forms is really more a phenomenon of the 1970s."[80] In his study of the early Philip Glass Ensemble, David Chapman argues that the problem common to the minimalist disputes is one of "friendships and collaborations collapsed over questions of who influenced whom and who deserved credit for what technical innovations,"[81] as well as subsequent efforts "to assert mastery over their shared history."[82] Glass comments further on what this specific generational shift was in his conversation with Duckworth:

GLASS: I'm not the only person of my generation who became a composer/performer. We really came back to the idea that the composer *is* the performer and that's very, very valuable. For one thing, we became real people again to audiences. We learned to talk to people again. As a group we lost our exclusivity, the kind that had been built up through years of academic life. I personally knew that I didn't want to spend my life writing music for a handful of people. . . .

DUCKWORTH: Do you have any idea why that change happened in your generation?

GLASS: We all went through the cultural crises of the sixties. It was civil rights, pop music, and drugs. . . . We saw our friends work in the field of popular music, living in a very connected way with their culture, and many of us wanted to have the same connection in our work. We wanted to be part of that world, too. It didn't mean writing popular music; that wasn't possible for people like myself. I have no training in it, and I have no inclination to do it. But it did mean that we saw the role of the artist in a much more traditional way—the artist being part of the culture that he lives in.[83]

Glass most famously addressed this distaste in his famous quote about the Boulez scene in Paris as dominated by "crazy creeps"; less frequently commented upon, though, is his writing in *Music by Philip Glass* about the minimalist grounds for escaping the serialist tradition. Serialism "produced a very abstract and, to most ears, 'modern' sounding music," Glass recognized, but "its intellectual rigor and sheer difficulty for creator, performer and listener made it seem almost automatically worthwhile, regardless of how it actually came out. *After the premiere of a new piece, it was not uncommon to hear the remark, 'It's actually much better than it sounds.'*"[84] This comment is very near to the concerns raised in "Music as a Gradual Process" that I discussed in Chapter 1; Glass's critique of the generation preceding him, the feature that forced him into rebellion against it, was less the actual sound of it than the discourse surrounding it, in which it was possible for an audience of insider listeners to dismiss the taste of another audience members by saying the music is *actually* better than what it sounds like, *if only you knew how to listen through*. His concern was with the production of a difference between what the audience *heard* and what the composer or critic claimed it *was*. Much the same, as he tells Duckworth, he did not want to spend his life writing music that no one would listen to. Glass is critiquing the normalized mode of listening highlighted by the generation prior, based on "secrets of structure" as the locus of valuation—he is critiquing the entirely normalized *abrutir* of contemporary music listening.

Much of this is well-trod ground. Indeed, we could relate these critiques to the idea of "presence" that Chapman highlights in Glass's music as a central thematic in concert reviews during the 1960s and 1970s. Chapman builds from the work of the art historian James Meyer, for whom minimalism is specifically a genre constituted in polemic. "Presence, as interpreted by Meyer, described the viewer's embodied experience of an artwork, the powerful impression of a work on its spectator, and the active articulation of the proximity between the viewer and the object being viewed."[85] Indeed, in a 1972 interview, Glass related the idea of presence specifically to volume following similar developments in rock music (and, by all accounts, the Theatre of Eternal Music), where volume is seen as an encompassing, space-based means of ensuring that "the sound" is a singular phenomenon to which everyone in the performance space has equal access—presuming there isn't a "secret" agenda in play, disadvantaging the listener in relation to a privilege generated for the composer and performers (or composer-performer).[86]

The point, then, is that Glass very much views his involvement with minimalism as part of a generational movement that has as much to do with Young, Riley, and Reich as with civil rights and pop music—as, further, with the general "antiestablishment" or "antiauthority" movement of the late 1960s. That Reich calls this a "smokescreen" aimed at hiding his indebtedness to the other big four minimalists is surely possible; but what might also be possible is that Glass is less willing—and less expected to by interviewers, for some reason—to engage in a form of positioning based on combining what Chapman calls, drawing on Taruskin, the "race to the patent office" with a pedagogic focus on technical developments and one-upmanship.[87] Indeed, as Chapman argues, Glass's entire career is about collaboration: the influence of Riley and Reich is only one early stage of a career that saw him collaborate with literally dozens of librettists, stage producers, poets, and musicians.[88]

All of this work points to the fact that, when it comes to Glass, community and collaboration are the central critical themes to address—we see much less scholarly work focused on formalist analysis or separating him from his colleagues through ahistorical ideas about composer biography, and much more work on the ensemble and its makeup.[89] Perhaps because his career is so heavily focused on collaboration, Glass is less willing to carve up any point in his career through reference to the pedagogic myth or *abrutir* that Reich and Young so willfully turn to. In not doing so, the drama and intrigue of the metaphysical tradition abruptly ends with him.

What should we make of Reich's and Young's critique that Glass refuses to acknowledge the paternity of his ideas? How should we interpret this critique in light of these two composers' beliefs that the history of Western art music always happens progressively, through a concentration of existing ideas that are then elaborated upon by each composer recognizing his roots? How do we refute their obsession with history as list of notable firsts? If the institution of pedagogic authority is intended to fill the vacuum created by minimalism's critique of composerly authority, and if this is the moment of confiscation and defanging of the "collective" (perhaps: generational) politics of minimalism, then Glass is the only one who does not engage in this form of policing. The community of minimalism, read this way, is an economy of exchange among the big four grounded in a togetherness of influence and exchange that creates distinction and distance between them when not properly acknowledged. Glass becomes a dead end in this economy. Surely there is a composer for whom Glass could claim to have concretized or clarified a particularly messy set of ideas—and such a claim would extend our big four into perhaps a big five or six. The underlying logic that upholds this articulation of four composers known as "minimalists"—from Mertens through Strickland to Duckworth and Schwarz and Potter—is that they were originally part of a community broken by the relative (un)willingness of members of that community to "give credit where credit's due." The currency of this community is pedagogic articulation of paternity as a means of negating the former (auto)critique of the composer's privilege, a privilege that Reich and Glass both argued was earned at the audience's expense.

Four Organs and *Phase Patterns*

I would like finally to briefly consider the origins in programs and sketches of two 1970 pieces by Steve Reich that are less often called upon as part of upholding the metaphysical narrative of minimalism: *Four Organs* and *Phase Patterns*. I contend that these two pieces draw attention to the open network of exchange going on in 1970 among the big four minimalists, in such a way that it undermines the monodirectional line of influence narrative that has long been at the center of the metaphysical narrative of minimalism, and which I am arguing finds its basis in the hierarchical authority of the pedagogic relation. In this way, through considering the origins of these paired works for electric organs, I want to argue for early minimalism as relying on a dispersed and nonhierarchical image of influence and pedagogy. Such a dispersal—a disarticulation of the monodirectional line of influence—opens up minimalism without recentering the big four constellation.

Both pieces were premiered in one of Reich's major early concerts: the 7 May and 8 May 1970 performances at the Solomon R. Guggenheim Museum in New York billed as "An Evening of Music by Steve Reich" (Figure 10).

In that program, *Four Organs* is dated "1/70" and was performed by Steve Chambers, Philip Glass, Art Murphy, and Steve Reich on electric organs and Jon Gibson on maracas. *Phase Patterns*, dated "2/70," was performed twice, once as a "warm up performance" and then following the intermission as the concert's second half; the performers were Steve Chambers, Jon Gibson, Art Murphy, and Steve Reich.

In his program notes for *Four Organs*, Reich calls that piece "the result of working with an electronic device," the Phase Shifting Pulse Gate, which he had developed in 1968–1969 with Larry Owens, a technician at the Bell Laboratories.[90] The idea for the composition came from the Pulse Gate, but Reich quickly abandoned the system due to its unreliability and lack of musical interest. As a result, the only electronics involved were the electric organs. The piece itself is based on "a short repeated chord where individual tones . . . extend gradually out like a sort of horizontal bar graph in time." He continues, "Eventually all tones [are] held for an extremely long time creating a sort of slow motion music." To create this long-duration music inspired by his abandoned Pulse Gate idea, Reich "briefly thought about a large group of brass instruments," but, eventually, "Electric organs were used *because they were available* and because they have strong attacks and releases that can be clearly heard through all the sustained notes." Both pairs of instruments are interesting—Reich had never worked with brass instruments to that point, and only rarely since, as his orchestral sound is most often defined by strings, percussion, keyboards, and woodwinds, with the near total absence of brass.[91] I am inclined to think of the initial idea—particularly in that it was focused

Thursday, May 7, 1970   8:30 PM   Friday, May 8, 1970

THE SOLOMON R. GUGGENHEIM MUSEUM

PRESENTS

AN EVENING OF MUSIC

by

STEVE REICH

Phase Patterns (2/70) (warm up performance 8:10 - 8:30 pm)

    Steve Chambers, Jon Gibson, Art Murphy, Steve Reich - electric organs

Piano Phase (1967)

    Art Murphy and Steve Reich - pianos

Four Organs (1/70)

    Steve Chambers, Philip Glass, Art Murphy, Steve Reich - electric organs

    Jon Gibson - maracas

          --- intermission ---

Phase Patterns (2/70)

    Steve Chambers, Jon Gibson, Art Murphy, Steve Reich - electric organs

Figure 10. Concert program from "An Evening of Music by Steve Reich" at the Guggenheim Museum, May 1970. Paul Sacher Stiftung, Steve Reich Collection.

on long tones—as having been influenced by the use of brass in Young's revived Theatre of Eternal Music in the late 1960s, including players like Garret List, Rhys Chatham, and Ben Neill. Sumanth Gopinath underlines Reich's recognition of the proximity of *Four Organs* to Young's work through its early parodistic titles.[92]

More directly, however, why were electric organs *available*? Reich had never composed for them before; indeed, following *Four Organs*, and *Phase Patterns* of 1970, the only other work to feature the instrument is 1973's *Music for Mallet Instruments, Voice, and Organ.* I contend that we can tie the availability of organs at this point, as well as Reich's push to use them, to his friendship with Philip Glass and, more importantly, their frequent tours together at the time. Indeed, the Guggenheim series also included music by Glass.[93] The program for Glass's performances featured three organ-dominated pieces performed by Glass, Gibson, Reich, Murphy, Richard Landry, David Behrman, Beverly Lauridsen, and James Tenney, including the premiere of *Music in Fifths*, *Music in Contrary Motion*, and *Music in Similar Motion*. In the Guggenheim program for "Live/Electric Music," Glass's biography immediately identifies him in relation to the instrument: "Philip Glass, *who plays the electric organ*, was born in 1937 in Baltimore, Maryland." In Glass and Reich's joint conversation with Tim Page from 1980, Glass brings up their relationship specifically in terms of pieces for electric organs. Glass says, "It's so clear we are dealing with two different personalities. Ten years ago, when you had something like *Music in Fifths* on the one hand and *Four Organs* on the other, there wasn't an awful lot of other music around to compare it to."[94]

The fruitfulness and frequency of their professional and personal entanglements at this point are attested to in Reich's agendas at the Sacher Foundation. November and December 1969 are full of plans to rehearse with "Phil" as well as with "Jon" and "Art" in the lead-up to the Guggenheim performance. Entries on 3, 12, 14, and 21 December specify rehearsing *Four Organs* at "Phil's." Rehearsals intensified in 1970, as 3, 4, 10, 11 January all include entries for rehearsal at Phil's, leading up to entries for Glass's concert at the Guggenheim on 16 and 17 January. Entries for 19 and 24 January include buying an organ and picking up an organ, and on the twenty-fifth Reich makes himself a note to copy out *Four Organs*, which he then xeroxed on the twenty-seventh. The rehearsals of *Four Organs* continue throughout February and March. In April he has a note to himself that Phil will be coming by to pick up an organ. Leading up to Reich's own Guggenheim concert on 7 and 8 May, as well as the joint concerts by Reich and Glass at the Walker Art Center in Minneapolis (in which Glass performed on *Four Organs* as well), Glass hosted several rehearsals at his loft. This suggests that during the period from the winter 1969 through the spring of 1970, Glass and Reich were involved in an intensive series of rehearsals, centered at least in part around the use of electric organs in Philip Glass's loft. Reich bought his own—presumably for composing at home—days after the first performance of several of Glass's early organ-driven pieces at the Guggenheim, and dates the score of *Four Organs* January 1970, the month of Glass's concerts.[95]

Phase Patterns, first sketched during the same period, has its own relationship to collaboration and effaced dedication. Paired with *Four Organs* as a study of extended duration and slow harmonic change, *Phase Patterns* focuses exclusively on the use of the rudimentary percussion pattern called paradiddles—left-right-left-left right-left-right-right. These patterns, so familiar to Reich as a percussionist, are transferred to the keyboard and phased against themselves. Reich's sketchbooks reveal the rapid development of the piece. An entry on 27 January 1970 titled *Pattern Studies* shows paradiddles in two hands on keyboard; on 10 February similar sketches are given the title *Phase Patterns*. On 27 February, Reich titles a sketch "*KEYBOARD DRUMMING for Art Murphy*." Entries from 8 and 11 April show Reich working through several potential patterns of alternating left and right hands on a sustained chord, including one that develops from LR to LLR LRLRLR to LLRLRR LRLR with an annotation suggesting that it "tends towards Phil's music."[96] He finally moves toward the title *Phase Patterns for Art Murphy* and dates it, retroactively, "2/70." Reich notes that the resultant patterns suggested in the score were developed collaboratively during rehearsals by Reich, Steve Chambers, and Art Murphy.

These directions were carried over into the score published by Universal Editions in 1980. But the piece's title had been abbreviated in a fashion becoming all too familiar. In contrast to the original manuscript title referencing Murphy, the published score is titled simply *Phase Patterns*. The simple effacement raises complex questions: What is the difference between a dedication and a title? Or, following Cardew's writing about Cage's pieces for David Tudor, can something that reads like a dedication in fact be an instrumentation?[97] It's difficult to pinpoint whether the dedication was removed at the same point in 1970 (it is not included in programs, even at the premiere) or whether it was kept in place until its publication a decade later. Perhaps *Phase Patterns* and *Four Organs* explain why Reich claims that he was only advising Glass on his compositions until early 1968: beyond that point, the two were in more sympathetic collaboration, though he never feels the need to directly state that. What is worth noting is that *Phase Patterns* was developed in close collaboration with Chambers and Murphy, whose credit in developing the patterns is maintained in the notes to the score. Reich was clearly under the direct influence of Glass's organ-based and arithmetical-additive processes while writing. *Phase Patterns* could perhaps be relabeled *Phase Patterns, or Keyboard Drumming with Art Murphy after Rehearsing with Phil Glass*.

Conclusion: Minimalism, Pedagogy, *Abrutir*

That La Monte Young influenced Terry Riley, and Terry Riley influenced Steve Reich, and Steve Reich influenced Philip Glass has been tracked, over and over, in histories of minimalism. There's no real reason to deny this. What I hope to have shown is how what Rancière calls the pedagogic myth is implicated in the metaphysical narrative. This leads to an uncritical historiography dependent upon elisions of authorial responsibility, a reversion to Romantic norms of authorship, when a redistribution of authorship was precisely the field of play. While I have most centrally critiqued Reich's claims about his role within this trajectory, this is not to suggest that he is more at fault or more wrong about his position than the others—whether his fellow big four or composers and even artists more broadly. No, the reason Reich ends up being singled out in this chapter is that he merely brings up the issue more frequently, and with greater consistency, than any other relevant composer. It seems misguided, perhaps disingenuous, to make a recurring autobiographical talking point of one's own influence on another composer by frequently returning to an effaced dedication to yourself, particularly when the same thing has happened in your own career as well. Still, it's not particularly interesting to point out that someone is being disingenuous or hypocritical—these should not be the beginning or end of critique in themselves. Broader conclusions can be drawn from the examples above.

Philip Glass clearly had an influence on Reich, as Mertens and Potter have argued, and as I believe I have shown by redirecting the proposed relationship between the two of them as put forward most often by Reich. Looking at the performances, publications, and recorded output of the minimalists between late 1969 and early 1971 points to further resonances among them. La Monte Young and Marian Zazeela released their first LP, singing along with sine-wave drones, as the *Black LP*; Reich released his first LP with Shandar of *Four Organs* (the live recording with Glass on one of the organs from the Guggenheim) and *Phase Patterns* (recorded live at UC Berkeley; Glass was not present for that trip); Glass recorded and released his first LP, of *Music with Changing Parts*, later in 1971; Terry Riley began performing primarily solo organ concerts for several years after 1970, including the live performances in April 1971 (in Los Angeles) and May 1972 (in Paris) that were released as *Persian Surgery Dervishes* in 1972; Riley and John Cale, former members of the Theatre of Eternal Music, also released an LP together called *The Church of Anthrax* in 1971 (recorded 1968) that has held little or no place in the history of minimalism.⁹⁸ Almost all of these recordings, with the exception of the Young and Zazeela LP, prominently feature electric organs.

My goal here is not to suggest that our histories are wrong because Glass influenced Reich more than the other way around; such accounting-ledger history is not very interesting, either. The important question is: How did we get from an indistinct simultaneity of organic and organ-driven, indistinct moments of collaborative rehearsal and exchange to a clean-cut, hierarchical succession claimed as evidence of normative propriety, priority, and paternity?

Above I noted Reich's removal of both the names Terry Riley and Brother Walter from the official cataloged title of *It's Gonna Rain*, and his removal of Art Murphy from *Phase Patterns*. I similarly considered the terms of Philip Glass's inclusion of a reference to Reich in *Two Pages*. In all cases, there was an implication that including references to other composers or performers in the title was a form of, as Riley said in another context, giving credit where credit's due. That is, the inclusion of the name of a composer-performer-colleague-collaborator, during the peak of that collaboration, is typically assumed as evidence of a direct debt for stylistic emulation or borrowing. While a compelling assumption, this reading raises major problems. There is no generic convention that would lead one to assume that the inclusion of a name other than the author's at the head of a score is evidence of a debt; indeed, there is no generic convention for how to "properly" cite another composer's influence on one's work within the format of a score. There are of course many methods of intertextual allusion in literate Western art music: we can think here of stylistic parody or direct quotation, as in Berio's *Sinfonia*, or the direct, named inclusion of references to compositional influences—here Ligeti's *Selbstportrait mit Reich und Riley (und Chopin ist auch Bewegung)* seems the ideal exemplar. But there is no *convention*, no clear citational practice in play. Including citation is not one of the strengths of the medium of the notated musical score. But nor are scores an ideal means of representing a collaborative compositional practice, as the early minimalists recognized.

This returns us to the initial problem: What were those names meant to do, and why were they removed? What importance did they commemorate, and what threat did they pose? I am especially drawn to Potter's offhand suggestion that, perhaps, Glass simply wrote "for Steve Reich" on his copy of the score as he handed out the parts for *Two Pages*. If so, are there parts "for Art Murphy" and others? If this were the case—and indeed it seems plausible to me—this was no titular dedication, but a simple means of handling part-labeling when the performers are not "Violin 1" or "electric keyboard 2" but, in fact, your friend Phil, sitting right there. This problem has already been broached in the previous chapter: What can we make of the inclusion, in the "score" for *Day of the Antler*, of not "3-string viola drone" but "JC" for John Cale? We could make the problem bigger: How does one sign a score at all when most of the work is happening in rehearsal and on tape? Are composers obligated, as archival evidence toward potential copyright disputes, to sign the tape as it spools off the recorder? What is the difference, authorially—indeed *legally*—between the "Time-Lag Accumulator" and "*Frippertronics*"? Does placing Robert Fripp's name on it remove any credit to Brian Eno? What about credit to Riley? And isn't phasing associated with Steve Reich? Why, when it comes to the *machinery*, is Riley still the association, even though Reich's name is tied to the phasing process? The poor French Radio technician . . .

This is all to say that there is *much* in a name when thinking through authorship. Names do not seal off authorship in a neat, contained package—rather, they pose its foundational problem. Practices of naming, distinct nominations, are very often at play in attempting to disentangle the early authorial politics and polemics of minimalism. But at no point have I leaned on disentangling as a goal. Rather, I want to complicate the oversimplified efforts to disentangle that result in published scores from the collaborative, stoned, and collectivist-politics-leaning moments of early minimalism. A clear historical awareness of what "minimalism" is—if indeed one insists that it be anything at all—perhaps requires more the quick flip of a pen, of why someone would write "for Steve Reich" on top of a score before handing it off in a first rehearsal, than it does the undertaking a deep formal analysis of the piece's rhythmic modules and melodic patterns to establish paternity. We too often allow such questions of authorship to immediately turn to absurd reductions—if the performers are coauthors, what then of the printers and the pulp mill workers? Or the donors who provided the capital to build the venue? In early minimalism, in the particular piece of paper that Glass handed Reich and its historiographic staging, we are in something at once messier and more immediate. We do not need abstract extremes and absurd extensions; we need to dwell in the indistinct gap.

Names, names, names—it's all about names. What happens when we write a name, and where? Names are different depending on where we write them—is the name bold, right up top? Is it *italicized, below the title,* in clear homage? Is it offset, to signify authorship of the sounds—or rather, the directions for producing the sounds? Do any of these matter if it's not in the program or on the record? The last two chapters have argued that the prominent early minimalists worked extensively in collaboration, often "writing" their music to magnetic tape in rehearsal before, or rather than, writing it in scores. Whatever long historiographical sweeps we want to write onto these events to explain their development, it seems clear that the early political rebellions of minimalism were successful if we judge only by the fact that those musicians involved became *very* self-conscious about being seen as overly dependent on their friends. The early efforts of the American minimalists—in parallel with similar events in rock, free jazz, theater, performance art, happenings, dance, and radical politics—were perhaps *so* successful at finding functional and even perhaps mundane methods of undermining their own priority that, when it began to take any hold, they panicked and retreated to strong authority.

Again, all of this is making much of a relatively minor fact—that the metaphysical history of minimalism is held together and ordered into a coherent singular narrative, a monodirectional line of transmission of influence, by its dominant practitioners inscribing a hierarchical, pedagogic relation where once there was a mess of names, citations, shared organs, borrowed portable tape players, and collaborative performances. Where there were composers out for walks in San Francisco rather than locked in an office or the library. The imposition of pedagogic authority in the vacuum left by the absence of compositional authority will be a pivot for the remaining chapters. In suggesting that Young, Riley (to a much lesser degree), Reich, and Glass (to a slightly lesser degree) enacted a confiscation of the egalitarian politics of what we call minimalist music, I am highlighting both the egalitarian potential of that music and the means by which it has been historically turned into something other: a formalist compositional style, defined by a set of sonic characteristics that were merely the means to a confiscated and defanged political end. Reich and the other minimalists sought out tools to reassert priority, and thus drew themselves back into the modernist art music lineage whose authorial politics they sought to destroy. This was not inevitable in fact, but perhaps maps too easily onto how like to structure our fictions.

Four

Indistinct Minimalisms

Punk, No Wave, and the Death of Minimalism

—————

Minimalism has gone on to influence rock on the one hand and composers like John Adams on the other. But if you want to say minimalism as a school is dead, I'd say "hear, hear, but I'm not dead."
  Steve Reich[1]

We didn't think of ourselves as minimalists. We thought of ourselves as living in a world of music where composers and performers were one, and where the audience were right in front of us.
  Philip Glass[2]

There is history precisely because no primeval legislator put words in harmony with things.
  Jacques Rancière[3]

Minimalism died in the late 1970s. It's hard to precisely date the change, but in the same moment that the music was nationally recognized as an accessible style of American composition demanding audience attention, the name itself was widely judged inadequate for a music overcoming its prior, unfortunate commitments. Within those judgments it circulated all the more.

The shifts away from earlier austerity were visible everywhere. Philip Glass and Steve Reich, the two composers most closely associated with the style, had each turned to large-scale commissions for traditional orchestras and opera companies. In the *New York Times*, John Rockwell wrote that Reich's most recent piece *Tehillim* included "variation of tempo, a freer harmonic palette, and specific examples of word painting." If he's writing such music, "Can Mr. Reich really be called a 'minimalist'?"[4] Reich is happy to declare the movement dead—but only while noting that he isn't, and that minimalism's impact can be heard in the music of John Adams, on the one hand, and in rock, on the other. Writing a year earlier in *High Fidelity*, Tim Page foregrounded the inadequacy of the name and some possible alternatives: "Minimalist music? Pulse Music, if you prefer. Pattern Music. The *New York Times* has called it 'trance music'; critic Richard Kostelanetz refers to 'modular music.' Philip Glass, one of the leading figures in the field, likes to call his work 'music with repetitive structures'; the rock crowd grooves to 'space music'; and detractors have decried the 'stuck-record school of composition.'"[5] Page's "Minimalist Primer" eventually concedes to "settle upon the most popular, if not the most apt, label for this style."

How are we to read his presentation of all of these, potentially more appropriate, synonyms? First, they suggest that properly naming a compositional style is difficult, but possible, work; and second, that "minimalism" is to be read as dismissive or slanderous. In 1977 Joan LaBarbara had dismissed the label for precisely that reason, saying that the label minimalism was "purely laughable to label such rich and complex music."[6] John Adams, Reich's preferred inheritor of minimalism's estate, had much the same complaint: his music, "Romantic, classical, minimalist, all at the same time," is "a little too rich" to be labeled minimalist.[7] These proclamations of death and inadequacy nevertheless did not stop *Time* magazine from declaring 1982 "the year of minimalism."[8]

Each of these accounts, written between 1977 and 1982, insists that minimalism is something to be gotten over. It is ignorance, negativity, austerity—even, we can extrapolate from LaBarbara and Adams, impoverishment. But *High Fidelity*, *Newsday*, and *Time* introduce minimalism to a national audience not because the music is ignorant, negative, and austere, but rather as a success story: the composers of ignorance, negativity, and austerity have grown up and come to their senses! Certainly another name could have been proposed for this music at the moment of its arrival to national attention. But the fact that the name generates so much handwringing is perhaps the point. Minimalism arrived not only as an exciting, new compositional style: it also a moral and historical lesson about abandoning youthful naivete, radicalism, and ignorance. Capital-*M* Minimalism was announced to national audiences precisely as a celebration of having overcome its being early. "Minimalism is dead" should perhaps rather be read as "(Early) minimalism is dead—say hello to Minimalism!"

All of these (early) M/minimalism(s) must be read as homonymic, and the discourse of minimalism as a battle over homonyms.[9] Homonymy provides one overshadowed genealogy of Rancière's use of the (near synonyms) "disagreement" and "dissensus." Indeed, the short-lived discourse of homonymy in his work precedes those more popular concepts as terms of art in his work. Published immediately prior to *Disagreement*, Rancière's *The Names of History* sets in motion a reading of French historiography through placing in tension disjunct meanings of a disciplinary homonym: *histoire*. Whereas English and German distinguish between fictional story and factual account, "The French language designates lived experience, its faithful narrative, its lying fiction, and its knowledgeable explanation all by the same name."[10] This poses a problem for "homonym hunters" who insist that a rigorous *science* of history requires precise definition of terms and ardent, unequivocal language. Therein lies the founding paradox of history as a discipline: "The confusion of language was in fact needed to measure the dilemma in its rigor: . . . the difference between history as science and history as narrative was necessarily produced in the heart of narrative, with the latter's words and use of words."[11] That is, while historical scholarship often polices historical uses of language in contemporary statements of distinction, it retains a proximity to literature—to storytelling—in its medium (words) and their inescapably ambiguous usages.

How do we tell apart histories and stories? Rancière uses the term *poetics of knowledge* to name "the set of literary procedures by which a discourse escapes literature, gives itself the status of a science, and signifies this status."[12] History, he argues, is a result of the conjunction of science and nonscience, fact and fiction. Opining this conjunction leads too many historians into elaborate narrative frameworks aimed at escaping the danger of narrative in constructing the historical facticity of their account.[13] And indeed the language of the *account* is fundamental here too: Rancière often notes that *logos*, as reason or speech, is not only speech but also its account. That is, the stagings or emplotments of logic, reason, language, and speech as recounted after the fact are inseparable from reason itself.[14] Hence the place of staging, of teaching, of historiography in his work; hence, too, the skepticism toward articulated gaps between presentation and representation, transitivity and intransitivity, discourse and metadiscourse, and so on. There is history as a discipline, he argues, precisely because words are not in precise "harmony" with the things they refer to. These tensions and paradoxes are what produce not only historiography, but also the objects of histories: disagreements, misunderstandings, appropriations of language to render a counterfactual, failures to properly articulate policy, revolts against unjust laws, punning critiques on protest placards, and battles over the implied, presumed, and unthought meanings of our most ambiguous (that is, our most important) words.

Homonymy plays a key role here. The normative practice of historical science is to examine the documents of history to distinguish the "true," or "proper," or "correct" usages of a term like "minimalism" from those that are false, improper, or incorrect. We build a metadiscourse and a method around such distinctions. In a later essay, "The Use of Distinctions," Rancière calls back to his discussion of homonymy as fundamental to his political, aesthetic, and historiographical conceptions, and retroactively redefines disagreement as "a conflict over homonyms."[15] He continues, "There are two ways to deal with homonyms. One is to proceed to purify them, to identify the good name and the good sense and disperse the bad. Such is often the practice of the so-called human and social sciences, which boast that they only leave to philosophy empty or definitely equivocal names."[16] We can think here of key terms in philosophy like truth, love, or justice. "The other way considers that every homonymy arranges a space of thought and of action, and that the problem is therefore neither to eliminate the prestige of the homonymy, nor to take names back to radical indetermination, but to deploy the intervals which put the homonymy to work."[17] To think through homonyms means to privilege not masterful, scientistic explanations of surfaces and depths or causes and effects, but distributions of sensibility as apportioned by a given usage in a particular historical context.

Such a conception of homonymy could be a broad principle for historical work, as is made clear in Rancière's discussion of disciplinary names like "history," "politics," and "philosophy" as homonyms.[18] In the case of minimalism, however, I want to make the case that more is at stake. I want to tie Rancière's notion of homonymy (as setting up and "inhabiting the gap"[19] between terms) to my earlier discussion of (early) minimalism as productive of indistinctions. That is, where many important terms can be historiographically staged as homonymic, I want to insist not only that minimalism is served by this Rancièrian method, but more importantly that minimalism provides an exemplary instance for building upon it. This is because minimalism is precisely about setting up and operating indistinctions: between composition and performance, rehearsal and concert, writing and recording, composing and listening, composers and bands, and so on. In this chapter, I am also interested not in the *distinction* that Reich suggests between "rock" and "John Adams," but rather another *indistinction*, this time between "punk" and "minimalism." Minimalist music sets as its task the staging of such indistinctions, and staging musical indistinctions is productive of minimalist music. This is the challenge that it offers to (art) music historiography. In light of this production of minimal, proximate relationships, we need to seriously question the efforts to classify and distinguish within it or, as in the case of this chapter, to insist upon its death as a means of arguing that it has ceased to be what it was (early minimalism) in favor of becoming what it is (Minimalism).

From Rancière, then, in this chapter I borrow a conceptual framing of historiography as staging disputes over homonyms. My question is this: How did "minimalism" circulate as an undifferentiated label in the years prior to becoming universally and consensually recognized as referring to the (inadequately named) Minimalist music of Young, Riley, Reich, and Glass? Against existing narrations of such a question, I do not distinguish between good and bad uses of the word, but rather insist that they are all homonyms of each other: that is, that everyone is using the same name but meaning a different thing by it. Such a rendering of speech and writing relies not on truth and falsity, but on different distributions of sensibility. This is not a gesture of throwing up my hands in the air in favor of relativism. Rather, I want to insist that the term circulated broadly and is consistently found as an operator in naming various indistinctions mobilized across sounds, venues, and figures in downtown New York of the late 1970s. Most importantly, none of the critical applications examined below will be negative accusations or dismissals, in contrast to the above concerns about the term's inadequacy. That is, in the moment before Minimalism arrived as a singular discourse of celebrating getting-over-being-minimal, minimalism was a positive label of various practices of performing indistinction on the downtown scene. Minimalism moved quickly from being dismissed as "early" to being lamented as "dead." My claims about homonymy should not be reduced to a cynical suggestion that interpersonal communication is impossible; rather, the whole point is the miraculous fact, constantly affirmed in everyday life, that we manage to communicate even across such layered and incommunicative misunderstandings. I am reminded here of the discussion of Young and Conrad in Chapter 2. There my point was not that Conrad was purely right and Young purely wrong; rather, I think the remarkable thing is that the Theatre of Eternal Music managed to function for three years with many members differently (mis)understanding the nature of what they were doing together.

To present my reading, I turn to yet another pair of composer-collaborators: Glenn Branca and Rhys Chatham. Few would challenge their minimalist credentials, but they have played little part in understanding minimalism's discursive arrival, and certainly not in the conventional narratives of music history courses. For my part, they were a contingent choice: I explored their reviews as part of an initial framing of media portrayals of collaborators prior to their (inevitable) disputes. I spent little time in earlier chapters working through the nature of the authorial disputes and none on resolving them. Here I pay even less attention: the reasons for Branca and Chatham's falling out play no part here. Instead, they are figures that help locate a discourse in its place while also following its broadest circulation. The two worked together frequently in the late 1970s and early 1980s, and each was frequently acknowledged as a leader of the downtown scene. Tracking their crossings leads me to all manner of indistinctions. These play most importantly on Reich's distinctions in the epigraph to this chapter. Minimalism should be buried, he says, but not before counting its relevance and impact in the autonomous, compositional minimalism of John Adams on the one hand, and on a heterogeneous style like rock music, on the other. Chatham and Branca draw us into a world not of either-or, but of both-and; not of distinction, but of indistinction, between two coterminous, emergent discursive labels: punk and minimalism.

Where can we point to an exemplary blurring of these chronologies? In 1976, the same year that many histories insist that the term "minimalism" came into common usage in art music criticism, the Ramones played over forty shows at CBGB and other clubs in support of their first album, released on 23 April. The next day Steve Reich and Musicians premiered *Music for 18 Musicians* at Town Hall. I am not claiming that either directly influenced the other, that we should suggest they are musically the same, or that either could possibly be seen to precede the other (as both went through extensive rehearsal and performance well before these "official" release dates). Instead, I simply contend that such contrast calls to attention why, when albums like Reich's *Music for a Large Ensemble* or Glass's *North Star* were released in 1977 critics might have raised flags about them being particularly "minimal." This is even truer when they appeared on record store shelves alongside the first Ramones LP in the spring of 1976, or in comparison to *No New York* produced by Brian Eno (discussed below) in the fall of 1978. Perhaps most importantly, as I will show below, in the summer of 1976 and the months and years immediately following, it would become increasingly difficult to know whether New York critics were referring to Reich or the Ramones when they labeled a performance or recording "minimal." Such homonymic blurring has played no part in music-historical genealogies of the term "minimalism" in large part because such writing begins from a teleological drive toward tidy, taxonomic classification. But as I will show, by 1978 it had become far more common to label a punk show "minimal" than a concert by Glass at Carnegie Hall.

We should take the rejections and distancing from "minimalism" that were so prominent among composers and critics not as yet another instance of an ahistorical, transcendent dismissal of a genre name as insufficient to the complexity of a composer's output. (As Reich likes to note, Debussy disliked the term impressionism.) Rather, I want to suggest that such rejections are more in line with what we should call—redirecting the term from Johann Girard's history of minimalism—a "double rejection."[20] For Girard, the two rejections were minimalism's foundational refusals of both serialism and chance. For my purposes, the rejections are not only historical but also political. Reich, Glass, and others were not only distancing themselves from the authorial politics of their own early music; they were also refusing the critical discourses that articulated a connection between their music and that of the Ramones, Teenage Jesus and the Jerks, Talking Heads, Theoretical Girls, and other bands being labeled as "minimal" far more often than were Reich or Glass in the New York music press at the time. Choosing to follow Branca and Chatham in their movements through the downtown New York scene means voting in favor of following minimalism's production of indistinction. Keeping a close eye to both the presence and the absence of the word "minimal" in New York music press during the late 1970s, particularly in reviews related to Branca and Chatham, helps clarify what the emergent, major discourse of Minimalism covered up, and where those blurring indistinctions do not carry over. This chapter's real dispute, then, is less that between Branca and Chatham than that between various indistinct minimalism(s) and the hegemonic image of a distinct, zombified, big-*M* Minimalism.

Building "Minimal" Consensus

So how did "minimalism" initially appear in contemporary criticism? As with any discursive label, it did not spring fully formed or consistently applied in the early years, which has led many scholars to thoroughly trace its early development.[21] A handful of critical events have become canonic, many of which are closely tied to the (slightly earlier) development of the term in the visual arts: Barbara Rose's essay "ABC Art," which ties Young's music to minimalist visual art;[22] Jill Johnston's 1964 review of the first Theatre of Eternal Music performance;[23] and John Perreault's 1968 article on Young are prominent early examples.[24] In his negative review of an early performance of *Four Organs*, Donal Henahan used the term, Edward Strickland writes, "more specifically than Perreault's relatively casual adjective, though still not in a specifically denominative manner."[25] Michael Nyman's first interview with Steve Reich, in 1970, is often connected to Reich's 1972 *Artforum* interview with Emily Wasserman, in which he concedes that "there is some relationship between my music and any Minimal art" in that an artist like Sol LeWitt "will set up an idea and work it through rigorously."[26] Pride of place frequently goes to *Village Voice* critic Tom Johnson, who Strickland argues "first applied [minimalism] explicitly and directly to the music as a movement or shared style in" September 1972 in his article "La Monte Young, Steve Reich, Terry Riley, Philip Glass."[27] Johnson further stabilized the term by referring, in an often-cited usage, to the tape music of Charlemagne Palestine as "perhaps the most extreme form of musical minimalism" he had yet encountered.[28] A few months later, John Rockwell, another New York critic who will be of central importance below, noted that Glass's music relied on an "austerely minimalist aesthetic"—though he was referring to the fact that his new piece, *Music in 12 Parts*, might in fact be a *betrayal* of this aesthetic.[29]

Historians have been rather consistent in their narrations of these appearances. Strickland contends that, despite this flurry of early applications, the frequent usage of *minimal/ism* by Johnson, Rockwell, and Nyman around 1974 "did not cause either a terminological or musical revolution" because the "music itself had yet to attain mainstream acceptance as classical music."[30] Instead, it was only with the popular and institutional successes of 1976—Reich's *Music for 18 Musicians* premiered at Town Hall on 24 April, and Glass's *Einstein on the Beach* at the Metropolitan Opera on 21 November—"that mainstream critics began looking in earnest for a label . . . and Minimalism . . . slowly became a household word, at least in more progressive households."[31] Strickland is clear on this point in developing his method for sorting through the archive: while the word appears more or less concretely, more or less assertively, and more or less frequently from the mid-1960s on, it only takes on a strong denominative consistency following the major 1976 premieres by Glass and Reich, and then often as a retrospective label for the style that the two had left behind. That is, as the term began to appear in heavy circulation, it was already being dismissed: "By the time the term was affixed to the music, the period of strict Minimalism was *long since over* and the composers had evolved in *distinctly non-minimal directions*."[32] Early, then dead.

The conductor Paul Hillier's stance in his introduction to the 2000 Oxford edition of Reich's *Writings on Music* is characteristic of the more recent treatment of this period. "By the mid-1970s," Hillier writes, soon pointing specifically to 1976, the style of music based on

> steady-state tonality, a fixed rhythmic pulse, and unremitting focus on
> a single, slowly unfolding pattern . . . had earned the epithet "minimal-

ist" . . . , although the composers most deeply involved were already beginning to produce works of such size and stature that both the label and the dismissiveness with which it was so often applied began to look mean-spirited and, worse, misguided.[33]

Indeed it is the exact years in question, 1976 to 1982, from *Music for 18 Musicians* and *Einstein on the Beach* through to Reich's *Tehillim*, Glass's *Koyaanisqatsi*, and *Time*'s "year of minimalism," that have been treated as the obvious stopping point in many of the major scholarly histories of minimalism.[34] Indeed, it's a difficult period for many historians who refuse to get over the universal importance heaped onto the (radical, or swinging, or hip, or countercultural) 1960s. Regardless of the supposed freedoms resulting from breaking with metanarratives inaugurated by "postmodernism," Kristin Ross has noted that the early 1980s marked the moment when "consensus first comes to be taken for granted as the optimum political gesture or goal."[35] Moreover, such consensus was very often introduced and carried by figures formerly associated with radical politics, but who had become repentant for their earlier radicalism (see the Introduction).

Historians have sought to impose consensus upon the diverse usage of the word "minimalism." Much like the discourse of "purity" around *Pendulum Music* (see Chapter 1), this historical consensus most often takes the form of sorting through the archive of available reviews to narrate the arrival at an unequivocal meaning. Scholars like Keith Potter, Peter Shelley, Edward Strickland, and most recently Christophe Levaux have uniformly fallen into the same trap: that of believing that minimalism is what it is, that it could be found where it was, and that history should be the process of narrating how it got there. Despite the valuable archival and historical contributions each draws from his idiomatic readings, they each more and less write this evidence within a narrative of minimalism becoming itself somewhere around 1980. Levaux's recent book drastically expands upon these possibilities by reintroducing dead-end labels like "theatre of mixed means," "music with roots in the aether," and "solo ensemble music" for early tapes and live musician pieces.[36] Even still, articulating the definition of a label like minimalism under such assumptions necessarily begins from drawing a line partitioning "proper" and "improper" usage. Within this regime of archival investigation, any piece of evidence can be split into one of two categories: first, pieces of criticism that use the term "minimalism," but require qualification in that they do not precisely align with the meaning of the term that we expect today;[37] and second, pieces of criticism that accurately reflect the aesthetic of minimalism as we today understand it but call it something other than minimalism.[38]

While these and other historians carefully follow the nuances and subtleties of reception, there is a general methodological fault in trying to build up the discourse around the *eventually* dominant figures and applications of closely related terminology—that is, in expecting to find minimalism exactly where we know it to be.[39] This method produces striking aporias in the archival search. For example, while scholars frequently note that Johnson's first review was of Reich's *Drumming* premiere in 1971, that he grouped together Young, Riley, Reich, and Glass in 1972, or that he labeled Charlemagne Palestine's music a radical form of minimalism in 1974, no scholars has remarked on Johnson's very strong application of the term in March 1972.

Rhys Chatham was hired by Woody and Steina Vasulka as the Kitchen's first music programmer at the end of 1971 at the age of nineteen, and held the position until 1973, and then again in 1976–1978 following stints by Arthur Russell and Garrett List. During the first months of his programming, Chatham put on several concerts featuring his own music, including one that drew a review from Johnson in the *Voice*.[40] The 9 March 1972 article, titled "A Surprise under the Piano"—only three months after the review of *Drumming* that began Johnson's career at the *Voice* (and which did not include the word "minimal" in any form)[41]—reviews Chatham's concert "Music with Voice and Gongs." The closing piece for four amplified gongs, Johnson writes, "allowed [the gongs] to do their own beautiful thing, with a minimum of human tampering." While the adjective "minimum" here is a general descriptor, it is closely followed by the proclamation that Chatham's music was "a radical new kind of minimalism which almost negated the whole idea of composition." Here, the close proximity of two applications—"minimum" as a descriptor, and "minimalism" as a stylistic label—encourages consideration of the concept's consistency. Indeed, the second usage recalls Johnson's frequently cited claim—from two years later—about Palestine's tape music as "the most extreme form of musical minimalism" the critic had yet encountered.[42]

What is *minimal*, across both usages in the article on Chatham, is not the sonic materials; instead, it is that *the composer's interventions in the sound are kept to a minimum*, and that this refusal to tamper created a music in which the traditional concept of composition was "almost negated." Indeed, it is the *only* early, explicit usage of the term that is immediately followed by a definition of what Johnson means by the term, and several years before the early usages that Johnson himself prioritizes in his volume of collected writings.[43] This helps distinguish quite clearly the "minimal" (which he often applied to Palestine, Spiegel, Behrman, and Chatham) and the "hypnotic" (Young, Riley, Reich, Glass) in Johnson's writing. For Johnson, minimalism has more to do with authorship (or its near negation) than with formal features of the sounding results; though minimal authorship is surely audible in the sonic product, emphasis is placed on the composer's minimal involvement in producing that sound.

Of course, "minimal" came up in a number of contexts during the mid- to late 1970s. For Bernard Gendron the aesthetics of "minimalism" played a key role in Lester Bangs's conception of punk, which Gendron summarizes in relation to three themes: "sheer aggressiveness and loudness," "minimalism," and "defiant, rank amateurism."[44] While Gendron's outline of the Bangs/punk aesthetic as a whole is important, his understanding of minimalism in particular helps in considering the interrelated senses of the "minimal" in circulation in music in late 1970s downtown New York. Gendron writes:

> As a label, "minimalism" entered art world discourses rather late, only in the mid-1960s, when it became a favorite aesthetic buzzword in painting and sculpture reduced to bare-bones abstraction. . . . By the early 1970s, "minimalism" was being applied to the stripped-down, repetitive pattern-oriented music of Lamonte Young [*sic*], Terry Riley, Steve Reich, and Philip Glass—*not to their liking, one might add* [Gendron here cites Strickland's overview of the term]. By the mid-seventies New York rock criticism, operating within the hothouse atmosphere of the New York art world and increasingly receptive to Bangs's punk philosophy, was actively incorporating the art label "minimalism" into its discourses about the CBGB scene.[45]

Bangs's punk philosophy tracked the development of a freer, noise-oriented, and less song-based form of rock music emerging from the Velvet Underground and the Stooges.[46] This music straddled an entirely different relationship between artfulness and populism than the one explored by groups like the Who and what Bangs called "lumbering sloths like Led Zeppelin." Gendron reads this distinction through an "art/pop dialectic" by showing how the term "minimalism" functioned in the "promotional jargon for the CBGB underground . . . [as] the productive dissonance of art and pop." The group that appeared as the "ultimate and paradigmatic minimalists"—producing this indistinct dissonance between art and pop—was, for critics at the time, the Ramones. Within their music, the term "minimalism" served a dual discursive function:

On the pop side, "minimalism" implied simplicity and adherence without ornamentation to a basic universal rock framework, which in turn implied accessibility, familiarity, and eminent commerciality. . . . On the other hand, "minimalism" is clearly an art term betokening a certain self-conscious approach to musical materials—a certain conceptuality, certain views about history and tradition, even a certain detachment.[47]

There is a problem with Gendron's reading, however. None of the critics that he cites directly uses the term "minimalism"; it is Gendron's own term to summarize a particular aesthetic value within the punk scene, which he sees as the relationship to a "universal rock framework" that refuses the flighty song forms, improvisation, solos, and jams of the dominant stadium rock bands of the time. (This distinction is heavily racialized, with many of the new-wave and no-wave bands entirely erasing any African American influence from their music, in contrast to most rock music of the time.)[48] The first time "minimalism" appears in the primary citations in this section of Gendron's book is in a quotation from Tommy Ramone, cited decades later in Clinton Heylin's oral "pre-history for a post-punk world": "Whenever we had to find someone to play with us, we'd use the Talking Heads. Even though the Ramones played hard and raunchy, conceptually there were a lot of similarities: the minimalism."[49] Later Chris Frantz of Talking Heads, reflecting on the exact same issue from the other side, is quoted as saying: "The Ramones, in their purist minimalism, could be viewed more abstractly 'not just [as] a band,' but as 'a real good idea.'" Indeed, minimalism, "with doses of irony and parody," Gendron writes, "became the recognized aesthetic trademark of the Talking Heads as well as of the Ramones."[50]

Nevertheless—and Gendron surely knew this, but did not directly need to quote these sources to make his admittedly more philosophical than historical case—these two bands, alongside many others, were frequently labeled minimalists in the rock press of the late 1970s. This was particularly true of English publications like *Melody Maker* and *New Musical Express*, which used the concept of "minimalism" to clearly distinguish a feature of the American punk scene from its English counterpart. Reflecting on this difference, Michael Watts, writing from England in September 1976, argues that New York "punk is Minimalism (I think it means making a virtue out of very little)," in contrast to the aggressive assault of the British bands.[51] When Talking Heads were put on the cover of the *Village Voice* following their third-ever concert in 1975, James Wolcott wrote that they are "one of the most intriguing off-the-wall bands in New York. Musically, they're minimalists."[52] As outlined above, at this point the term had not yet gained any precise consistency as an identity for composers. The title of the article—"A Conservative Impulse in the New York Rock Underground"—suggests that minimalism in rock is a backward-looking mellowing of bombastic 1970s rock.

The British context was similar. In the summer of 1977, Nick Kent of *New Musical Express* wrote that Talking Heads had immediately taken their place among "Television, Patti Smith, the Ramones, and Heartbreakers" as part of the CBGB scene in New York. He continues, "Convenient tags like 'punk' and 'art-rock' found themselves strange bed-fellows in numerous articles consummated by the inevitable bandying of the term 'minimalism.'"[53] Kent joins British colleagues in using minimalism to contrast the current New York punk scene from the "gashed-up rock" of a few years earlier by acts like the New York Dolls. Minimalism is defined as a "new austerely dressed-down form of rock" of which Talking Heads were the dominant practitioners. Mick Farren, also writing from England, offers a similar perspective. He refutes the belief that the Ramones draw on the noisy legacy of the New York Dolls, MC5, or The Who; rather, Farren claims, their music recalls "the Shangri-Las, the Ronettes" and all the rest of the "baroque" school of early sixties, Phil Spector pop. The difference is that "they've taken that music, and . . . they've removed the arrangement, the harmonies, the twenty-piece orchestra, the introduction, the coda, and even the melody." He continues, "*This is minimalism in its highest and purest form.*" He concludes, recognizing one of the central critical problems of the coming years, by noting that "one of the crosses the minimalist has to bear is that the lumpen public always tends to assume that his constant efforts to reduce everything to its basic components is a symptom of stupidity and lack of talent."[54] The British press continued its effort to make sense of the New York rock scene even into 1980, when an article in *Melody Maker* again referred to "the infectious minimalism of the Ramones [that] has been with us for six years now."[55] Talking Heads and the Ramones became the dominant models of this self-conscious, intellectualized version of American punk as minimalism. Perhaps most importantly, the term is applied sincerely, without claiming its inadequacy; that is, it is a more direct and literal application than was the case, around the same time, of "minimalism" among the big four.

"Minimalism," as I will continue to show, meant a lot of things throughout the 1970s in New York. In the early years, it referred to a style of visual art in which an idea was set up and allowed to rigorously run through a process, which critics immediately recognized as heavily influential on Reich (via

Sol LeWitt) in particular.[56] Around this same time, it became an important adjective for critics like Johnson and Nyman, who used it rather consistently to refer to music involving little contrast between materials such that most of the material is present at the outset, as well as music in which the authorial voice is defined by as little tampering as possible in the resultant sound or formal structure. When rock critics picked up on the term, it was used, as Gendron notes, to reference the self-conscious conceptualism of the visual arts, as well as to stripping down song structures to their bare bones. It was only after this punk usage that the term took on consistency as the proper name of a genre defined by repetition and drone, as exemplified by emergent household names like Steve Reich, Philip Glass, Terry Riley, and, shortly thereafter, John Adams. But more than any of these uses, what's important is how, at each step, we find the term "minimalism" used to mark indistinct junctures, moments of impurity and indifferentiation. We must avoid the trap of staging such moments of indistinction as sloppy steps on the way toward a pure, metaphysical conception; rather, each indistinction exacerbates and intensifies the preexisting ones. Minimalism, that is, does not need to be made distinct, but rather registered as an operator of indistinction.

What is most important for me is considering the indistinct blurring between these two usages of the term: not that there is a world of art where it holds one meaning and a world of pop in which it holds another, but that these two worlds were essentially the same. The word "minimalism" names a discursive gap and the practice of inhabiting it. The "distinctive" feature of minimalism I am drawing out, if it must be seen that way, is "not between two principles of [mutual] exclusion, but between two principles of co-existence."[57] These two worlds existed within the same venues, called to the same critics and performers, and staged a real-world denotative conjunction. The historiographic obligation is to find a way for writing to inhabit that gap rather than beginning from dividing the scene into distinct zones and hybrids, notable precursors and traceable influences. Criticism of Chatham and Branca can help animate that buzzing, minimal gap rather than resolving it. Their selection was contingent. I am not putting them forward as exceptional figures not given their due, but rather as figures who draw our attention to how different emphases empower trajectories of minimalism living through and beyond the era of its imposed "death." I want to show that, while authors for major publications like *High Fidelity* and *Time* always tied mention of minimalism (vis-à-vis Young, Riley, Reich, and Glass) to the inadequacy of the term, downtown critics like Johnson, John Rockwell,

Greg Sandow, and Jon Pareles, when writing about Branca or Chatham and their broader circle, frequently labeled music "minimal" without any cynical distance—that is, without feeling the need to reject the term as insufficient or derogatory. It did not name an imposed austerity or ignorant regression but a new principle about how composition, performance, and authorship could be understood.

Rhys Chatham's Minimalist Education

As Johnson's review above already shows, reading criticism of Chatham from the 1970s adds a new dimension to the discourse of "minimalism" in play at the time. Indeed, Chatham was central to what minimalism was and would become in the early 1970s—not only through his compositions, but also in his modes of performing, curating concerts, and sharing resources. For my part, I recognize Chatham as the first composer to have been pedagogically steeped in the early music of Young, Riley, Conrad, Reich, Glass, and others while they were all still involved in collaborative early minimalism. Like each of them, Chatham's turn toward minimalism was a specific rejection of an earlier attachment to academic serialism.

This rejection began at a 1969 Terry Riley concert in a series called the Electric Ear.[58] The intermedia performance was well attended, and even drew a positive review from the notoriously conservative Harold C. Schonberg in the *Times*. There the eminent critic referred to Riley as "a pianist-saxophonist-composer-electronics specialist who has become one of the heroes of the new movement."[59] There is no mention of "minimalism" or anything "minimal"; indeed, Schonberg's one complaint is of the maximal volume pushed beyond the pain threshold. He writes that "[Riley's] thing is repetition of patterns to the point of hypnosis," adding, "His left hand . . . must be made of one of the new unbreakable synthetic plastics." Schonberg's review calls my attention to where New York and its music scene stood at that moment: plastics were new, repetition was new, high-volume concerts were new, as was a non-proscenium venue that included a state-of-the-art "color console" for throwing elaborate psychedelic projections onto and behind the performer—but it was all becoming prevalent enough that the *Times* had to send its chief classical music critic.

A 1981 profile of Chatham by John Rockwell singled out the importance of this concert for the young composer. Chatham is quoted as saying, "In 1968 [*sic*], the Electric Circus had a Monday evening series of new-music concerts called 'The Electric Ear.' At the time, I didn't even like tonal music, but I heard Terry Riley, and that was [a] big influence."[60] Chatham further discussed the event when I spoke with him in 2014.

> I went to hear Terry Riley. I was this young composer and I thought, "I'm gonna hear some really good noise!" And I got there and saw this long-haired guy with red hair and striped bell-bottom pants playing circus organ! And I was absolutely disgusted . . . because at the time, tonality was completely out. If you wanted to be a hip composer, it had to be dissonant. So I went downstairs and asked for my money back. It was five dollars to get in, which you can imagine what five dollars was like for a seventeen-year-old in 1968 [*sic*]. . . . And they wouldn't give it to me, so I said, "Aw, what the heck, I'll go back and listen." And I listen, and I said, "You know, this isn't so bad!" Of course it was *Rainbow in Curved Air*—like a long, hour-and-a-half version. And then there was an intermission and then they played *Poppy Nogood* with David Rosenboom playing viola. And all I can say is I walked in there a serialist and I walked out converted as a hardcore minimalist.[61]

Following the Riley concert, Chatham became involved in Morton Subotnick's studio at New York University, where he met composers Maryanne Amacher, Charlemagne Palestine, and Ingram Marshall. "And so, there was Charlemagne doing these pieces of long duration, and I said, 'Well, I like pieces of long duration too.' I had just been to see the Terry Riley concert. And Marianne was into music of long duration too." He continues,

> Composers back then, on the downtown scene, couldn't play at McMillan Hall at Columbia because we weren't doing the right type of music. And neither was Philip and neither was Steve. And so the way all those guys handled it, Philip and Steve before Charlemagne and me of course, and La Monte and Terry ten years before anybody— the way we handled it, we realized we could do the concerts in people's living rooms in SoHo.[62]

Chatham set out to develop a music series to provide himself and his friends a space to perform their music, and found the space to do so at the Kitchen. "I modeled the series I did at the Kitchen on Thais Lathem's series Monday nights at the Electric Circus"—the same series in which he first heard Riley (and minimalism) two years earlier.[63] It was thus out of that first minimalist experience that Chatham became a "minimalist"—something that he viewed as not only an aesthetic orientation, but also a practice of programming, institutional relations, and performance practice; in the 1981 profile with Rockwell, he retroactively labels Riley's performance at Lathem's series a "first epiphany."

Chatham's first stint as a concert programmer began in October 1971 and leaned heavily on the parallel influences of La Monte Young and Tony Conrad. The 4 October concert featured works by Laurie Spiegel alongside pieces by Chatham with titles like *Composition Equalizer, Composition 15.iv.71*, and *Journey of the Sine Wave Generator and the Square Wave* that clearly reflect Young's influence not only sonically but in titling practices (Figure 11). He subsequently booked Young for a concert on 13 December 1971 (Figure 12). Because the Kitchen could not afford to pay Young's high fees, he was offered 100 percent of the door sales. As Chatham recalls it, Marian Zazeela insisted that they accept the offer, as the pair were particularly cash strapped at the moment. Young's concession was to put on a "performance" that was simply a listening session to the couple's recent *Black LP*. "So we had the record player and La Monte put the needle on and we listened to the record. And on one side it was a version of just Marian and he and the Moog synthesizer playing *The Tortoise, His Dreams and Journeys*, and on the other side was the gong piece. And the concert finished and Marian was very pleased: 'Well, La Monte, we got our grocery money.'"[64]

The Kitchen had become the home of the 60 Hz hum. On 11 March 1972, the Kitchen provided space for the first performance of Conrad's *Ten Years Alive on the Infinite Plane*, featuring Conrad on "violin, intervals from the just intonation families of 2, 3, 7, 11, and 17," Chatham on "long string drone," and Laurie Spiegel on "pulsing bass."[65] A few months later, on 25 May, "Rhys Chatham & Associates" presented the New York premiere of "Dr. Drone in Concert performing his quiet version of 'composition in the key of 60 cycles.'" The piece again shows the overlapping influences of Conrad and Young during a period when the two were still on good terms; indeed, the work seems a direct outgrowth of the Theatre of Eternal Music, which Young had reformed with Chatham as one of the singers. Labeling the music "in the key of 60 cycles" recalls Conrad's writing from *Film Culture*: "Outside the domain of 60 cycle current, our music will fall less resonantly on the city ear, the most tonal of all cultures."[66] The poster from the Kitchen proudly announces—the only instance of such an announcement I have ever seen—a program note written by Conrad for the concert. We should certainly take this as a sign of Chatham's enthusiasm for Conrad's theoretical sanction (Figure 13).[67]

```
Electronic Music Concerts   Monday nights at the Kitchen

October 4.....Works of Laurie Spiegel and Rhys Chatham
1) "Harmonic Piece".......L.Spiegel
2) "Tombeau"                    "
3) "Pieces of 3"                "
4) "Composition Equalizer"  R.Chatham
5) "Composition 15.iv.71"        "
6) "Composition 30.ix.71"        "
7) "Return to Zero"..........L.Spiegel
8) "Journey of the Sine Wave Generator
and the Square Wave" ( 3.ix.71)....R.Chatham

October 18.... Works of L.Spiegel, R. Chatham, and Jesse Miller
1) "Before Completion"....L.Spiegel
2) "Harmonic Composition"..."
3) "Mines"..................."
4) "Composition 15 iv71"....R.Chatham
5) "Roma".............. J.Miller
6) "Canyon at Sunset" ....."
7) "Sojourn" .....L.Spiegel
8) "Tombeau" ......."
9) "Composition 30 ix 71"....R.Chatham
10)"Journey of the Sine Wave
Generator and the Square Wave"..Chatham
11)"Return to Zero"...Spiegel

October 18...All works by Mr. Emmanuel Ghent
1) "Battery Park"
2) "Danger High Voltage"
3) "Phosphone"
4) "Fusion."
5) "Fission"
6)"Super Nova"
7) "Our Daily Bread"
8) "Lady Chatterly's Love"
9) "L'Apre Midi d'un Summit Metting"
10) "Source"

October 25.... Experiments with flute and violin
played by Rhys Chatham and Dimitri Devyatkin, respectively
modulated through a Putney synthesizer by Woody Vasulka

November 1... works by Rhys Chatham
1) Out of the Forest...
2) Green Line Poem #1 and #2
3) Green Line Poem, with Gong and Microphone, played by
Anya Allister and Karen Haney, respectively
```

Figure 11. Concert program from "Electronic Music Concerts Monday Night at the Kitchen." Featuring music by Rhys Chatham, Laurie Spiegel, and others. October 1971. Courtesy of the Kitchen Archives.

Figure 12. Poster for "The Kitchen Presents: Preview of the New LP Recording [by] La Monte Young and Marian Zazeela," 13 December 1971. Courtesy of the Kitchen Archives.

For all its associations with Young and Conrad, Chatham would have first encountered the 60-cycle drone at the Electric Ear. "Time is suspended," Harold Schonberg wrote in his review of Riley's performance. "One idea—either ingenious or Machiavellian, depending on how you look at it—occurred in the second piece. There Mr. Riley pulled a plug from one of the amplifiers to create an open circuit. This low-pitched sound—around a B-flat?—kept going throughout the course of the composition, the longest pedal point in history."[68] Schonberg's ear is surprisingly accurate, if his technological awareness was less so: the 60 Hz drone that would have resulted from his open circuit falls only slightly above the B-flat three octaves below middle C. In

Rhys Chatham & Associates present:

n.y. premier - DR.DRONE In Concert

performing his quiet version of
··composition in the key of 60 cycles··

video projection by Hrut Herjolfsson

with program notes by Tony Conrad

Thursday   25 May 1972   midnight

 240 Mercer St.

Figure 13. Poster for "Dr. Drone in Concert" at the Kitchen, 25 May 1972.
Courtesy of the Kitchen Archives.

his program note, Conrad encouraged his readers to tune in to 60 cycles: stick
your finger in a socket ("it's more a shock to people watching") or "transmit
it through the air. Use your ears as transducers. . . . Join the most constant
universal life event on our continent. Hum at 60 cycles."[69]

Clearly Chatham was a student of the Theatre of Eternal Music school,
tuned into the punk-Pythagoreanism of open-circuit hum. The 60 Hz drone
was perhaps the defining aesthetic of music curation in the Kitchen's first
years. Young and Conrad spent the summer of 1972 in Kassel, Germany, as
participants in Documenta V, where both the *Dream House* (with Conrad
hired to maintain Young's oscillators), and Conrad's film work were presented.
When the performances were done, Conrad headed to Wümme, where he
made his record *Outside the Dream Syndicate* with the progressive rock band
Faust.[70] Chatham recently claimed that he felt slighted at the time, as he had
been involved in developing the music with Conrad and Spiegel as *Ten Years
Alive*. In a 2008 interview, Chatham told Alan Licht that he was "really jeal-
ous . . . and a little pissed off" about Conrad recording the album with Faust.

"Because we had developed the music as a trio—Tony, Laurie Spiegel, and myself. And then Tony went on tour and that record with Faust came out, and I was so sad. But I got over it really quickly. I liked what they were doing so much and I still listen to the album with great pleasure."[71]

Tom Johnson was impressed with both the new venue and its precocious young music director. He profiled Chatham in an October 1972 piece titled "Someone's in the Kitchen—with Music."[72] There Chatham is described as "a 23-year-old [*sic*] composer," and "remarkably open-minded," though "not the ambitious type that you might expect to be organizing concerts."[73] The Kitchen is described as "simply a space where composers can organize their own concerts," in contrast to the institutionalized contemporary music venues and performance organizations around New York. The major contribution was in the concert format, as particularly highlighted by events in the upcoming second season, and in particular the "one-man" events by composers like Laurie Spiegel, Jim Burton, Judith Sherman, Garrett List, Phil Niblock, Tony Conrad, Alvin Lucier, and others. This "one-man format," Johnson explained to his readers, was a welcome contrast to the typical art music program consisting of pieces by several different artists—a format in which "many remarkable ideas have gone by almost unnoticed, simply because they were stuffed into the middle of a concert which contained a potpourri of conflicting styles."[74] In contrast, the Kitchen allows artists to craft their own presentation context, giving their music (often drone-based, or duration-oriented, or repetitive) the space and time required to best experience it. As in Riley's *In C* premiere, or the Theatre of Eternal Music loft concerts, composers now had a venue that supported novel presentation of not only music, but also authorship. What's more, the composers were in almost every single case involved in the performance—a situation unheard of in uptown venues.

In 1973 Chatham passed the music director job to the cellist and composer Arthur Russell so that he could focus on his own music (Chatham would later take up the position again from 1976 to 1978). Chatham decided that he "had to break away from La Monte" because the pieces that he was writing "sounded very very much like Charlemagne Palestine or La Monte Young." In the spring of 1976, Chatham had what he would call his "second epiphany," following the first one at Electric Ear; in this case, the composer Peter Gordon (of the Love of Life Orchestra) brought Chatham to see a Ramones concert celebrating the release of their first LP, *The Ramones*; the concert was probably in April or May 1976.[75] As Chatham had been working extensively with Young, Conrad, and Palestine during the period, and writing his own drone-inspired electronic music, his first experience of the Ramones was ironically one of harmonic complexity: "Those guys, their music was highly complex. They were playing two more chords than I was. They were playing three, I was only playing one."[76] The Ramones "epiphany" became an experience through which to clarify his own compositional voice; he realized a common trend among the composers he was interested in: "La Monte . . . had been highly influenced by a different kind of music, by North Indian classical music. Steve was influenced by jazz and had studied Ghanaian music. Philip was highly influenced by process art and by Ravi Shankar. And I said, 'What can I do?'"[77] Chatham immediately borrowed a Fender Telecaster from the composer Scott Johnson and began learning how to play electric guitar.[78] Minimalism, Chatham reaffirms, places in resonant adjacency musical and artistic resources formerly imagined as "distant" or external, at least within the associated composers' pedigreed backgrounds.

The two epiphanies—Riley and Ramones—position Chatham's compositional career as a meeting of what we would today call "punk" and "minimalism," though neither term was yet in concrete circulation. Chatham was primed for the Ramones concert as a result of prior listening experiences going back to the Electric Ear concert. He heard the Ramones as "complex"—against all discourse of the time, which labeled their music as the peak of punk rock "minimalism"—because he had been working with one chord since, after listening to Terry Riley, he became a self-described "hardcore minimalist." Chatham made the connection clear as early as 1981 in his conversation with Rockwell: "I had never been to a rock concert in my life, and I loved what [the Ramones] were doing. There seemed to me a real connection between the minimalism I had been involved with and that kind of rock."[79] That Chatham clearly and loudly identifies as a "minimalist" is central—and that he was doing so in 1981 even more so. As in my reading of Reich writing *It's Gonna Rain* "after listening to Terry Riley" (see Chapter 2), the foundational mythology of Chatham as a composer forms around a double epiphany in which he was converted into the identity "minimalist" after hearing Riley, which allowed him to hear the Ramones *as minimalist*. I say *as* minimalist in a double sense: that is, both Chatham himself listening as a minimalist, and that he heard the Ramones as fellow minimalists. For Chatham, minimalist had become an identification of an entrained listening positionality.[80]

The importance of Chatham's role as programmer cannot be overstated, even before his compositional career took off. The Kitchen was the central institution for forging, in the early years, what Benjamin Piekut might call an "actually existing" minimalism. While Branden Joseph does not specifically mention it, the "death at BAM" surely implies leaving behind not only private concert venues like Glass's loft at Chatham Square, but in particular artist-run institutions like the Kitchen where Young, Conrad, Chatham, Spiegel, and Palestine performed under Chatham's direction, while Reich workshopped his *Music for 21 Musicians and Singers* in May 1975 under Russell's directorship.[81] Chatham's musical tastes—converted overnight by an encounter with Riley's repetitive form of composer-performance amid the 60 Hz drone—set the tone for music curation at the Kitchen, and drew together the nascent "minimalist" scene of early 1970s New York. Nevertheless, it is only when his Ramones epiphany truly sets in, and his engagement with volume and electric guitars brings him into contact with the rock scene and colleagues like Glenn Branca, Jules Baptiste, Jeff Lohn, Wharton Tiers, and Robert Longo, that Chatham becomes notable as a composer in his own right, rather than just a precocious young organizer.

Bands at Artists Space

In the 8 May 1978 *Village Voice*, Robert Christgau's addition to the "Voice Choices" column was headed "ARTS SPACE NEW WAVE ROCK":

Showcasing some of the horde of third-generation New York bands to have surfaced recently. Schedule: Terminal and the Communists May 2 (before this issue goes on sale); Theoretical Girls and the Gynecologists May 3; Daily Life and Tone Death May 4; DNA and the Contortions May 5; Mars and Teenage Jesus and the Jerks May 6. Except for the May 6 groups (both of whom have struck me as arty and empty), I like all the bands I've seen enough to catch them again, and the word-of-mouth on the others is intriguing. Those who seek finished music should stay away; otherwise, check it out.[82]

Alongside the poster for the event, whose capitalized heading "BANDS at Artists Space" suggests novelty to hosting rock acts at an art gallery, this announcement garnered excitement in the downtown music and art scene—despite the fact that none of the artists listed on the program had released a record. That Christgau calls the music "third-generation" suggests it is a "third wave," following on early adopters like Television and Patti Smith, and then the Ramones and Blondie. After the release of Brian Eno's LP *No New York* later that year—discussed below—this short-lived third wave took on the nihilistic label "no wave" in subsequent histories of underground and experimental rock. I would like to consider how this scene intersected with minimalism. Perhaps more than the cross-fertilizations of punk as minimalism highlighted by Gendron, no wave gives discursive counterweight to musicological efforts to construct genres as discrete entities beholden to well-defined criteria that always precede their impacts. That is, the image of no wave as a melding of punk and minimalism overdetermines the historical priority of any of those three names.

Artists Space was founded in 1972 by arts administrator Trudi Grace and critic Irving Sandler. Much like the Kitchen a few blocks away—which opened only a few months earlier, and with a similar mandate and funding from the New York State Council on the Arts—Artists Space was founded by artists to support "the needs of artists who were involved in the production and presentation of work outside the context of an existing institutional structure."[83] In this sense, both venues were closely tied to the impulses that developed the loft jazz scene, again in the exact same neighbourhood, as discussed by Michael Heller. Loft jazz and no wave shared very similar musical and institutional origin stories, including developing out of the desolation of downtown New York, and relying on artists' capacity for self-determination in live-work venues like Ornette Coleman's Artists House at 131 Prince Street, just around the corner from Artists Space.[84]

The 1978 Artists Space festival grew out of a regular event among many of the Buffalo-associated artists now known as the "Pictures" generation—including Robert Longo, a close frequent of Chatham and Branca—who frequently held Battle of the Bands evenings at the loft space owned by Paul McMahon and Nancy Chunn at 135 Grand Street. These battles were "raucous competitions in nonmusician musicianship that made the punk bands of the moment seem like virtuosi."[85] That many of these "bands" featured conservatory-trained musicians and composers from Juilliard or Mills College by no means deterred from the anti-everything aesthetic. Many of the "musicians" involved in the scene were artists from other media, as the gallery's publicity material for the festival makes clear: "This area of music has lately received much attention by artists, both as listeners and as performers. The series is in keeping with Artists Space policy of presenting what is currently of interest in the art community."[86] Indeed, no wave can most easily be defined as the sonic result of avant-garde theater, performance, and visual artists forming amateurish, antispecialization "punk" bands.

In his oral history of no wave, Marc Masters describes the indistinction no wave bands produced between artists, artistic media, and output in the downtown scene at the time. Glenn Branca, one of the scene's early leaders, told Masters:

> I wanted to make art, and it was so cool that you could make art in rock clubs. You can't imagine how exciting that was to people. There was this whole new scene of young visual artists who had grown up listening to rock music, who had come to New York to do visual arts, to do painting, to do conceptual art. And they heard these bands that were clearly coming from the same kind of sensibility, and all they could do was imagine themselves up on that stage playing this fucking *art music*.[87]

The designator *art music* is surely a careful choice on Branca's part: he is not referring to "Western art music" but rather to music, made by visual artists, that was one product of their artistic practice. Other no wave musicians have made similar claims. China Burg of Mars says she got into bands because "it's very up front sleazy. It's not this world of pretension that the fine arts can be so entrenched in."[88] Pat Place of the Contortions argues that the music scene was "way more exciting to me than what was going on in the art world . . . in performance art and conceptual art."[89] Her bandmate Don Christensen said, "I came to New York basically to be a painter, [but] I got seduced by the CBGB's scene and meeting musicians and having a good time."[90] Branca later discusses the constitution of audiences: "It was clear there was this audience made up of people just like me[:] they were visual artists or theatre artists or performance artists."[91] The filmmaker James Nares told Masters, "Different disciplines came together. There were filmmakers, artists, musicians, poets, everybody. Everyone seemed to have a common purpose." In a quote that closely echoes Tony Conrad's 1965 claim that John Cale was "by night sawmill and by day a frightening rock 'n' roll orchestra,"[92] Nares continues, "We would be making a racket in a studio one day, and shooting a movie the next."[93] Lydia Lunch of Teenage Jesus and the Jerks agreed: "Everybody was doing everything. You painted, you were in a band, you made films, you wrote songs."[94] For many artists involved at Artists Space, the "band" was a new medium that supplemented film, paint, or theater as a collaborative enterprise for artistic production. Artists thwarted their own training, talent, and expertise in favor of the indistinction between disciplines and media, such that an antivirtuosic antimusic became a form of antiart broadly rather than specifically a musical project.

Following on the popularity of this -music among the artists, Artists

Space organized the "BANDS at Artists Space" series. The festival's legendary status results from indirectly producing one of the best-known documents of the period: the Brian Eno–produced LP *No New York*, which supplemented the record industry-preferred punk label from "new wave" to an anti-institutional and antiart *no wave*. While the festival featured ten bands, Eno's LP, released in fall 1978, only included four short songs each by four of the bands—DNA, Mars, Teenage Jesus and the Jerks, and Contortions.[95] Much debate has circulated as to how the four represented bands were chosen, and has produced particular mystery around the "other" bands—most of whom never even got into the studio. *Pitchfork*'s review of the 2005 reissue of *No New York* credits the close interrelationship among the four recorded bands as the principal reason the other artists were left off: "Original DNA member Gordon Stevenson left the band to play bass for Teenage Jesus & the Jerks. DNA's name came from a song by Mars. Lydia Lunch and James Chance were dating—he quit Teenage Jesus in '78 to do his own thing. Bands who weren't as entrenched in the loop—Red Transistor, Static, Theoretical Girls [only the last of whom played the Artists Space festival]—were left off the comp."[96]

Other means of introducing distinctions between the bands have been proposed. Bernard Gendron argues that Eno simply dismissed some of the now lesser-known bands because of a distinction that was as much geographic as generic:

> Both [Branca and Chatham] appeared at the original Artists Space festival, Branca with Theoretical Girls and Chatham with the Gynecologists. But from its first days, no wave proved volatile in its designations and divisions. It did not take long for a split to appear between the East Village groups closer to the pop scene at CBGB's—Teenage Jesus, the Contortions, among others—and the SoHo "art fags," such as Branca and Chatham. The East Village groups soon were perceived as central to the no wave movement and the SoHo groups only marginal to it. This separation was permanently fixed in 1979 [*sic*] with the release of the *No New York* album, that canonical no wave compilation, which only featured the East Village bands.[97]

Simon Reynolds's history of postpunk relies on the same practice of division, suggesting that Theoretical Girls and the Gynecologists were left off simply because they were more associated with the SoHo scene.[98] Like Strickland making a case for why Young wrote the Theatre of Eternal Music's drones based on the work that Conrad and Cale would later do (see Chapter 1), Reynolds further bases his argument on proleptical perspective when he argues that Theoretical Girls "boasted no less than two composers in its lineup, Glenn Branca and Jeffrey Lohn." To suggest that Theoretical Girls was excluded from the collection because Branca was a composer is to proleptically introduce divisions between the scene that did not necessarily exist at the time. It is to use the results of that scene as evidence of its formation. It is only as a result of the Artists Space festival and the indistinct interrelation of various "minimalisms" in downtown New York that Branca was ever able to become a "composer," a claim that I will elaborate upon in the next section. In all cases, the distinction between composers and bands, or composer-led bands and "actual" collective bands, plays a key sense in how the scene is retroactively cut up into distinct camps.

Perhaps the most startling absence in these readings is that Branca and Chatham were not only in the 3 May groups, Theoretical Girls and the Gynecologists. They both also performed on 4 May, Branca alongside Barbara Ess, Paul McMahon, and Christine Hahn as a guitarist in Daily Life, while Chatham performed a version of his *Guitar Trio* as Tone Death. Branca and Chatham were thus members of four of the ten bands, though none of them made it onto *No New York*.

Many of these groups ended up being very short-lived. Existing writing tends to accredit this to the no wavers being particularly "volatile," thus mapping a biographical parallel onto the austere sound. But I think something less contentious is in play: these groups were never formalized *bands* in the first place. The band names were a means of positioning this music as an art project, perhaps turning each composition or compositional style into a stable political formation. Accordingly, the Static and Daily Life are largely the same people, performing under different concepts; the same is true of Tone Death and the Gynecologists. They can perhaps be more likened to the title of an art show or museum event—they form, draw work and artists together, take a name, and are gone again. But presenting this music as performances by *bands*, regardless of how contingent or momentary, and in rock music spaces, was central to the material practice of no wave and, by extension, Branca's and Chatham's early careers. Taking a name was perhaps the fundamental performative gesture here as a means of playing with genre, authorship, and audience expectation. In doing so, Branca, Chatham, and their friends and collaborators marked indistinct slippages between proper and collective authorial names.

Looking at contemporary reviews of the festival from the *New York Times* will help clarify the actual position of these artists at the time. Much like his British colleagues discussed above, Rockwell distinguishes New York's "underground" scene from the one in London, insisting that the former involves "a more deliberate attempt to create art out of rock, a closer connection between young rocksters and experimental artists."[99] Most importantly, he writes, "Sometimes the bands are ones that have also played the C.B.G.B./ Max's circuit . . . sometimes they are more obviously experimental. . . . But usually—and here's where things get really interesting . . .—*you can't tell the difference.*"[100] Rockwell lists the bands involved in the festival without interpellating individual "composers" out from the band of which they are members, though he does mention that "like all such groups their memberships appear to be in a constant state of flux." Turning to the keyword throughout all of this, Rockwell describes Mars as performing a "tightly controlled and generally interesting brand of *minimal rock*" and Teenage Jesus and the Jerks as "content[ing] themselves with *minimalist instrumentals.*" He closes by warning—against all contemporary perspective on how shocking no wave was in its time—that the "*minimalism* . . . of both bands suggest[s] that the whole New York underground scene is in danger of falling into a new orthodoxy as rigid as anything that may have preceded it." It is quite clear that Rockwell is not referring to Reich and Glass, and that no contemporary reader would make that mistake. Perhaps more importantly, when he needs a catchword for stagnant, downtown orthodoxy, *minimalism* is the clear choice.

A longer piece in the 2 June *Times* developed many of these ideas. First discussing the several years of "rock-art" that had come out of British "art-school graduates" and progressive rockers, Rockwell searches for yet another means of distinguishing these acts from bands like the Velvet Underground, Patti Smith, Television, and Talking Heads—all performers central to the punk aesthetic that Lester Bangs and others were outlining: "Rock has always been a populist medium, and that populism has tended to express itself in commercial terms. . . . [But] today there is a whole crop of bands in New York that either have no pretensions whatsoever to commercial success or, if they do, are operating in a realm of total delusion."[101] For Rockwell, the distinction between rock and art has always been that rock is inherently populist—"commerciality incarnate"; now that there are bands about whom this decidedly cannot be argued, he seems to be asking, how are we to redraw distinctions? Again, indistinction is the principle in play, rather than a problem to be sorted out: this indistinct experimental sensibility is a result of avant-garde artists from painting, theater, performance art, film, and sculpture pervading what would have (or should have) simply been another "rock" scene. That the noisy music made by these bands can be heard as "rock" is every bit as conflicted as is the capacity to hear it as "art." After noting that "Mr. Eno is now producing a documentary collection of some of these bands," Rockwell introduces the ones he considered notable: "These bands go by such as names as Theoretical Girls, Tone Deaf, Teenage Jesus and the Jerks, Mars, D.N.A., the Contortions and many more." They not only perform at "such punk haunts as Max's Kansas City or CBGB's" but also at venues typically set up for "experimental 'classical' music, loft jazz, performance art or video," including Artists Space and the Kitchen, which have been offering "rock nights more and more often" (under Chatham's second stint as director, post-Ramones epiphany).[102] The distinction, it seems, between rock and art, or between pop and experimentalism, has been minimized so far as to raise questions about the very terms of that distinction. Critics and historians too often take it as their job to articulate new lines of fracture.

In reviewing the Artists Space festival, Rockwell does not single out Branca by name from Theoretical Girls (as any author writing after the fact would), though he does write that "Rhys Chatham, who's the Kitchen's music director and a long-time SoHo composer, is in Tone Deaf." Returning to the art-pop binary still in place, and capturing a strong contemporary definition of no wave, Rockwell writes:

> This sort of rock is itself so uncommercial that even most rock fans would be confused by it. . . . Much of the music of this sort carried *the notion of minimalism to new extremes*. A few lonely chords are pummelled away with furious strumming while a drummer pounds out a repetitive beat with merciless, humorless insistence. Tuning seems to strike most of these bands as a silly frill, and the vocals are generally toneless screams. But amid the silly posturing some fascinating ideas can emerge. Theoretical Girls got into some unusual shifting planes of instrumental color at the Kitchen, balancing gritty blocks of aural texture in an eerie, affecting way.[103]

Allow me to draw out several key features of these reviews. First, Branca is not mentioned at all by name, though Theoretical Girls is clearly the band that most caught Rockwell's attention; Chatham is the only individual interpellated from any of the ensembles, and there only as a potentially valuable contextualizing name among readers of the *Times*. Second, commentary on the music focuses on specifically the *lesser-known* bands from these performances: Rockwell is not interested in discussing James Chance's infamous mischief (including getting into a fistfight with *Voice* critic Robert Christgau at the festival—the other major reason why the Artists Space festival makes it into most histories of punk), but rather focuses on Theoretical Girls' "unusual shifting planes of instrumental color" and Nina Canal (of Gynecologists and Tone Death, and soon to be in the all-woman band Ut) who "came on stage with a little girl and sang duets with her to a half-rock, half-harmonium accompaniment that was very beautiful. But also very, very far from the commercial arena."

These performances—and no wave as a genre—introduce an important disruption into the musical discourse of "minimalism" in late-1970s New York experimentalism. In writing that the no wave groups "take the notion of minimalism to a new extreme," it's impossible to tell whether Rockwell is referencing the concerts by Talking Heads and the Ramones at CBGB, Reich at Carnegie Hall, or Arthur Russell, Tony Conrad, and Charlemagne Palestine at the Kitchen. It is in these moments that homonymy carries its most important historiographic impact. Anyone reading this review might be inclined to suspect that the minimalism taken to new extremes is that of Reich, Glass, Young, or Conrad. But we have little reason to suspect that—or at least absolutely no reason to prioritize that assumption over the belief that he was referring to the Ramones or Talking Heads.

Indeed, Rockwell reviewed Philip Glass's first concert ("At Last") at Carnegie Hall that same month; Robert Palmer wrote in a preview of that concert that Glass's music has been called "solid state, minimalism, [and] trance music." He continues, "The aesthetic of minimalism, repetition, and structural lucidity is now an important aspect of the punk and new-wave movements in rock," as evidenced by the fact that Glass had recently been seen hanging out with Brian Eno at CBGB.[104] Nevertheless, when Rockwell reviewed Glass's concert—his second article in the 2 June 1978 issue, along with the above "The Rock World and the Visual Arts," in which he described so many of the Artists Space bands as minimalists—he did not describe Glass or his music as "minimal," highlighting instead a disappointing shift uptown as Glass hired professional singers, unamplified, and turned his own electric organ way down: "The result was extremely quiet for a Glass piece" and, to someone who had followed Glass's small space ensemble development of *Music in 12 Parts* and other pieces, "a little disconcerting."[105] (The review reveals the drastic changes in taste that the minimalist aesthetic effected over the course of the decade; in a 21 February 1973 review of a Glass concert at the Kitchen, Rockwell opined that Glass had his "Music for Voices" performed by the Mabou Mines dance troupe—"it would be interesting to hear it sometime with a trained choral ensemble."[106] By contrast, in 1978, he writes that "the Smith Singers supplied a nicely full-bodied choral sound, but it can't be said that they were all that radically superior to the dancer-singer-actors of the original cast."[107])

No matter which idea of "minimalism" Rockwell had in mind when he claimed that it had been taken to a new extreme (Ramones? Reich?), the central fact stands: the howls, yelps, incessant detuned strumming, and neurotic percussion of the Artists Space bands had produced a new extreme of how "minimal" music could be—both in material and in authorial intervention. No wonder that, in the New York press of 1978 or 1981, it became difficult to call a European orchestral commission by Reich or a concert by Glass at Carnegie Hall "minimal." And no wonder those composers were rejecting that label for their own work.

Glenn Branca, Illiterate Symphonist

Chatham's role within the downtown scene is already visible by 1971 and 1972, when all of the canonic early minimalists were still working together to varying degrees in collaborative agreement. His eventual collaborator and friend Glenn Branca only arrived in New York several years later, transplanted from Boston, where he had founded the Bastard Theatre. The two quickly became close collaborators. Like La Monte Young, Branca was rather secretive about his career and personal life, rarely granting interviews or sharing archival documents with researchers. Branca died of throat cancer in 2018; in the months prior, he sold a number of signed posters on eBay that provide a glimpse at the chronology of events in which Branca and Chatham performed side by side. There was a concert held at the Kitchen a few weeks before the Artists Space festival featuring two bands each with Branca and Chatham: Daily Life and Theoretical Girls for Branca, the Gynecologists and Arsenal for Chatham (9 April 1978); there was an early Static concert on 13 June 1978 that featured Branca's *Instrumental for Six Guitars* (though the poster does not specify that it is his own composition) and probably included Chatham as one of the guitarists; a 29 January 1979 show at Hurrah's featured both Branca (backed by Anthony Coleman, Mike Gross, Frank Shroder, and Stephen Wischerth) and Chatham (with Jules Baptiste, Robert Longo, and Wharton Tiers) listed by name as composers. Some external evidence comes from a scanned page from the 1979 itinerary of the booker at Tier 3, which shows Branca penned in for 5 December and Chatham for 6 December.[108] Further, for Branca's first solo gig—at the Kitchen, discussed below—in January 1980, the program claims that Chatham played guitar in *Instrumental for Six Guitars*, and existing recordings and commentary from both suggest that Branca performed frequently in Chatham's *Guitar Trio*.[109]

My major concern in this section is to argue, simply by accumulation, against the model of hybridity often relied on in discussing these artists. Branca's and Chatham's collaborations reveal a close blurring between the worlds of no wave and new music composition, often again falling under the label minimalism or, at times, "minimal rock"—a label John Rockwell in particular used during the late 1970s to label performances like theirs. Reviews take on the form of comparison between Branca and Chatham as composers, as critics insisted on articulating a distinction between the two, always grounded in reference to their backgrounds: Chatham the former serialist, Branca the long-standing punk. In particular, I am opposed to the discourses of "accreditation" relied on by both contemporary critics like John Rockwell and later historians like Bernard Gendron, in which it is assumed that individuals can only reproduce the conditions of their background.[110] Instead of arguing that Branca and Chatham are different in their very similar music because Chatham is at heart a classicist and Branca is at heart a rocker, I think it necessary to consider the larger network within which this distinction is articulated. That is, what about their scene has made it possible for these crossovers to occur so easily, so discretely, and so indistinctly as to keep critics on their toes in feeling the need to articulate a distinction for them? Reading reviews of concerts that they were both involved in further develops my claim about the indistinction developing between composer and band following the Artists Space festival. I lastly present reviews of Branca's early symphonies in the New York press, as critics began to regularly label Branca the hero of the downtown scene, and even the greatest composer living—despite the fact that he was musically illiterate and did not write traditional scores for his ensemble.

Of course Chatham is a classicist who studied serialism as a teen, tuned pianos, and so on before turning to the Ramones and loud guitars; of course Branca cannot write music. These are differences, and I do not aim to efface or deny them. My argument is more mundane: that these background distinctions cannot be the focal point for all analysis, and that perhaps in making them such, we have long missed something far more fundamental and interesting about this scene and Branca and Chatham as only two actors within it. Rather than considering this a chiastic, dual process of accreditation, of world-crossing and hybridity, we should perhaps consider something both simpler and more theoretically interesting: under the label minimalism, a composer could form a punk band, and a theater artist could become a prominent symphonist. It is not that either crossed from one discrete camp to another; rather, it is that this minimalist scene, in this place at this time, had created such indistinction and dislocation that there was barely a gap to cross. Arguments grounded in preexisting domains subsequently hybridized rely on the same ahistorical reifications as does examining the era prior to authorial disputes as if the collaborators are always necessarily on a collision course with proprietary battles. These modes of prolepsis are absolutely standard when historiography begins from searching out causes that will rationalize effects.

John Rockwell's June 1979 review of a no wave concert outlines the indistinction between composer and band that the word "minimal" was used to mark at the time.[111] In "Rock: 2 of the No-Wave," Rockwell writes that the scene had moved on from lofts and art galleries to assert itself in the same venues that "spawned the new-wave [punk] scene of just a few years ago." The titular use of the label "no wave" implies a balance between two political formations: there is the impulse toward the tradition of art music, of sole authors, with recognition that they are attempting to present their work under collective names; and there is the simultaneous observation that these performances are noisy, distorted, and performed on electronic instruments by bands well versed in and more associated with rock music. While Chatham was performing under his most recent band name, Melt Down, and Robin Crutchfield (formerly of DNA) with Dark Days—recall that "these ensembles tend to exchange members from gig to gig"—Rockwell presents the proper names Chatham and Crutchfield as those of composers, and the pieces they performed were read as works: "Mr. Chatham's first effort Tuesday was the same piece he'd done at the Kitchen festival of new music recently: one chord strummed in a rhythmic ostinato with light percussive accompaniment, illustrated by Robert Longo's handsome slides." "Minimal" comes up repeatedly, objectifying this indistinction between composers within bands, or bands formed by composers: "It's easy to mock the no-wavers, who reduce rock to such minimalism that to some it might seem there's nothing there at all. But minimal painting can look simple, too, and at its best no-wave rock focuses the issues of musical creation and perception in a remarkable way."[112]

The recent "Kitchen Festival of new music" Rockwell references was New Music, New York, which subsequently toured for years as New Music America, becoming one of the dominant forums for 1980s American experimentalism. The biggest names at New Music, New York were surely Glass and Reich, but it also featured major downtowners like Tony Conrad, Meredith Monk,

Garrett List, Jill Kroesen, Tom Johnson, George Lewis, Laurie Spiegel, Jon Gibson, Charlemagne Palestine, Annea Lockwood, Gordon Mumma, and Barbara Benary. In his review of the festival, Rockwell singled out Phill Niblock, Charles Dodge, David Behrman, Rhys Chatham, Frankie Mann, and Laurie Anderson.[113] While many of the New Music, New York artists might today be at least peripherally labeled "minimalists," the term barely comes up in the article. Niblock's piece "sounded like the inside of some cosmic organ"; Behrman's "blended humanism and electronics in a specially charming way"; Anderson "confirmed her status as about the most charismatic performance artist we have who uses sound extensively." In fact, the only appearance of the term "minimal" is in reference to Chatham, who "did a minimal-rock piece that really fused those tendencies superbly."[114] Chatham's performance—of *Guitar Trio*, which he performed extensively throughout 1977–1979 with bands including Tone Death at Artists Space—occurred on the final night of the festival, 16 June, alongside pieces by Anderson, Gordon, Lohn, Mann, and Ned Sublette. While Branca was not included as a composer in the festival—why would he have been?—he was a member of the band Lohn formed for the evening, alongside Wharton Tiers, Margaret Dewys (already performing their own shows as the Static), Julius Eastman, and Scott Johnson.

The distinction between Glenn Branca, the composer, and the Static, the band, was still lost on Tom Johnson in a review of the Static's first seven-inch record in September 1979. While he writes that the new band is "an experimental rock trio headed by Glenn Branca," he does not explicitly hear the music as Branca's writing, though he does provide the first accurate description of what is now Branca's well-known compositional style: The band's song "'My Relationship' revolves around a curious kind of chord change. The two guitars alternate between a unison and a two-note cluster, while the drummer pounds out a beat that is extremely insistent, even for rock. The song isn't all that 'static.' In fact, it changes tempo once and even builds to a climax before its three minutes are over."[115] In that Johnson's review recognizes the group as "headed by" Branca, but still hears the music as by the Static, it differs sharply from Rockwell's review of the Dark Days and Melt Down concert. A few weeks later, Rockwell wrote about an evening of short pieces by "emerging composers" on the SoHo scene at the Kitchen; he bemoans its quality: while "two or three top-notch successes can redeem a concert like this . . . only one piece had much luck." Branca's "limply titled 'Untitled'" was "another of the minimal-rock efforts the Kitchen likes to present" and "made one want to hear more of Mr. Branca's music."[116]

Later in November, the magazine *New York Rocker* published an essay by Branca on his colleague Rhys Chatham. Branca wrote the single-page piece from a dual position of upholding Chatham's academic pedigree while pushing for his recognition as a rocker in his own right by the magazine's dominant audience. "Over the past two years," Branca writes, "Rhys Chatham has been performing 'Guitar Trio' in clubs, galleries and new music spaces around New York under the successive names Tone Death, Meltdown, and New Americans." Branca continues, "The piece has varied in length from six or seven minutes to thirty minutes, and has undergone many changes of personnel and instrumentation. At the Mudd Club, Rhys added two trombones; at Hurrah, three percussionists, bass, and twelve-string guitar; at the Kitchen, a full orchestra. But the standard set-up is three six-string guitars and drums." Whether this is true—I have come across no mention of a full orchestra performing *Guitar Trio*—is less relevant than the rhetorical position Branca takes on the music. "Although this music can certainly be seen as innovative or modern, the final effect is still that of vicious, uncompromising rock music. *This* is what [Lou Reed's] *Metal Machine Music* should have sounded like."[117] Branca's appraisal is clearly aimed at pointing out *Guitar Trio*'s capacity for wide programming at punk clubs (Hurrah's), art discos (the Mudd Club), and avant-garde spaces (the Kitchen), and simultaneously questioning the grounds upon which such distinctions are made.

While Branca was attempting to offer his colleague the punk rock credibility he needed, he was eager in his own right to be seen as a composer. Greg Sandow wrote several reviews in 1980–1981 that aimed to distinguish between the styles of Branca and Chatham. Two months after the piece was published, Branca's first solo concert took place at the Kitchen in January 1980 (Figure 14), before touring to other venues including Hallwalls Gallery in Buffalo. In contrast to his work with the Static, the program featured pieces titled so "limply" as to assure audiences of their artful nature and not risk a possible misunderstanding as popular music: *(Instrumental) for Six Guitars*, Nos. 1, 2, and 3 from *5 Lessons for Electric Guitar*, and *(Untitled) 1979*. Sandow's review combined Branca's 16 January Kitchen concert with performances by Rhys Chatham at the Mudd Club on 10 January and Hurrah's on 29 January.[118] The review is titled "Classical Music for Loud Guitars," and headed by a Deborah Feingold photo of Branca and Chatham in front of a graffiti-covered wall (Figure 15). "Glenn Branca and Rhys Chatham write some of the most challenging classical music in town," Sandow writes, before adding dubiously, "for their rock bands." Where Chatham's classical background holds him to a "rapt and impassive" performance style, "the members

of his band (Jules Baptiste, Robert Longo, and Wharton Tiers) . . . thrash at
their instruments more wildly."[119] In contrast, Branca is compared to Reich
and Glass, though Sandow is concerned about the limits imposed by his
musical illiteracy: "Sometimes Branca's musical structure is a little rough. . . .
Chatham is the only member of either band who reads music; the compli-
cated scores have to be notated informally and taught to the players by rote."
He closes this review by noting that while "Chatham . . . has made a con-
scious effort to become a rocker . . . Branca . . . [has] always been involved
in rock." The comparisons continue in a 17 September review. There Sandow
writes of being that he was surprised to see people dancing, and decided "that
Chatham's stuff might be rock after all," before Chatham, "stung, perhaps, by
put-downs from rock critics . . . decided that his music . . . is really, at heart,
classical." Branca, on the other hand, surprised Sandow with a newly updated
version of *Lesson No. 1* that leads him to describe as "frighteningly good, one
of the best composers alive."[120]

On 17 April 1981 at the Kitchen, Chatham put on a concert titled "Drastic
Classical Music for Electric Instruments." Sandow reviewed the performance
a few weeks later as a case study in the relationship between the new music
scene and academicism.[121] Sandow uses Chatham's concert to argue for the
strength of the rock/classical hybrid in the downtown scene and as particularly exemplified by Chatham: "Rhys Chatham's music is too loud and too
exciting to be academic. The excitement's partly physical—from high volume
and a rock and roll beat—and partly intellectual." While some find it "brash
and punky," Sandow hears it as "severe and classical."[122] Alongside "Glenn
Branca, Peter Gordon, [and] the members of DNA," Sandow argues that
Chatham "is writing the newest new music around," and that it is "aggressive and triumphant" in the face of the "older new music" (the reference is
clearly to minimalism), which is "often soft, playful, or meditative." In the
two Sandow essays and Rockwell's "no wave" review, we see much the same:
critics attempting to sort, amid a number of concerts in 1980 and 1981, the
distinction between minimalism in rock, in "classical" music, and the terms of
any minimal-rock hybrid.

Sandow was right in his prediction about the shock Branca's music
would provide for the new music scene as he settled into his role of—rather
traditional—composer. Between 1981 and 1983, Branca composed and performed his first three symphonies: *Symphony No. 1 (Tonal Plexus)* (1981), *Symphony No. 2 (The Peak of the Sacred)* (1982), and *Symphony No. 3 (Gloria): Music
for the first 127 intervals of the harmonic series* (1983). While Kyle Gann has
suggested that critics were bothered by Branca's pretension in labeling the

THE KITCHEN
CENTER FOR
VIDEO, MUSIC
AND DANCE

GLENN BRANCA January 16, 1980 8:30 p.m.

Program

Film by JOHN REHBERGER (2 1/2 min)
(Performance from evening of short pieces at 33 Grand St., Spring 1978)

"LESSON #2" (From "5 Lessons for Electric Guitar") - 6 min.
Naūx, Glenn Branca - Guitars
Frank Schroder - Bass
Anthony Coleman - Piano
Stephen Wischerth - Drums

"SHIVERING AIR" (12 min)
David Rosenbloom, Glenn Branca - Guitars
Frank Schroder - Bass
Anthony Coleman - Piano
Stephen Wischerth - Drums

"LESSON #1" - 7 min.
David Rosenbloom, Glenn Branca - Guitars
Frank Schroder - Bass
Anthony Coleman - Organ

INTERMISSION

(untitled) 1979 - 11 min.
Harry Spitz - Sledgehammer
David Rosenbloom, GlennBranca - Guitars
Anthony Coleman - Piano
Stephen Wischerth - Drums

"(Instrumental) For Six Guitars" - 14 min.
Jules Baptise, Mark Bingham, Glenn Branca, Rhys Chatham,
Paul McMahon, Wharton Tiers - Guitars
Stephen Wischerth - Drums

HALEAKALA, INC.
59 WOOSTER
NEW YORK,
NEW YORK
10012
(212) 925-3615

Figure 14. Poster for Glenn Branca, "Loud Guitars," at the Kitchen, 16 January 1980. Courtesy of the Kitchen Archives.

Rhys Chatham and Glenn Branca: rockers?

Figure 15. Photo of Rhys Chatham (l) and Glenn Branca (r) in front of a graffiti-covered wall. Photo by Deborah Feingold, printed in the *Village Voice*, 25 February 1980.

pieces "symphonies,"[123] major paper critics like Rockwell and Sandow who had been following Branca's career had little issue with the change and, other than criticizing Branca's understanding of large-scale form or notation—and thus labeling him a "primitive" directly or opaquely—were excited by the quick rush of work. In the first review of one of the symphonies, John Rockwell calls the work "ambitiously entitled," before conceding that Branca is no exception among the long line of "composers [who] have been violating the orthodox symphonic form for 150 years now."[124] Rockwell is simultaneously untroubled by including the work within the symphonic tradition and, what's more, considers it "the acme of what recent New York art-rockers have yet accomplished." Only eighteen months into the decade, Rockwell concludes by claiming that Branca has "the talent, organizational skills and charisma to establish himself as the glamorous leader of the lower Manhattan experimental scene of the 80's."[125]

In May 1982, the *Times* assigned the review of Branca's second symphony to its chief rock critic, Robert Palmer.[126] Perhaps caught on the work's subtitle, *The Peak of the Sacred*, Palmer notes that Branca's "transcendentalist strain," which goes "back through La Monte Young to Ives, Ruggles, and other American tinkerers," is brought "into the foreground" in the second symphony.[127] Immediately after praising the work for being more "rapturously lyrical and hymnlike than much of the *Symphony No. 1*," Palmer nevertheless argues that "Mr. Branca is running short of ideas. There was little in *Symphony No. 2* . . . that one hadn't heard in his earlier pieces." He continues, turning to the primitivist line, "Mr. Branca may eventually have to learn more about conventional music notation in order to avoid painting himself into a corner." The article then suddenly changes on a dime:

> But what a corner! The sound of all those guitars, overtones bouncing around the room, sonic masses forming and dissolving like curtains of rain, is still utterly invigorating. And Mr. Branca has made remarkable strides in his ability to control dynamics, foreground-background relationship, and other fine-tuning aspects of his presentation. He is an inspired American original, and one can imagine him winning a sizable nationwide audience in the months and years to come.[128]

The tone is distinct from the preview of the second symphony that Rockwell wrote a week earlier, in which he praised Branca's "music of massive sonic grandeur."[129] Like every one of these articles, Rockwell raises for the reader the problem of placing Branca within a genre: "What . . . are we to make of Glenn Branca? . . . Whether this is 'serious' or classical or rock or all three, Mr. Branca is the leader of the most vital new trend to transform downtown new music since the minimalists." Rockwell disagrees with Branca's contention that "there's no adherence to any kind of classical structure," writing, "while there is no sonata-form, there is certainly the sectional juxtaposition of contrasting moods that characterizes the modern, post-Mahler symphony." Despite Gann's claims (which are likely true in some other contemporary publications), Rockwell, as at least one major critic, was perhaps even more defensive of the use of the term "symphony" than the self-conscious Branca in the early years, arguing for its consistency with historical application. Nevertheless, Rockwell asserts that Branca's "development might seem to be impeded by his inability to read music with any fluency"; while his music is written down, it is "in a kind of shorthand that does not correspond to conventional notation." Branca is thus "a prime example of the postliterate avant-gardism that has sprung up in the electronic era—an era in which the recording studio and electronics provide the 'permanent' documentation that written notation used to provide."[130] For both Palmer and Rockwell, Branca

is not a minor character on the downtown scene: he is the best composer living and primed to be the "leader" of the experimental 1980s, continuing the
legacy of the composers who can now be labeled without qualification "the
minimalists."[131] Perhaps most importantly, in the wake of those minimalists,
it is now possible for an illiterate composer to create transcendent, important
work by writing purely to electronic media rather than staff paper. This situation would have been unthinkable two decades earlier and, importantly, has
remained so within prominent didactic music histories, where the existence
of scores remains a primary boundary to mark inclusion/exclusion within a
teachable canon.[132]

That Johnson, Rockwell, Sandow, and others were so closely tracking
genre shifts among Chatham, Branca and others at the Kitchen (often as
"minimalists" or "rock-minimalists") at the exact moment that the national
"middlebrow" press defined minimalism for readers as a style without ade-
quate label, is revealing of those major publications' interest. Of course, for
Time or *High Fidelity*, the goal is to present their readers with up-to-date
information on trends moving out of the vanguard and into mainstream
acceptance; rather than following an aesthetic into the run-down lofts and
art galleries of late-1970s SoHo, they turn the best-known and most successful members of that style into representatives and spokesmen of that aesthetic. That tracking the style in its early development is beyond the scope
of *Time* is of course not news to any historian of an avant-garde. Indeed, by
definition, the appearance in middlebrow press is typically taken as a sign of
that vanguard's death, which is of course what many (including those magazines) proclaimed. Perhaps the death of minimalism is the necessary criterion
for its public emergence as Minimalism. As Kristin Ross has argued, this sort
of turn to spokesmen from within a pluralist and vibrant movement is a "tried
and true tactic of confiscation" of a political message; it is even more helpful
in dismissing an effective critique if those spokesmen are listened to primarily for their "trumpeted renunciations."[133]

In contrast to following the big names, pursuing "actually existing minimalism" as evident in an event like the Artists Space festival reveals the
multiple paths that a musician within the late-1970s downtown scene could
follow. For Chatham, it was an entry into the punk scene authorized by
the connection Branca forged between *Guitar Trio* and Lou Reed's *Metal
Machine Music*; for Branca, the formation of Static allowed enough indistinction between his "limply titled" minimalist works and his rock songs to allow
him to slide into the role of "composer" of transcendental symphonies. These
two cases raise important issues of generic and biographical constraints: Are

we to consider Chatham as having successfully become a punk? Or is he forever stuck in the position of a serialist aiming to escape the status of poseur? In contrast, is Branca—perhaps one of the most prolific contemporary symphonists—a "composer" or a "rocker"? As Rockwell wrote in his early review of no wave, it doesn't matter. The distinction between composer and band had been so minimized by the time of the Artists Space festival as to be irrelevant. These artists were inhabiting that minimal gap, that buzzing indistinction, though critics and historians rely on methods that widen it and recreate distant binaries. After a decade of composer-performers leading their own ensembles, focusing on in-rehearsal development and recordings rather than scores, and playing in lofts and art galleries rather than concert halls, it had become entirely possible for Glenn Branca, the illiterate symphonist, to be proposed as the uncontested leader of the downtown compositional vanguard. It had simultaneously become unclear to critics how to position this music generically for their readers. When bands are in artists' spaces, composers are performing in clubs, jazz musicians are in live-work lofts, and so on, critics and audiences have been deprived of the clear, institutional boundaries that define genre at least in part by venue, concert etiquette, audience makeup, and record label affiliations. To follow Kristin Ross's description of May '68, perhaps downtown experimentalism, too, was a crisis of functionalism produced by physical dislocation. To begin from putting participants back "where they belong" is not only to undervalue the shifts that had taken place, but to police the history of why and how these artists staged their indistinctions in the first place.

Coda: Aluminum Nights

In this chapter I aimed to make the case that minimalism, in the era of its death, was not only alive and well—it was more importantly a productive, determined, and positive politics or aesthetics of making music. We must recognize this in sharp contrast to the perspective of American national press at the time, the confiscatory claims of its biggest names, and even the historiographical narrative that Branden Joseph calls the "metaphysical history of minimalism." The contemporary rejections of (early) minimalism that instated Minimalism as a household name relied on two interrelated parts. The first was the already mentioned double rejection: Reich, more prominently than anyone else, rejected both his own earlier critique of art music authorship *and*, as I hope to have shown in this chapter, the possibility of any association with the musics like punk and no wave more frequently labeled minimalist at the time. But a second rejection played a role as well. Where I have made a case for Chatham and Branca proudly self-identifying as minimalist and their reason for doing so, the composer John Adams came to prominence as the leading figure of a second generation of minimalists even as he rejected the label as inappropriate. In *Newsweek* in 1984, Adams himself claimed that the label was insufficient for his music, which is a "a little too rich," while willfully acknowledging that when people hear minimalism they think of his music. A list of suggested minimalist records describes his music as "Romantic, classical, minimalist, all at the same time," and the profile of Adams lists his most immediate associations: with Harvard, the Boston Symphony, the San Francisco Symphony, and the New York Philharmonic. Peter Goodman takes the inclusion of Adams as good reason to call upon the opinions of senior, institutional composers on Minimalism.[134] For Adams's teacher Leon Kirchner, minimalism is the "white noise" at the end of history, written by "the entropy composers" who are "humanistically negative." Not Adams, though: "He has in his repertoire a rather commanding memory of past music and past harmony." This in contrast to Glass, whom he characterizes as "lobotomized Bruckner." For Charles Wuorinen, minimalism only gained any traction because of the sleight of hand of publications like the *New York Times* that were serving an audience of listeners who are "almost completely illiterate musically."

Against the use of minimalism as a name of either negation or ignorance, events into the 1980s at the Kitchen make clear the ongoing and expanding value of the name to mark insides and outsides. At the ten-year anniversary gala in 1981, minimalism was the dominant reference point for critics. Two evenings of music were collaboratively curated by former Kitchen curators Rhys Chatham and Garret List alongside the current curator, George Lewis. Running through the performers involved, John Rockwell lists, among many others, "the Philip Glass Ensemble, which plays Mr. Glass's popular Minimalist music . . . Maryanne Amacher, a Minimalist composer . . . , [and] Steve Reich and Musicians, who like Mr. Glass's ensemble, specialize in the Minimalist music of their leader."[135] Jon Pareles took the opportunity to coin a litany of new hyphenate-minimalisms:

> In the course of the 70s, minimalism—those simple repeated patterns—
> escaped the avant-garde and found itself an audience. Although some
> minimal procedures germinated in the 60s, the Kitchen . . . has been
> closely associated with the growing respect accorded Glass, Reich,
> and fellow travelers including Laura Dean, Michael Nyman, Eno, and

others. As art music goes, minimalism has definitely hit the bigtime. Instead of playing for 200 people at the Kitchen, Glass and Reich can each sell out Carnegie Hall annually. . . . Perhaps because minimalism dovetails with the drone of rock and the repetition of funk . . . there's no culture shock between pop and this facet of the avant-garde. The presence on the benefit program of the Raybeats (surf-minimalism), Bush Tetras (hard-funk minimalism), Love of Life Orchestra (atonal jam-funk minimalism), Lydia Lunch (abrasive minimalism) and Red Decade (suite minimalism) showed how much cross-fertilization has occurred.[136]

For all its work of indistinguishing, then, part of turning early minimalism into Minimalism might also rely on splitting it into a variety of hybrid forms. Minimalism was not dead, Pareles seems to suggest—it had fractured into a multitude, or a contagion present in contemporary musical culture, but that cannot be located in any singular sound. Minimalism could be hyphenated to label nearly any musical practice associated with the Kitchen—with the notable exception of the Black artists on the program at Aluminum Nights. While George Lewis is named as one of the specifically nonminimal highlights, Leroy Jenkins, Fab Five Freddy, and Julius Hemphill and K. Curtis Lyle are not mentioned, perhaps because they were impossible, in the context, to bring under the article's thematic heading, "minimalism." Each of these artists has clear social connections with the institutions and figures of minimalism—not least the Kitchen—which might have made their inclusion as some kind of hyphenate-minimalism just as reasonable as it was to label Lydia Lunch or Red Decade. I am not sure it would be helpful to extend the label "minimal" to Fab Five Freddy, though, or the performance of *The Collected Poems of Blind Lemon Jefferson* by Lyle and Hemphill (now available as an archival recording from 1971). But it seems striking that only the white artists on the program are credited with minimalism's use of "simple repeated patterns" drawing in part on the "repetition of funk." Is funk minimalist? Maybe as it makes an appearance in Love of Life Orchestra or the Bush Tetras. The band of four sisters from the south Bronx performing as ESG certainly ties into not only funk but minimalism, and punk, and they released an album on 99 records in the summer of 1981 alongside Glenn Branca, the Bush Tetras, and no wave staples Y Pants. The ground for making such connections is fertile in sound and relation, but hardly in writing.

The collective working practices, rhythmic orientation, rejection of notation, and grooving, repetitive forms that minimalism is credited with introducing to art music are, of course, all closely associated with transtlantic Black musical practice. Part of the problem is that for these white critics and in this predominantly white scene, these signifiers of Black musical practice did not register as experimentalist gestures, or as stylistic novelties, when encountered in Black performance. In his later role as a scholar of experimentalism, George Lewis has discussed the Eurocentricity of the downtown avant-garde that he attempted to disrupt in his programming at the Kitchen. Responding to Sally Banes's argument that African American culture was a viable cultural resource appropriated by white colleagues, Lewis insists upon the issues of structural racism and white privilege in play in those dynamics. He quotes Jon Panish, who writes that "it was precisely because these Euro-Americans stood in a superior social and political position vis–à-vis African American culture that they could appropriate or exploit these resources."[137] Many scholars have pointed to the instances of appropriation immediately audible in the music—Reich's use of Brother Walter's voice in *It's Gonna Rain*, African rhythmic appropriations in *Drumming*, Young's or Riley's Hindustani vocal practices—but it seems evident that these are one dimension of minimalism's dissensual practice of creating resonant adjacencies. I think here of Young's performances of blues and gospel piano in the early 1960s (and again in the 1980s and 1990s as part of the Forever Bad Blues Band). Recalling what Lewis labels as a foundational binary opposition between composition and improvisation in pan-European conceptions of music,[138] it is only in relation to his background as a Berkeley-trained musician and emerging leader of the downtown, interdisciplinary avant-garde, that Young could sit down at a piano and turn repeated blues progressions into an avant-garde gesture. We must wonder: What would have happened if a Black artist like Ornette Coleman or Archie Shepp—two people who could certainly have attended some of those loft performances—sat down at a piano in the moments after a Fluxus happening and began playing blues progressions over and over?[139] Would it register as a challenge to anything? Could it have been imported into the history of modernist ruptures within the continuum of the avant-garde such that it could be used as evidence of progress toward an entirely unrelated concept like drone? The tragedy of that situation is that the discourse of modernist rupture and originality insists that it is only through its appropriation from its originating artists that something like a blues progression becomes a radical gesture.

Published just weeks prior to Aluminum Nights, Robert Palmer's 1981 interview with Brian Eno further underscores the way that minimalism is not "unmarked" in its whiteness, but rather names white appropriations of Black musical culture in this moment in New York. Palmer describes Eno as some-one "who seduces rock musicians into unproductive intellectual byways," and as "a bridge linking the rarefied world of today's concert music to the cutting edge of rock."[140] Eno is "not unaware of his role as a carrier of avant-garde concepts and techniques into the popular consciousness. To his detractors, his willingness to perform this function makes his music essentially deriva-tive, but his ends are not the ends of most 'serious' composers." Reich's *It's Gonna Rain* is singled out for its "serious" influence on Eno, but Palmer is careful to point to a rock relationship through his collaborations with Robert Fripp of King Crimson on "dreamy, slowly developing drone music" like *No Pussyfooting* (1973). Likewise, Eno's "recent interest in African music" has had a huge impact on his work. Across these named influences, we encounter each of the major points of attention we might today associate with mini-malism: Reich or Riley's tape-phasing pieces (often based on Black voices or popular musics), drone-oriented musics drawn from a system identical to Riley's time-lag accumulator (and inspired by the tambura's role in Hindu-stani music), and the influence of African drumming. Nevertheless, the only appearance of the word "minimal" in the piece on Eno is in reference to Talk-ing Heads; Eno's influence as producer and collaborator is one that confused some of the band's fans, as the group "has evolved from its beginnings as rock minimalism into a densely layered, African-influenced brand of funk." That is, minimalism in this instance names the white, punk-affiliated origins made complex and unrecognizable by the inclusion of Eno's newfound taste for African-inspired funk. Rock is the minimal "inside" into which Eno, as a "carrier of *avant-garde* techniques," has introduced new, decidedly non-minimal ideas—even though they are the key compositional features that early minimalism drew upon. Palmer's approach to Eno is strikingly similar to Pareles's discussion of Aluminum Nights above when he writes of how minimalism "dovetails with the drone of rock and the repetition of funk." Minimalism is here, in 1981, a signifier of stripped-down, arty, angular white rock but specifically in its relation to minimalism's major stylistic appropria-tions from Black musical practices, whether in Reich's and Riley's tape pieces so often based on Black voices and musics or in direct borrowing from Afri-can drumming.

Like the music itself, the name minimalism was far from dead in early 1980s New York. It was at once a frequently used critical term for labeling a growing stylistic trend, a term for dismissing the ignorance and arrogance of those developments, and the name under which the repeating, funky, dron-ing, collectivist white appropriations could continue onward while ensuring the exclusion of Black artists making similar sounds: on the one hand, John Adams, Charles Wuorinen, Steve Reich, and *Time* magazine telling us that minimalism is dead and reminding us to turn our attention to the latest in orchestral minimalism; on the other hand, Branca and Chatham, the Kitchen, no wave bands, artist spaces, and loft venues all experiencing a discursive peak of the positive application of the name "minimalism" as having precisely to do with those features of early minimalism I have repeatedly highlighted. Recalling the historiography of homonymy, we must not see the death-of-minimalism thesis as a false appearance covering up the true depths of early minimalism. Rather, this is a dispute taking place in the form of a conflict over names—who has the right to it, who wants to claim it, who needs it to be a negative disparagement and who a positive identity, where it cannot travel and who might want nothing to do with it. Names, Rancière reminds us, are not taxonomic devices but poetic operations. That is, they are tools used to gather others around, not in line with distinct criteria for classification, but with felt connections. These uses of language to name a crowd, free of a scientific reason for sharing a name, immediately produce those who want to partake and those who insist that it is not a valid identity in the first place. On what criteria do these people group themselves together? What stylistic traits are consistently shared across *Pendulum Music*, the Theatre of Eternal Music, a DNA song, and a Branca symphony? How can we cohesively list the stylistic and formal traits that will make of them a classification?

We can't—minimalism names a working practice of authorship that begins from indistinctions that undermine the conditions of validity or eligibility concerning such identifications. Music histories do not need a "minimalism" simply to remind us of the possible historical "pendulum swings" that allow a return to diatonicism at mid-century. Music history, in the singular, draws from minimalism tight-knit connections between indistinction and ignorance, radicalism and impossibility, authorship and necessity.

The important thing is how we tell stories. Minimalism names a proximity: it is relational rather than absolute. It does not need to be an imposition of austerity or ignorance such that artists lessen their ideas down to a "minimum of means" with which to compose a piece. It is not a "lobotomy." We can instead read into it a localized refusal of concrete forms of musical authorship at mid-century, grounded as they were in outdated modes of heteronomous authority through delegatory documents. It stages near proximities, producing blurring, buzzing, homonymic indistinction between contingent, adjacent pairs. It is a practice of rehearsing-writing together, of listening together, of inviting the audience that is also the performers into a concert space that is also a rehearsal space and a living space. It indistinguishes and is thus a challenge not only to taxonomic ideologies of musical classification, but also to historiographies that begin from distinguishing and sorting similar historical objects into their proper place, narrating stories of pure beginnings and failed ends, or insisting that for any action a singular subject must be named. Music historians have chosen to tell the story of this challenge to normative art music practice as one of failure by relying on historiographical stultifications, and by attaching the story to a handful of subjects already willing, by the time the histories were written, to apologize for their earlier naivete and convictions. There is another story that can be told here, from these same sounds, figures, and materials—but it relies on attending to indistinctions, inhabiting the minimal gap between relations, and formulating a historiographic method willing to sit with the hum.

Conclusion

The Names of Minimalism

In Branca's and Chatham's circulations through downtown New York, I recognize a renewed form of early minimalism—one in which supposedly rigid, concrete distinctions between categories of composing, performing, and listening are redistributed, placed in such minimal proximity that questions of authorship, nomination, historiography, genre, and pedagogy are thrown into new light. Minimalism names such a principle of indistinction as it grows out of the working practices and authorial politics of figures like Conrad, Young, Reich, Riley, Glass, and others. As I have argued, early minimalism is not a chronological concept—it is not about the first piece, or whether it ended in 1968 or '76 or '82—but rather one that redistributes our attention to working practices, authorial challenges, and productions of indistinction between the two. Critics, composers, and historians have been nearly unanimous in insisting that the period of Branca's and Chatham's activity marks the death of minimalism. Against this death, we should ask how Branca and Chatham each retrospectively understood their relationships to "minimalism."

When I asked Chatham about his understanding of minimalism, he told me: "The big minimalists in the early to mid-1970s were La Monte and Terry, and Charlemagne [Palestine] was huge with *Strumming Music*. Those performances were absolutely amazing. And Philip and Steve. And these guys were all either my fathers or my uncles. I essentially had a student relationship with them. I felt like a student when I was before them."[1] The power dynamics involved here—calling upon both filial relationship and the heightened, pedagogic rhetoric of being "before them"—recall those discussed in Chapter 3. Chatham differs from those accounts, however, in that he was less a direct peer and collaborator with Conrad or Young than, as he notes, a student: he tracks direct relationships to each of the major figures of minimalism as an artist he was inspired by, whom he programmed or performed with, despite being of a younger generation. "Uncle Phil" and "big brother Charlemagne" were neighbors and collaborators; everyone involved called upon the others when they needed performers, space, or instruments. Chatham refers to this form of mutual aid as "sharing services," work that would have been central to his role as music programmer at the Kitchen during both of his stints. His connection to the performative and political practices of early minimalism are direct and tangible: he was often there, at the Kitchen, perhaps organizing chairs, sound checking, or otherwise supporting performances.

As a next-generation minimalist, Chatham names "the great debt that we owe" to the minimalists as turning to performing their own music. He told interviewer Rob Young of *The Wire* in 1999 that Young, Conrad, and Palestine were his early "role models," and that it was through speaking with and listening to them that he "broke out of the idea of a composer as a kind of dictator who tells musicians what to do and bosses them around." He continues, "Along with Terry Riley, it was Charlemagne, Tony, and La Monte who turned me on to the idea of being a composer-performer in a real-time context, working with a group of musicians to arrive at ideas rather than sitting alone in a room at one's desk with a pencil, eraser, and manuscript paper."[2] When I spoke to Chatham in 2014, he made similar claims: "A lot of us saw Terry playing *A Rainbow in Curved Air* and *Poppy Nogood and His Phantom Band*, or we saw La Monte perform with the Theatre of Eternal Music in all its various forms, and we got the idea, 'Hey! If we want to have our music performed, we best perform it ourselves and get like-minded people to perform it with us.'" He continues, "A lot of those people ended up playing in each other's bands simply to get the music out."[3]

I was struck at the time that Chatham's conception of personal debts all went directly to a DIY aesthetic of putting on your own shows, performing your own music, forming your own band. His rejection of the composer at a desk recalls Conrad's earlier concerns around burying the role of the score as a document of delegation, and the troubling relations of production that led the Theatre of Eternal Music to take up collectivism in the first place. In such a framing, to valorize the sounding, formalist techniques productive of minimalism is to return the style to its desk, to pen and paper, and to (mis)take the effects for the causes—indeed, to historicize them as such. How, Chatham and his colleagues in the late 1970s asked themselves, can we find a way of "writing" our music, or of communicating with audiences, that is not similarly stultifying? That does not rely on the delegations of the score? That recognizes collaborative development rather than making the composer "a dictator who tells musicians what to do?" The method of composers forming *bands*—and the way that this opened up spaces and opportunities for non-musicians to form bands that could barely be distinguished from them—was the first step in the great, successful *afterlife* of the challenges raised by Conrad and Reich; it was a next form of early minimalism.

Where Chatham focuses on bands and performance—what we could broadly call organizing—Branca places different emphases. In a 2012 interview, David Todd asked Branca, "Do you feel like your work is minimalism?" Branca responds:

> I mean, yeah, it's minimalism. I've tried to tell people, "I'm a minimalist." Period. End of story. I'm not a postminimalist, I'm not a postmodernist, I am a minimalist, and I feel as though my work should be seen in that context. I'm not doing what Philip Glass is doing, I'm not doing what Steve Reich is doing, or La Monte Young, or Phill Niblock, or Charlemagne Palestine—there's a long list of good minimalists whose work is different from mine. But what I'm doing is definitely minimalist, the way I see it and the way I think about it.[4]

Writing plays a role for Branca as well—here it is less about escaping the dangers of delegation within one's band-organization. Rather, Branca's concern is a nearly spiritualist one about the failures of writing in relation to experience as definitive of minimalism:

> There's music within music. That's what the message of minimalism is. There's music that you haven't written down that goes on while the music that's been written down is playing. And it's both psychoacoustic and . . . well, it's both acoustic and psychic. It's something that happens not only inside your ear but inside your brain.[5]

Minimalism for Branca—more like Glass than the other figures he names—is tied to scored, compositional writing. These scores are unconventional, though—as many critics noted, Branca never learned to "write music," and instead created elaborate graphs and taught his performers by rote as he conducted from the podium, most often with cigarette in mouth, thrashing wildly in a terrifying, visceral ecstasy. Beyond the "illiterate" practice of these scores, Branca's scores, moreover, do not even represent the music. They create yet another form of indistinction—between the practice of writing and the proximate tension with the inability of the writing to capture the ringing harmonic complexities that are the primary goal of Branca's music. These complexities cannot be written down or even approached directly. Rather, they must be accumulated collectively. It perhaps takes a composer who does not "write music" in a traditional sense to recognize this play of insides and outsides, withins and withouts.

The long arc of these chapters prioritizes a few key themes in the reorganization of composerly activity in the 1960s, and around minimalism in particular: the movement away from recording as scored notation to recording both the "work" and the composition-rehearsal process on magnetic tape; composers' decision to perform their own work, most often by forming bands; the rejection of stultification in both formal structure and live presentation by focusing on repetitive and/or droning sound and performance in lofts and art galleries rather than concert halls. Composers saw themselves working in parallel to contemporary radical movements in refusing heteronomous authority, delegation, inequality, and paternalistic conceptions of property, exchange, intelligence, education, and privilege, as each was grounded in inherited, normative conventions of authorship in musical composition. I used the term *early minimalism* to label these relationships of music, performance, recording, and pedagogy that are definitive of the music that we call minimalism, despite the fact that the name is too often associated with formalist criteria as reflected in a small handful of artists' idiomatic compositional styles. My choice of *early minimalism* aspires to place the classic works of minimalism in their materialist historical context as tied into collaborative and collective efforts to work around the normative implications of art music authorship. I hope to have raised key questions about the narrative conceptions through which musicology to date has staged a continuous historiography of art music into the present by rendering those classic minimalist works as "early," framing minimalist authors' critiques as obviously impossible, and thus reasserting, more strongly than ever, the necessity of singular authorship as conceptually prior to any compositional activity. We need to take these challenges seriously both to ground them in their material contexts and to be vigilant about offering a prehistory to parallel movements in our own time.

I had several intentions in calling this book the *names* of minimalism.[6] Most immediately, I was interested both in the big names we associate with minimalism, and in the generic or stylistic nominations under which their music found its cohesive articulation. In a more theoretical register, I was also eager to link *authorship* and *historiography* as both dependent on names. Individual authors' proper names need not be the only subjects of music histories, as is broadly and passively assumed in art music historiography. The names can be of authors in dispute over names, bands and collectives coming together to declare themselves a "we," and improper names like Poppy Nogood or Dr. Drone that attest to efforts to reframe individual creative outputs. Finally, I was eager to attend to the historiographic value of *homonymy* in the construction of insides and outsides, as well as the dispossessive poetics of naming. I consider naming dispossessive in opposition to a common assumption in music studies, that expanding the terms of inclusion is an inherently inclusive gesture rather than an often colonial and dispossessive one. Most immediately we can think here of the assumption that calling any sounding practice "music," in a music history context, is inclusive and benevolent, regardless of whether or not the name "music" has discursive purchase in the context. Closer to home, I have raised my concern throughout that expanding repertoire lists under the name "minimalism" is anything other than a parasitic effort to maintain the viability of minimalism.

In these final pages, I would like to attend one last time to questions of homonymy in music historiography, before turning to a discussion of *metonymy*, with particular attention to both Gary Tomlinson's writing on Aztec song and mid-1960s structural Marxism around Jacques Rancière, including in his dispute with his teacher Louis Althusser. I conclude by turning to the imbrication of naming and dispossession, homonymy and metonymy, in early minimalism and in (music) historiography more broadly.

Minimalism, I admit, has been used throughout this book with willful indiscrimination. As I suggested briefly in the introduction, music histories of minimalism have all insisted, without using my terminology, that *early minimalism is early*. To free us of redundancy, this has been reduced simply to *Minimalism*. This reduction fails to account for the fact that the two earlies are yet another instance of homonymy—they mean differently, and their buzzing proximity is key to recognizing how we have (mis)understood minimalism. It bears repeating. The first *early* signals that minimalism did not simply emerge as a fully formed Minimalism: there was no such cohesive designation until minimalism was declared dead in the early 1980s. What was dead, then, was the dissensual challenge of early minimalism, to be replaced by a triumphant, singular, consensual Minimalism that could now be linked to the longer tradition of Western European "literate" musical modernity. "In no longer being what it was," Rancière wrote in a different historiographical context, "[it] has finally become what it is in itself."[7] The second *early* is the mechanism, the alibi, by which we did not need to acknowledge that early minimalism: the second early says that now that these composers have moved on from the naivete of early minimalism, we have a mature, repentant Minimalism. The second *early* means ignorance; it is a stultification that insists that one was correct to be skeptical of early minimalism, and that all of the embarrassing parts have been carved away to leave us a few (still potentially embarrassing or unimportant) stylistic contributions: long durations, drone, harmonic stasis, repetition, diatonicism, gradual process, audible structure, and phasing.[8] I used (early) minimalism to remind us of the buzzing tension between these two *earlies* rather than dismissing them as redundancies.

That early is a homonym, in a Rancièrian sense, points to other recent priorities in the literatures of settler-colonial and Indigenous political theory. In his study of the history of "dispossession" as a term of art in critical theory, Robert Nichols writes of the settler-colonial mechanisms by which "property" as a legal concept is rendered from the land as part of a recursive process of dispossession.[9] This process has the frustrating result that, when Indigenous peoples and their allies try to reclaim land, they are driven into a conceptual conundrum: they must attempt to claim "ownership" over land that they refuse to recognize as "property" in the first place. That is, Indigenous claimants are pushed into a legal and philosophical aporia by cynics who insist that Indigenous battles over the land negate the very terms on which they must make their case. This has been a recurring problem "for racialized and colonized peoples (and their allies), who seek to leverage a critique of these ongoing processes but often find they must do so in a manner that is constrained by the dominant vocabularies available to them," precisely because the dominant vocabulary is one of dispossession aimed at rendering prior epistemologies invisible or unrecognizable.[10] Nichols labels this problem one of recursivity, arguing that it is an ongoing tactic used by the defenders of white, settler-colonial philosophies of property.

While Nichols does not use this language, I consider the tactic historiographic in its inscription, rather than purely structural or theoretical. Discourses like art music history thrive on narrative forms that track events of challenge and revolt by internalizing them within their normative concepts and logics. As a result, those who would challenge those terms find themselves either having to articulate their arguments from "outside" the proper language of the debate—and thus risk the accusation that they're talking about something inappropriate to the conversation at hand—or to raise an immanent critique that returns the entire conversation to the field of play of the dominant ordering logic.[11] Settler coloniality dispossesses and displaces by *re-placing* on Indigenous places. In discursive contexts, settler coloniality—and more directly here, the white, heteropatriarchal logics of universal property and exchange that uphold it, including the fantasy of singular authorship—often builds and replaces within the language in question, making it difficult or impossible to refer to the term in the way that it *used* to mean. I think here of the Ts'msyen scholar Robin Gray's writing about song rematriation; where many might insist that "ownership" and "property" are inherently colonial conceptions, Gray reminds us that Indigenous conceptions of ownership exist, but they most often point toward responsibility, stewardship, and connection rather than exclusionary private property.[12] Such discursive replacements mean that relationships of homonymy become clear sites of concrete struggle: disputes can come down not only to (mis) appropriations of existing terminology, but, even more, that appropriations of key terminology toward new ends can be an effective tool of revolt and critique.

Within such homonymic trajectories, the historical language of anachronism and the desire to hunt out moments in which language is "misused" become incredibly loaded. Historiographic aspirations to perfect, taxonomic distinction in such moments must be understood as instances of taking sides. Such distinctions are not inherently generous or benevolent scholarly gestures toward further clarification and edification. Just as often these gestures are dispossessive. When as music scholars we choose from among not only the names of composers but also potential genre names (solid state music? record stuck in the groove music?), we are covering up contested claims over terminology in favor of precise taxonomic classifications driven by insistence on distinction—which means carving up pre-existing indistinctions. This is often the method used when confronting archival documents in pursuit of the history of "proper" uses of the name "minimalism"—such archival hunts not only refer to the archival language, but also hold that language in compounded tension with what we already *know* minimalism to have become. It is a search to find proof that what we know is what we know. This desire to universalize knowledge, as Dylan Robinson has argued, is not a universal value, but a tool of settler coloniality; it is not about truth or factuality, but about guaranteeing the precise circulation and exchangeability of language and concepts outside of their grounded and particular foundations.[13] Robinson writes of such practices of "listening for" in music pedagogic contexts that it "satiates through familiarity (to feel pleasure from the satisfaction of identification and recognition) but also through certainty (to feel pleasure from finding the 'fit' of content within a predetermined framework)." He continues, "Hungry listening is hungry for the felt confirmations of square pegs in square holes, for the satisfactory fit as sound knowledge slides into its appropriate place."[14] Such distinctions are about the fantasy that all ideas always apply, if only we can carve away the misuses by ignorant actors—that there are square pegs and square holes awaiting their harmonious alignment, that words can exist in perfect harmony with things.

Like property and dispossession for Nichols, authorship is a slippery concept in musicology. We tend to imagine authorship as an a priori condition, a legal fiction necessary to and therefore preceding the work of "writing" music. It is often treated as a synonym for liberal subjectivity in its artistic dimension. As such, any critique of authorship that takes place in proximate relation with the work of musical composition—understood very broadly—is read as either incoherent or ignorant; claimants have failed to understand that they cannot produce in music without (first) being an Author. Someone like Tony Conrad, on the other hand, launches an attack from outside the proper realm of music (protest, picket, film, visual art) and is readily considered a prankster talking about something other than Music. Such a practice is difficult to even refute within the normative discourse of art music authorship; the only feasible responses are to ignore him or write from outside music history.[15]

We need critical conceptions of revolt that begin from recognizing the fact that critique often emerges simultaneously from inside and outside of the problem at hand. More precisely, we must recognize that the construction of insides and outsides is a narrative gesture rather than a scientific calculation. Revolt—politics, in Rancière's sense—exists precisely by playing on such (in)distinctions. When considering events of radical politics, we must recognize that it is often people involved in and indebted to the institution at hand—whether we want to call it Authorship, or Composition, or Western Art Music—that are best prepared to recognize its faults, exclusions, limits, and failings. One can certainly state these faults and perhaps contribute to polite reform, much as one can offer effective critique from "outside" with little direct involvement in a system. We are less prepared to discuss the mechanisms by which effective events of radical political activity in any "proper" domain can occur through *performing* the aporia, or fault, or gap from within it. Such actions are readily dismissed through the same problems of recursivity that Nichols highlights: "There's nothing to see here." When an immanent critique is effective, it tends to reorient the system just enough so as to be internalized by it. As a historiographic matter, then, the critique is staged as confused subjects raging against a phantom, or as naive or unnecessary because the system was on its way toward correction a few weeks, months, or years down the line. Ross and Rancière have each written of this as a fundamental aspect of the police conception of history—to render any political event as a hiccup in a broader teleology such that its partisans become delusional historical subjects fighting against systems that they failed to comprehend. We need to practice historiography in such a way that we become vigilant about such moments of egalitarian confrontation and recognize the concrete "calls to order"—which can even take the form of contextualizing the revolt—as the police concept of history in operation.

In this light, the police concept is the fundamental concern of Rancièrian historiography. How can we enliven these instances—often microscopic, or passing, or irrelevant—of politics as redistributions of sensibility as premised on the *assumption of equality of intelligence*? Very often eruptions of politics are immediately re-enfolded into the police. But it might be a *better* police. The skeptical perspective on instances of revolt in (music) history insists that if an instance of radicalism is not entirely "successful" (as measured by whom?), it was failed or pointless. Recall the ways that, in Chapter 1, *Pendulum Music* was regularly treated as an impossible model by referring to it, paradoxically, as the only *pure* instance of Reich's gradual process. The goal of a Rancièrian historiography is to develop discursive tools of vigilance regarding moments of effective egalitarianism so that, when we encounter them in daily life, we do not jump into the miserable role of police forces calling for order. I worry at times that musicology has equated "critique" with such instances of hunting out or constructing flaws in a radical claim. The whole point, we might say, is to stage even minor, remote, distant moments from the past in which equality was recognized. This is not to provide exemplary lessons for the present, but to attune our perception to recognizing and supporting these glimmers in our own contexts. Rather than hearing naivete, hypocrisy, cynicism, imperfection, or impurity in contemporary and inherently flawed radical praxis, perhaps history can be about training ourselves to hear its efficacies (alongside carefully and generously raising critiques in the right time and place, rather than making it the core aspect of our writing practice). An effective practical rule here is to learn to hear calls to order as signals of an effective moment of politics-as-equality still ongoing—one that we can redistribute our sensory relations to support and champion where appropriate.

My conviction throughout this book has been that capturing events of egalitarian potential is not about valorizing exceptional moments, but about recognizing our consistent refusal of any prehistory claimed by radical movements in art and politics. In the name of "critique," we consistently refuse the opportunity to weave the sensory tissue that might provide a precedent to eventual events of egalitarianism. I do not consider minimalism, or even early minimalism, an exceptional instance of effacing and destroying the privileges of authorship in Western art music. I do, however, think that the music-historical category "minimalism" names a repertoire and set of composers whose music emerges out of a valuable critique that we have had little interest in attending to. I have argued that we can register the efficacy of that critique in how consistently it is elided both by historians and by several of the composers themselves. That is, "Minimalism" names the products of early minimalism once the relevant political actions and authorial critiques have been elided as "early," reframed as lessons about how authorship *cannot* work. Reframing these critiques as inverted lessons takes place through narrative voice within a discipline in which narrative is often undervalued as merely the secondary report of the scientific work of primary musical and historical analysis. "The lesson of minimalism"—as a naive political formation that nevertheless resulted in a valuable historical "pendulum swing" that brings us back to diatonicism and simplicity from complexity—is not to be found in any particular sounding work or composer's writings, but rather in the dramaturgical trajectory that narrates, for example, the relationship between *In C* or "Music as a Gradual Process" and the early 1980s "death of minimalism." Must we take Steve Reich's rejection of his earlier ideas—in 1972, or 1981, or 2006—or his refusal that the essay could be a manifesto as proof that the ideas had become irrelevant?

I have spent little time discussing particular musical works in detail because, as I wrote in the Introduction, I don't think this problem is a musicological one. That is, it cannot be found dormant in the notes. Rather it is a methodological problem related to musicological assumptions about authorship as it knots together politics and historiography. This is the value of homonymy and of disputes—and of both as instances of dissensus. Musicology tends to prioritize defining conceptual terminology in relation to sonic and stylistic markers. To return to Nichols: "Meaning is assigned to terminology rather than reconstructed from the history of its uses."[16] Nichols's reading is not explicitly Rancièrian, but Rancière might add here that "the history of [a term's] uses" is precisely history, a discipline or a literature that exists as a contest over homonymy because "no primeval legislator put words in harmony with things."[17] The musicological method of giving terms meaning has the result that when we look at minimalism, we define a list of normative stylistic traits operative in and around (sometimes) the term "minimalism" and then build a reified fact around it. As a result, "what minimalism is" becomes largely about how subsequent composers carried on those stylistic markers related to those figures most closely associated with what we now already call minimalism. It is a history of minimalism as it has been told in music history texts, and thus minimalism as refracted through the conceptual distinctions (and class priorities) of music historians. I admittedly held rather close to the definitional events, figures, and musics of the normative style; my interest was in raising flags about making the musical criteria the definitive ones. Instead, I proposed those figures' disruptive proximities and disagreements as offering a new opportunity for staging a changing concept of authorship in the 1960s. This focus, I suggested, might provide us with the immanent tension and centrifugal force to break us out of our practice of mistaking authorship as, like liberal subjectivity, an a priori necessity that exists always prior to and inescapable from causal and intentional activities. Doing so drew out precisely how inconsistent the language of "minimalism" was in that moment—and, indeed, into the 1980s. Choosing the word "minimalism" from among all possible contenders was a dispossessive action—it rendered nearly invisible the historical fact that the term was more actively applied to punk and no wave at the time of its arrival as a term of consensus. As I argued in Chapter 4, the conceptual ahistoricism so often in play in music history has rendered the language such that when Steve Reich, for example, refuses the term, we read this as affirmation of a presupposed historical metanarrative: Debussy hated the term "impressionism," Reich hates the term "minimalism." We fail to recognize how such instances are, very literally, dispossessive: Reich was not making a claim about terminology from within a blank terrain; he was performing discursive dispossession, claiming negatively for himself what was still used positively in an uncomfortable adjacency to his work. He built by replacing.

The discursive construction of insides and outsides, and particularly how they are represented in discussions of revolt, critique, and egalitarianism, is fundamental in conclusively asserting what I consider politically and historiographically important about early minimalism as an object in music histories. I have argued throughout for early minimalism as staging proximities, contiguities, and adjacencies that become evident when we consider words like "history" or "minimalism" as homonyms. (Early) minimalism, I want to insist in conclusion, operates on a principle of historiographic metonymy, in opposition to the normative and hegemonic place of metaphor in Euro-American thought.

How do we distinguish metaphor and metonymy? The two are frequently paired as similar rhetorical figures. We know metaphor quite well—a conventional dictionary definition is as "a figure of speech in which a word or phrase literally denoting one kind of object or idea is used in place of another to suggest a likeness or analogy between them." Metaphors are absolutely standard in speech—we cannot function without them. On the other hand, literary theorists have for millennia had a hard time giving metonymy a clear and comprehensive definition. Sebastian Matzner recently accounted for this uncertainty, which exists even in its earliest known definition. In the first century BCE the Greek grammarian Trypho defined a metonym as "an expression that explains a synonym by a homonym."[18] Not very helpful. For more recent literary theorists like Roman Jakobson, metonymy is a variant on or subgroup of metaphor but distinct in that there is some sort of "real relationship" of continuity between the pair of words. This is a bit more helpful—it recognizes that metaphors rely on unreal relationships, the insistence on recognizing a similarity in unlike things. They play precisely on the need to fill the gap. But how do we define the *reality* of a relationship?

In *The Singing of the New World*, Gary Tomlinson relied on the metaphor-metonym dichotomy to help explain Spanish colonial misunderstandings of Aztec song in the Nahuatl language.[19] Nahuatl was nonalphabetic before Spanish contact, but it relied on pictographs as an inscriptive form. When colonizers began writing down the language in Latin characters, an entire view of reality was undone. Tomlinson links this to Nahuatl grammar: where most European languages can be distilled into their absolute smallest units that interact in often arbitrary ways beholden to a generative grammatical structure, Tomlinson calls Nahuatl an "agglutinating language"—it is created by adding prefixes, suffixes, and even infixes to build up complex compounds with no universal grammatical rule overriding their syntactic constructions.

Sentence-words and pictographic writing reflect what Tomlinson calls "a smaller distinction between linguistic denotation of things and the actions involving them."[20] Within the racist, colonial European thought of the time—Tomlinson outlines at length Derrida's reading of Rousseau in *On Grammatology*—pictographic languages like Nahuatl were read as evidence of a savage stage in a progressive teleological movement that would inevitably arrive at an Enlightened alphabetic writing. The Nahuatl language was made *early* as part of the colonial project. The real novelty of alphabetic writing is that it places speech in a relation between things and writing: you cannot move directly from a written word to a thing without going through the sounding medium of speech. In contrast, pictographs "inscribe the world in a palpable, substantial medium not itself distanced from the thing it encodes."[21] Where European alphabetic writing separates itself from the world and marks this transcendence as a metaphysical success story, pictographic writing is not set apart from or against the world—it is of the world, "its paint absorbed back into it," as Tomlinson writes.

The separation of things and writing is what reading is in Western thought. It runs on a structure that is modeled in metaphor as a grounding metaphysics of language. The first step in reading something is not to recognize a thing; it is to recognize a symbol, or inscription, or sign *requiring* reading. Reading, for Tomlinson and others, is as much about material presence as (material) absence. In transforming these songs, formerly based in pictographs and oral tradition, into something to be read, they are invested in a web of relationships that relies on Western methods of reading (after first inscribing, or assuming) distance. All of these are primarily, fundamentally, and indeed metaphysically based on assuming that *there is something there to be read into*—that words necessarily have something behind them. When we read, we assume and even invent an absence or a gap. Metaphor is the figure that lets us talk about this gap.

In mapping their European understandings of the purposes of song and poetry, Tomlinson notes that Spanish missionaries recognized the frequent appearance of the words for "flower" and "song" in Nahuatl song to metaphorical emblems of beauty. But these figures are not about disjunctions between, for example, a flower and a song as a metaphor to be recognized and overlapped as equivalent, meaning something about love or beauty or pain or loss or dignity. It is about connection, or metonymic participation:

> not a seamless merger of all things into all other things, to be sure,
> but rather a dovetailing of certain phenomena in the world between
> which Western modes of thought perceive gaps. Our effort should
> not be to divide Aztec flowers from Aztec song so we can put them
> together again in a metaphorical emblem. It should be to see, how-
> ever hazily, a perception of the world in which *flower and song were
> always already connected*; in which flower was in contact with song
> and therefore able to present it in some aspect, while song was adja-
> cent to flower and likewise able to present it; in which the question
> of the connections of parts to a whole stood in place of the question
> of relating unrelated things. Our effort, once again, should be to see
> a culture not of metaphors but of metonymies. These are the con-
> comitants of a material world seen as a varied, rich, but nonetheless
> narrowly integrated whole.[22]

Tomlinson, more even than Matzner in his literary study of metonyms, pinpoints the problem that Western thought on rhetoric has had with metonymy for literally millennia. The issue is not that we struggle to find perfect formal examples to distinguish metonymy from metaphor. It is that metonymy testifies to a different metaphysics of the world, of parts and wholes, that, by the time we try to outline formal examples, we have already left behind. Indeed, "the example" is a metaphorical construction. Within a world organized around metaphor, any metonym collapses into a confusing and indistinct subcategory of metaphor. Upholding metonymy requires a struggle against an innate, Euro-American understanding of part-whole or cause-effect relationships. That is to say, formally, metonyms are the exact same as metaphors—the challenge is to break with normative Western metaphysics of relationships as at a distance (a problem to be solved) in favor of a seamless cosmology of grounded relations. Things "dovetail" with each other in a worldview operating on metonymic relations. There is no need to argue that flowers are rhetorical *representations* of beauty; flowers and song are both voluminous things at hand. Song is an epistemological register that makes relationships of proximity audible. Metaphor is the regime of distance between things to be closed; metonymy insists on something like what Dene political theorist Glen Coulthard calls grounded normativity, "the position that land occupies as an ontological framework for understanding *relationships*."[23] Metaphor is ruled by causality and action; metonymy by participation and relation.[24]

This distinction between metaphoric *causality* and metonymic *participation* was lost on Rancière and his colleagues in Louis Althusser's seminar on Marx's *Capital* in 1965. Althusser called the seminar after he was approached by several students eager to read Marx together as a philosopher rather than an economist or political scientist. The group worked, Warren Montag writes, as a "kind of theoretical and political collective."[25] They set a goal to understand the mechanism by which Marx made political economy a scientific pursuit in place of the earlier "anthropological" and ideological thought of the figure Althusser called "the Young Marx." This collective famously authored *Reading "Capital"* in 1966, but not before yet another authorial dispute took place that splintered the group. During a session in which drafts of the papers were read, Jacques-Alain Miller was enraged to discover that Rancière had "stolen" his concept of "metonymic causality."[26] In his long contribution to *Reading "Capital"*, Rancière had used the term to help define the particular mechanism of what was unique in Marx's later, "scientific" writing.[27] Marx's understanding of capital as process, as relations of production, was founded on abandoning the anthropological model of subjective causality in favor of a structural causality that Rancière labeled (following Miller but initially without citation) metonymic causality. In this context, metonymic causality was understood as a form of structural causality in which the action of the structure (the cause) disappears into its products (its effects). Althusser called it simply "the absent cause," or "the existence of the structure in its effects" in opposition to the structure as "an essence outside the . . . phenomena which comes and alters their aspect, forms and relations."[28]

In his autobiography Althusser mentioned the dispute between Miller and Rancière, writing that he considered the whole thing ludicrous because concepts are common tools that "belong to everyone."[29] In his history of this period, Peter Hallward writes, "Perhaps it's no accident that this most anti-subjective concept, one conceived to help bury the old notion of authorial 'paternity' once and for all, should so quickly have become the object of such a quarrel."[30] Disputes abound in this period. Rancière was differently dismissive of this early writing, not because he was cynical about its arguments, but because he found his method too dominated by the structuralist fantasy of a rigid "science" as opposed to incomplete "ideology." Nevertheless, as Rok Benčin has shown, metonymy has continued to play a role in Rancière's thought: "Metonymy implies . . . a generalised displacement, in which anything can be revealed in anything."[31] This calls to mind most immediately Jacotot's system of universal teaching, where "everything is in everything," but Benčin is particularly interested in its role in Rancière's aesthetic thought: "As Rancière further elaborates the idea of the aesthetic regime in his later works, *aisthesis* takes on a slightly different meaning, one that is closer to metonymy."[32] Rancière writes that "politics in the first instance consists in the changing of places and the counting of bodies. In this sense, the political figure par excellence is metonymy, which gives the effect for the cause or the part for the whole."[33] Metonymy is the mechanism by which one can unfold relations of nonrelation as an endless chain of contingent, buzzing proximities, in place of well-ordered hierarchical structures premised on binaries of inside/outside, part/whole, cause/effect. Disrupting such reifications is the work of dissensus, as of homonymy: to constitute two wor(l)ds in the space of one.

Such an understanding helps in thinking through a total ecology of Rancière's work. As Davide Panagia shows, it is impossible to diagram out the conceptual relations among terms and concepts in Rancière's work on the model of a Porphyrian tree because there is no suggestion of causality or hierarchy among his terminology. Rather, we get something like chains or word clouds where politics equals equality equals dissensus equals displacement equals homonymy equals metonymy. Panagia labels this Rancière's "sentimental" style; his "*partager* is a distensive complex of interrelational adjacencies that procure a regard for the occurrence of an unforeseen."[34] A similar chain of adjacencies or appositions comes to mind for Ashon T. Crawley in his listening to Section XI of *Music for 18 Musicians*: "I still am about to cry yet again. And I think it's because of the breath, because breath means life means vitality means transfer means performance means blackness."[35] While Crawley was not drawing on Rancière, the two share an overlapping distrust of theory/object and cause/effect distinctions, one that I think is audible in the egalitarian poetics of early minimalism. Under an egalitarian method, terms are not causally related but adjacent, resonant, replaceable. Terms are often nearly synonymous with each other, even as the splitting of terminology into homonyms is his operative method or poetics. I hope we can continue to find ways to write—and to listen, and to teach—that prioritize the dramaturgical and scenographic adjacencies of buzzing homonymic relations, rather than a topography defined by surfaces and depths, causes and effects, expertise and ignorance, earlies and lates.

Metonymy, then, plays a key role in Rancière's work even beyond metonymic causality. Early on it was a source of dispute over propriety with a colleague, as well as the mechanism by which he began to find tools (later dismissed as too structural) by which to locate the particular mechanism of what made Marx's writing important. Rather quickly, he turned his attention not to Marx, but to workers' archives. As he told an interviewer recently, his idea

was to start from the meeting—and misunderstanding—between Marx and working-class political theory. My idea hinged on the *Manuscripts of 1844*. Roughly speaking, while Marx was writing these inaugural essays, what was happening down among the workers in 1844? What did Marx notice; what didn't he notice? That was always the idea: not to go back to the original origins, but to the origins of dispute and dissensus.[36]

Was there a danger, he seems to have asked himself, in treating Marx as *representative of* the thought of workers in the era of his earliest writings? In doing so, what do we lose not only about what workers were concerned with, but about the particular distribution of sensibility—the modes of reading, listening, speaking, writing—that autodidactic workers created in their daily lives? Most importantly, *what did Marx paper over?* That is, how was his discourse not simply a new contribution to workers' thought, but necessarily dispossessive of workers' discourses? How did what Marx has said about politics in the 1840s come to build on top of and replace what else *could have been said* about that period? Is there a counterhistory to tell in which Marx did not provide the visibility of workers' politics, but in fact displaced and covered up a more direct and relevant discourse that might have been in their own words? What other histories could we tell ourselves by using Marx's language as a hinge, a bristling, adjacent tension, out of Marx's own discourse?

I noted in the Introduction, in relation to May 1968, that (early) minimalism was not a collective revolt; it now seems necessary to note that (early) minimalism is not a precolonial musical practice set upon and misunderstood by colonial missionaries. It is rather near, though, in its practical formulation and daily labors, to the collective practice that led to *Reading "Capital"*. What minimalism shares with 1968 and, even more tangentially, with Tomlinson's reading of Nahuatl song is a principle of displacement that begins from insisting, against most academic modes of thought, that there is no gap between words and things, discourse and metadiscourse, science and ideology, rehearsal and performance, cause and effect, process and result, student and teacher, composer and performer, song and flower, theory and object. While we can certainly appreciate the efficacy of these headings in analyzing particular objects, discourses, relationships, or texts, each of these divisions happens purely in abstraction, most often as a first step toward introducing a problem for experts to solve, a means of stultifying, a rendering *early*. They are narrative inventions, not facts in the world. Early minimalism, as a metonymic practice, joined other instantiations of 1960s radical thought in seeking poetic and militant operations by which to insist that these distances need not be introduced in the first place. What is a practice of teaching that is nonstultifying, Jacotot asked? What is a form of causation that does not refer to an *anthropos*, a "bearer," the *Reading "Capital"* collective asked? What is a university in which students and professors are equals, the partisans of May '68 asked? What is a mode of composition that does not imagine the composer as progenitor and bearer of proprietary sound, minimalism asked? How can we refuse the distance between score and performance? Between composer and performer(s)? Between performing and listening? Rehearsal and concert? Writing and recording? What happens if we manifest a concert situation in which we insist there are no preexisting secrets, but only the collective orientation toward a shared listening experience? What if composers are in art galleries and anticomposers are in the street outside? How do we write that history?

Names do extensive work at the borders of authorship and historiography. Existing scholarship on minimalism, I have argued, has tended to make a metaphor of minimalism, as if naming it and its taxonomic criteria extracts it from the world of materials and things and sounds as a historical reality within a distinct world of music.[37] (Early) minimalism gives itself well to a metonymic reading for how it refuses distances, gaps, and binaries—or rather, for how it inhabits the minimal gap between them, providing the grounding that makes the relation real, historical, evident. Indeed, it gives the practice of inhabiting that gap a name in music history, though one that has gone unacknowledged to date. But such a structure of causality—or, as Tomlinson insists, not causality but *participation*—is readily available to all historiographic poetics. An attention to names as metonymies insists that words are tools in material battles—that they enter a scene and redistribute its resources, but can just as easily displace or dispossess. We need to take seriously the distinctions between proper and improper names. What differing authorial stake and historiographic politics are called upon when a sounding practice is credited to the Theatre of Eternal Music rather than La Monte Young? What indeed is the *place* of (im)proper names in authorship? How does "Steve Reich" mean differently on an essay or manifesto than "Steve Reich" atop a published, notated score? How are we to recognize the boundaries of inside and outside, or the narratological devices that draw one toward the other in resonant proximity? Early minimalism, like a metonymic historiography, stages indistinction and contingent relationships not as problems to be solved dialectically, but as structures to be exacerbated precisely in the narratological work of emplotment. The work that names do in such a field of relationship and participation must be different from what names are taken for within police histories of subjective causalities, intentions, authors, works, and properties. How can we differently understand the work of history, the work of musical *works* in art music, and indeed the boundaries and lessons erected in minimalism's name, once we acknowledge that we have moved well past these metaphorical fictions?

Notes

Introduction

1. In collaboration with documentarian Cathy Steffan, Conrad produced the public access television show *Studio of the Streets* beginning in May 1990. See Michael Cohen, ed., *Tony Conrad: Doing the City / Urban Community Interventions* (New York: 80WSE, 2014); and Corey Mansfield, "Animating the Periphery: Studio of the Streets and the Politicizing of the Buffalo Community through Public Access Television and Media Literacy," MA thesis, University of Southern California, 2014. Paige Sarlin writes that Conrad loved being a "minor celebrity in Buffalo—he was that guy on the steps of City Hall every Friday and that guy on cable every Tuesday for two years." Sarlin, "In Person, on Screen, in Context, on Tape," in *Introducing Tony Conrad: A Retrospective* (Buffalo: Albright-Knox Art Gallery, 2019), 248.

2. Branden Joseph, *Beyond the Dream Syndicate: Tony Conrad and the Arts after Cage* (New York: Zone Books, 2008); Benjamin Piekut, *Experimentalism Otherwise: The New York Avant-Garde and Its Limits* (Berkeley: University of California Press, 2011), especially Chapter 2, "Demolish Serious Culture!"

3. Cornelius Cardew, *Stockhausen Serves Imperialism* (London: Latimer New Directions, 1974). Reprinted by Primary Information, 2020.

4. The precise chronology here is unclear. It seems that Young does not often offer carbon copies of contracts; a telling exception here is the contract that he sent to Cornelius Cardew as part of a loan of the tape "Sunday Morning Blues." The contract is reproduced in John Tilbury, *Cornelius Cardew (1936–1981): A Life Unfinished* (Essex: Copula, 2008), 336. A 17 March 1983 letter to Betty Freeman points to the complexity of ownership of a copy of the December 1963 "the fire is a mirror" tape from the Theatre of Eternal Music. Freeman and Young exchanged several letters in 1987 about Young's planned multialbum deal with Gramavision in relation to Freeman's planned series with Angel Records. She had hoped to release some of his saxophone tapes (probably the early Theatre recordings) but was told this would be impossible. See Chapter 2, as well as Patrick Nickleson, "On Which They (Merely) Held Drones," *Journal of the Royal Musical Association* 147/2 (2022).

5. Brian Duguid, "Tony Conrad Interview," *EST* 7 (Summer 1996), http://media.hyperreal.org/zines/est/intervs/conrad.html

6. Conrad in Duguid, "Tony Conrad Interview."

7. These criteria draw early minimalism near to what Benjamin Piekut calls the vernacular avant-garde—though I get the impression that Piekut sees minimalism as marking the line where the vernacular avant-garde ends. (Riley *might* reasonably be included, Reich or Glass surely not.) See Piekut, *Henry Cow: The World Is a Problem* (Durham: Duke University Press, 2019), 387–407, and especially 392, where the Philip Glass Ensemble is named as a limit case.

8. Jacques Rancière, "The Use of Distinctions," in *Dissensus: On Politics and Aesthetics*, ed. and trans. Steve Corcoran (New York: Continuum 2010), 218. This is an unconventional definition of dissensus, which might surprise readers familiar with Rancière's work. I highlight the idea of homonymy as the battle ground of history from Rancière's book *The Names of History: On the Poetics of Knowledge*, trans. Hassan Melehy (Minneapolis: University of Minnesota Press, 1994). Shortly after, Rancière published *La Mésentente: Politique et philosophie* (Paris: Galilée, 1995), in which he introduced the language of politics and police, thus refiguring his thought onto disciplinary terrain prominently claimed by Anglo-American political theory. The latter book was translated as *Disagreement: Politics and Philosophy* (Minneapolis: University of Minnesota Press, 1998) by Julie Rose. As Samuel Chambers notes, the translation of the title misses the important French pun between mishearing and misunderstanding. See Chambers, *The Lessons of Rancière* (New York: Oxford University Press, 2013), 92–93. In the interview published as *The Method of Equality*, Rancière states that, as a result of this missed pun, he quickly put forward *dissensus* as a synonym for *la mésentente* because the English word "disagreement" risked incorrectly framing his work for English readers. See Rancière, *The Method of Equality: Interviews with Laurent Jeanpierre and Dork Zabunyan*, trans. Julie Rose (Cambridge: Polity Press, 2016), 83. "Dissensus" is thus a "a Latin word, even though it doesn't belong to the Latin tongue," meant to account for what was lost in translation as *mésentente* moved into English; I read his definition of disagreement as "a conflict over homonyms" in an effort to draw a closer connection between his most widely read work among political theorists (*Disagreement*), his later mobilization of dissensus in relation to art historical scholarship, and his very often overlooked writing on historiography, as in *The Names of History*.

9. Cecilia Sun writes of *In C*: "Many aspects of the hippie-bohemian picture I have just painted prove illusory. The group of avant-garde artists the premiere brought together never performed as a group again. The minimalist 'movement,' never forged into a cohesive musical community, has since splintered into warring factions over the very question of who invented the style." See Cecilia Sun, "Experiments in Musical Performance: Historiography, Politics, and the Post-Cagian Avant-Garde," PhD diss., UCLA, 2004, 152.

10. Joseph, *Beyond the Dream Syndicate*, 38–39.

11. Recent work on minimalism—and indeed across scholarship on experimentalism—has focused on figures robbed of their proper place in the story.

A partial list of these important studies must include the following: Brett Boutwell, "Terry Jennings, the Lost Minimalist," *American Music* 32, no. 1 (Spring 2014): 82–107; David Chapman's recent work on Art Murphy; several important *New York Times* profiles by Kerry O'Brien, including "A Composer and Her (Very) Long String Instrument," *New York Times*, 1 May 2020, and "Burning Pianos and Whispering Rivers: A Composer's Journey," *New York Times*, 8 November 2019. Extensive writing has appeared on the gay, Black composer Julius Eastman. See Mary Jane Leach and Renee Levine Packer, eds., *Gay Guerilla: Julius Eastman and His Music* (Rochester: University of Rochester Press, 2015); Ryan Dohoney, "Julius Eastman, John Cage, and the Homosexual Ego," in *Tomorrow Is the Question: New Approaches to Experimental Music Studies*, ed. Benjamin Piekut (Ann Arbor: University of Michigan Press, 2014), 39–62; and Ellie Hisama, "'Diving into the Earth': The Musical Worlds of Julius Eastman," in *Rethinking Difference in Music Scholarship*, ed. Olivia Bloechl, Melanie Lowe, and Jeffrey Kallberg (Cambridge: Cambridge University Press, 2015), 260–86. See also Sumanth Gopinath, " 'Black Forces': Julius Eastman Against Minimalism," in *We Have Delivered Ourselves from the Tonal—Of, Towards, On, For Julius Eastman*, ed. Bonaventure Soh Bejeng Ndikung et. al. (Berlin: Savvy Contemporary, 2020). I think also of Kyle Gann's recovery of Dennis Johnson's work in "Reconstructing *November*," *American Music* 28, no. 4 (Winter 2010): 481–91. Others could be added, but these share the impulse that our understanding of minimalism can be corrected or improved by extending its repertoire list; I am interested here in digging into its hegemonic form to ask about its unarticulated coherences around authorship, dispute, and, more implicitly, heteropatriarchal conceptions of whiteness *and* or *as* property.

12. Another key area of interest in minimalism scholarship has been on its extensive appropriations: of African drumming, Hindustani vocal music, Balinese gamelan, bebop (especially John Coltrane), free jazz, and African American popular musics. I make only passing contributions to this important conversation, but I hope that a comprehensive, critical accounting for minimalism's discursive and musical appropriations will appear soon. The most important work here is certainly from Sumanth Gopinath and Martin Scherzinger, both discussed in Chapter 3; note as well Gopinath's discussion of race and racism in Reich's work on Will Robin's podcast *Sound Expertise* ("Steve Reich and the Politics of Race," 15 September 2020).

13. The most substantial edited volume on minimalism is *The Ashgate Research Companion to Minimalist and Postminimalist Music* (Burlington, VT: Ashgate, 2013), edited by three of the key scholars of the style's history, Keith Potter, Kyle Gann, and Pwyll ap Siôn. While the editors set the task of breaking out of the singular focus on the "big four" minimalists, all expansions happen by recourse to technical and stylistic tools associated with them. That is, the inclusion of new composers is validated through reference to Glass's additive processes or Reich's phasing. The result is that the big four recede somewhat from the foreground but only by becoming the grounding definitional criteria.

14. Donna Haraway, *Staying with the Trouble: Making Kin in the Chthulucene*

(Durham: Duke University Press, 2016), 12. My thinking here is similarly influenced by Sara Ahmed, who describes how the "promise of diversity" risks the danger that "the sign of inclusion makes the signs of exclusion disappear." See *On Being Included: Racism and Diversity in Institutional Life* (Durham: Duke University Press, 2012), 65. I think here as well of Dylan Robinson's writing, including *Hungry Listening: Resonant Theory for Indigenous Sound Studies* (Minneapolis: University of Minnesota Press, 2020), but perhaps more explicitly in his open letter "To All Who Should Be Concerned," *Intersections* 39, no. 1 (2019): 137–44.

15. Cheryl I. Harris, "Whiteness as Property," *Harvard Law Review* 106, no. 8 (1993): 1707–91; and Aileen Moreton-Robinson, *The White Possessive: Property, Power, and Indigenous Sovereignty* (Minneapolis: University of Minnesota Press, 2015).

16. Joseph, *Beyond the Dream Syndicate*, 35.

17. James Meyer, *Minimalism: Art and Polemics in the Sixties* (New Haven: Yale University Press, 2001), 3. Michael Maizels, another art historian, also attends to minimalism's authorial politics. Maizels's work is especially valuable for how he breaks with all musicological self-consciousness to insist that, in many cases, minimalist composers were influential on minimal visual artists rather than purely the other way around. See *In and Out of Phase: An Episodic History of Art and Music in the 1960s* (Ann Arbor: University of Michigan Press, 2020).

18. Foucault reflected on shared features of 1960s revolts in "The Subject and Power" to articulate *relations* across relevant struggles. He lists several criteria: they are *transversal* in not being related to one country or location; they are concerned with *"power effects as such"*; they are *immediate* both in that participants focus on "instances of power closest to them," the "immediate enemy," and in that they do not expect an immanent solution; they "question the status of the individual" in challenging anything that "splits up community life"; and they focus on power as it appeals to the privileges of "knowledge, competence, and qualification" and are against all forms of secrecy and mystification as origins of those privileges. See Foucault, "The Subject and Power," *Critical Inquiry* 8, no. 4 (Summer 1982): 780–81.

19. Davide Panagia, *Rancière's Sentiments* (Durham: Duke University Press, 2018), 43.

20. I am hesitant to cite the best-known literature here, contemporaneous though it is to the period in question, by Barthes and Foucault. As Katherine McKittrick has argued, research that begins from Foucault will make Foucauldian conclusions. See *Dear Science and Other Stories* (Durham: Duke University Press, 2021), 23. The discourse of the "death of the author" is, nevertheless, relevant. Christopher Watkin recently outlined Rancière's relationship to that discourse, writing that scholarship grounded in the necessity of authorship (in the liberal subjective sense) has a hard time imagining otherwise; Watkin is thus critical of those scholars who fall back on "the tired old performative contradiction" critique in the face of (anti) authorial gestures. See Christopher Watkin, "Rewriting the Death of the Author: Rancièrian Reflections," *Philosophy and Literature* 39, no. 1 (2015): 32–46. Watkin restages Barthes and Foucault in light of his reading of Rancière's short essay "The Death of the Author or the Life of the Artist? (April 2003)," in *Chronicles of Con-*

sensual Times, trans. Steven Corcoran (London: Continuum, 2010), 101–5. Watkin and Rancière are insistent that the "death of the author" is not the end of (even individual) production in art, but the end of a consensus-oriented regime of authority that aspires to uphold the guarantee of its own validity. The death of the author—like the death of God in Nietzsche—does not mean there is no more author (or no more God); rather it marks a "new proliferation of author-figures," a plurality of modes of being authors, tied to a plurality of modes of reading or hearing the products of those authorships. Rancière turns to another historical homonym here: against historical grounding of authorship in nineteenth-century writerly culture, mass printing, intellectual property as "property," and so on, Rancière highlights how, during the same period, philologists were arguing over whether "Homer" was a proper name or an improper nomination by which to name collective production in writing. We can find skepticism toward the possibility of collective or collaborative authority alive and well in otherwise excellent recent literature on authorship such as Darren Hicks's *Artistic License: The Philosophical Problem of Copyright and Appropriation* (Chicago: University of Chicago Press, 2017). Hicks chooses Sherry Levine (as have Tony Conrad and Jacques Rancière for very different reasons) to note that, "Ironically, Levine is attempting to eschew authorship through acts of authorship, but she can't have it both ways." Watkin labels this mode of critique of antiauthorial practices the "tired old performative contradiction approach." In short, all of Hicks's legal, philosophical, and artistic examples are mustered toward refutation of the Barthes-Foucault-Rancière-Levine belief that authorship can be challenged immanently through its practice. Hicks (and others) view it as simple contradiction, label its partisans ignorant or hypocritical, and instead reaffirm the eminent dignity of authorship and intellectual property.

21. There is nevertheless a literature that considers dispute and disagreement in contemporary music. Cage and David Tudor, or Karlheinz Stockhausen and Victor Globokar, are notable here. See Martin Iddon, "The Haus That Karlheinz Built: Composition, Authority, and Control at the 1968 Darmstadt Festival," *Musical Quarterly* 87, no. 1 (2004): 87–118; Jonathan Goldman, "'How I Became a Composer': An Interview with Vinko Globokar," *Tempo* 68 (267): 22–28; James Pritchett, "David Tudor as Composer/Performer in Variations II," *Leonardo Music Journal* 14 (2004): 11–16. More closely related to my own work are Cage's disputes with both Julius Eastman (see note 11 above) and Glenn Branca.

22. A relevant text here is Alain Badiou's *The Communist Hypothesis* (London: Verso, 2010), in which he examines specific communist revolutions as individual, incomplete instantiations of a hypothesis about human communities.

23. Comprehensive bibliography of 1917 is well beyond the needs of this book. I am drawn, however, to China Miéville's *October: The Story of the Russian Revolution* (New York: Verso, 2018) for how it narrates, month by month, the events that took place between February and October 1917. His concern is to address the moments in the months in a year that have been fogged by their later developments. I am happy to report I do not need to deal with an early history that ends in violence; I call upon the parallel to consider the narrative means by which, in critical historiography, later events are rendered the inevitable destiny of their origins.

24. Allan Greer, *The Patriots and the People: The Rebellion of 1837 in Rural Lower Canada* (Toronto: University of Toronto Press, 1993), 3.

25. Ross has written frequently of the Commune and the Vendôme Column. The quotation is from *The Emergence of Social Space: Rimbaud and the Paris Commune* (New York: Verso, 2008 [1988]), 25; see also 5–8 and 38–39, where she quotes the anti-Communard Catulle Mandès describing tearing down the Column as a "youthful prank." See also her later book *Communal Luxury: The Political Imaginary of the Paris Commune* (New York: Verso, 2015), particularly 59–60, where she discusses how the event influenced William Morris's transformation of Trafalgar Square into an orchard of apricot trees in his 1891 utopian novel *News from Nowhere.*

26. E. P. Thompson, *The Making of the English Working Class* (New York: Vintage, 1966), 12.

27. Kristin Ross, *May '68 and Its Afterlives* (Chicago: University of Chicago Press, 2002), 158.

28. Althusser refers to the students as "infantile leftists" in a letter to Maria-Antonietta Macciocchi in *Letters from Inside the Communist Party to Louis Althusser,* trans. Stephen M. Hellman (London: New Left Books 1973), 312. Althusser is building on Lenin's 1920 essay "'Left-Wing' Communism: An Infantile Disorder." Rancière provides an important summary of the Althusserian response to May '68 in his first monograph, *Althusser's Lesson* (New York: Verso, 2011 [1974]).

29. See Kristin Ross's discussion of Sartre's critique of this trope in *May '68,* 165.

30. Jacques Rancière and Danielle Rancière, "The Philosophers' Tale: Intellectuals and the Trajectory of Gauchisme," in *The Intellectual and His People,* vol. 2 of *Staging the People* (New York: Verso, 2012), 81. Originally printed in *Les Révoltes Logiques* special issue "Les Lauriers de Mai ou les Chemins du Pouvoir," *1968–1978* (February 1978): 7–25.

31. Editorial, *Les Révoltes Logiques* 5 (Spring–Summer 1977): 6. Quoted in Ross, *May '68,* 128.

32. Ross, *Emergence of Social Space,* 5.

33. Davide Panagia writes, "The account of comprehension through communication in theories of consensus-oriented deliberation . . . insists that coherence, communication, and consensus are the only possible political goals, that antagonism is always dialectic, and that the movement of history is teleological. To make a fetish of agreement in this way is to turn a blind eye to a politics of resistance." See *Ten Theses for an Aesthetics of Politics* (Minneapolis: University of Minnesota Press, 2016), Thesis 4, "On Aspectuality." Kristin Ross insists that it is only in the intellectual climate of the early 1980s that "consensus first comes to be taken for granted as the optimum political gesture or goal." See Ross, "Historicizing Untimeliness," in *Jacques Rancière: History, Politics, Aesthetics,* ed. Gabriel Rockhill and Philip Watts (Durham: Duke University Press, 2009), 16.

34. Chambers, *The Lessons of Rancière,* 49.

35. I could raise many exceptions here—and this is part of the point. Philip

Glass's music is inherently and necessarily score based for its rapid-fire, unison rhythmic complexity. But in many other prominent American minimalist compositions—we can think here of not only Young, Riley, and Reich, but also Charlemagne Palestine, Julius Eastman, Dennis Johnson, Brian Eno, Laurie Spiegel, Ellen Fullman, and others—the music emerges primarily in relation to performance and tape, and most often in the absence of full scores. In short, much of the discursive labor of music-historical scholarship on minimalism has been about reconstructing or reinscribing (very literally) minimalism as if it had always been a score-based practice of art music composition. See Patrick Nickleson, "Transcription, Recording, and Authority in 'Classic' Minimalism," *Twentieth Century Music* 14, no. 3 (2017): 361–98.

36. Rancière, "Ten Theses on Politics," trans. Rachel Bowlby with Davide Panagia, *Theory & Event* 5, no. 3 (2001): n.p. Also published in *Dissensus*.

37. See Rancière, *Disagreement*, especially Chapter 3, "The Rationality of Disagreement."

38. Robinson, *Hungry Listening*, 82. While his name does not appear as frequently, Robinson's work stands alongside Rancière's in the pages that follow as a pervasive influence on the development of this project.

39. Jacques Rancière, *Aisthesis: Scenes from the Aesthetic Regime of Art*, trans. Zakir Paul (New York: Verso, 2013), xi.

40. Rancière, *The Ignorant Schoolmaster: Five Lessons in Intellectual Emancipation*, trans. Kristin Ross (Stanford: Stanford University Press, 1991), 46.

41. Rancière insists that his work is not "theory." See "A Few Remarks on the Method of Jacques Rancière," *parallax* 15, no. 3 (2009): 114. Disciplinary impositions of a division between theory, object, and method have also been a recurring concern in recent Black studies scholarship. I think here of Ashon T. Crawley, who writes, "To make a claim for *belief*—in and of Black Study—is to trouble and unsettle epistemological projects founded upon pure reason, pure rationality, in the service of thinking with and against how that which we call knowledge is produced and dispersed. . . . This refusal of disciplinary boundaries is important because disciplinary knowledges attempt resolution, attempt to 'resolve' knowledge." See *Blackpentecostal Breath: The Aesthetics of Possibility* (New York: Fordham University Press, 2017), 3. Similarly, for Katherine McKittrick, disciplines serve to "differentiate, split, and create fictive distances": "Around every corner, at every turn, disciplinary practitioners provide disciplined narratives that confirm the solidity of disciplinary knowledge and its categorical difference from other ways of knowing." See McKittrick, *Dear Science*, 36.

42. Rancière, *The Names of History*. A notable example here is Christophe Levaux's *We Have Always Been Minimalist: The Construction and Triumph of a Musical Style* (Berkeley: University of California Press, 2020), in which the stated goal is to treat minimalism as a "fact" that can be rendered through the processes of music history as a "science."

43. Rancière, "The Use of Distinctions," 208–9.

44. As Dylan Robinson recently framed it, such work of "pinning down" is cen-

tral to colonial thought and history, where knowledge runs on resources rendered singular to make them extractable, part of what Eva Mackey has described as the settler pursuit of certainty. See Robinson, *Hungry Listening*, as well as Mackey, "Unsettling Expectations: (Un)certainty, Settler States of Feeling, Law, and Decolonization," *Canadian Journal of Law and Society* 29, no. 2 (2014): 235–52. I think here as well of Robert Nichols's writing on dispossession discussed in the conclusion. See *Theft Is Property! Dispossession and Critical Theory* (Durham: Duke University Press, 2020).

45. This idea of drones as the pure origin of minimalism is pervasive in earlier writing on the style, but is most critically taken up by Joseph under the rubric of the "metaphysical narrative of minimalism" (*Beyond the Dream Syndicate*, 37), and by Grimshaw in his chapter "The Ideology of the Drone" in *Draw a Straight Line and Follow It: The Music and Mysticism of La Monte Young* (New York: Oxford University Press, 2011), 84–113.

46. Josef Woodard, "Hail! Hail! Gunther Schuller," *Musician*, October 1991, 28.

47. Mick Farren, "Notes on Minimalism (or Learning to Live with the Ramones)," *New Musical Express*, 21 May 1977.

48. Ashon T. Crawley, *The Lonely Letters* (Durham: Duke University Press, 2020), 35–36.

49. Panagia, *Rancière's Sentiments*, 38.

50. Quoted in Tim Lawrence, *Hold On to Your Dreams: Arthur Russell and the Downtown Music Scene, 1973–1992* (Durham: Duke University Press, 2009), 80.

51. On listening postures, see Kerry O'Brien, "Experimentalisms of the Self: Experiments in Art and Technology, 1966–1971," PhD diss., Indiana University, 2018, 83 and 98–99.

52. Indistinctions play a central role in Chapter 4.

53. See Nickleson, "Transcription, Recording, and Authority."

54. See Benjamin Court, "Racialising Amateurism: Punk and Rap," *Third Text* 34, no. 1 (2020): 49–61.

55. Crawley, *The Lonely Letters*, 36.

56. Rancière has argued that philosophy's first task is to defend its priority by ensuring that workers and artisans (in the Platonic sense) are rendered incapable of speaking philosophical or rational language. *In the Philosopher and His Poor*, trans. John Drury, Corinne Oster, and Andrew Parker (Durham: Duke University Press, 2004) most prominently, Rancière draws attention to the Platonic myth of the metals as an originating mythology of the necessity for people to stay in their proper place.

57. See Alexander Weheliye, *Phonographies: Grooves in Sonic Afro-Modernity* (Durham: Duke University Press, 2005), 7.

58. Author's conversation with Jill Kroesen, Skype, 11 December 2016.

59. I am thinking here of Bernard Gendron's exceptional *Between Montmartre and the Mudd Club: Popular Music and the Avant-Garde* (Chicago: University of Chicago Press, 2002). While critically attuned to such high/low blurring across the twentieth century, Gendron nevertheless turns to Branca and Chatham as models

of how "art" and "punk" combined in the no-wave moment. This reading is presented less critically by many music critics, as will be discussed in Chapter 4.

60. Rancière, *The Names of History*, 35.

61. See Brigid Cohen, *Musical Migration and Imperial New York: Early Cold War Scenes* (Chicago: University of Chicago Press, 2022), especially 195–98.

62. Timothy A. Johnson, "Minimalism: Aesthetic, Style, or Technique," *Musical Quarterly* 78, no. 4 (1994): 742–73.

Chapter 1

1. To name only a few, the essay appears in *Source: Music of the Avant-Garde, 1966–1973*, ed. Larry Austin and Douglas Kahn (Berkeley: University of California Press, 2011), *Audio Culture: Readings in Modern Music*, ed. Christopher Cox and Daniel Warner (New York: Bloomsbury Academic, 2017), and *Music in the Western World: A History in Documents*, ed. Piero Weiss and Richard Taruskin (Belmont: Thomson/Schirmer, 2008). It was originally published in *Anti-illusion: Procedures/ Materials*, ed. Marcia Tucker and James Monte (New York: Whitney Museum of Art, 1969), 56–57. My page numbers refer to Reich, *Writings on Music, 1965–2000* (New York: Oxford University Press, 2002), 34–36.

2. Rancière, "Ten Theses on Politics," Thesis 8.

3. See Robert Fink, "(Post-)minimalisms 1970–2000: The Search for a New Mainstream," in *The Cambridge History of Twentieth-Century Music*, ed. Nicholas Cook and Anthony Pople (Cambridge: Cambridge University Press, 2004), 542.

4. Reich, "Music as a Gradual Process," in *Writings on Music*, 35.

5. A particularly generous peer reviewer at University of Michigan Press went to great pains to insist on another important relationship on parallel terrain, that between performers and virtuosity. I agree with this point, and hope that another author will pursue it at length. For this reviewer, the fact that in early minimalism the performers were often close associates of the composer was key, as was the fact that Reich might ask Jon Gibson and Philip Glass to play percussion rather than hiring "professional" percussionists. Any sense of "virtuosity" in this music, as Reich told Emily Wasserman in 1972, is the result of all instrumental parts being exactly equal timbrally and texturally. Early minimalism runs on this concern for equality of parts, and prioritizing interpersonal relationships; as Reich says, "The virtuosity is in their ensemble relationship with each other." I feel that this argument is the reviewer's more than my own, and am grateful for this generous recognition of an extension of my own claims. See Emily Wasserman, "An Interview with Composer Steve Reich," *Artforum*, May 1972.

6. Milton Babbitt, "The Composer as Specialist," in *The Collected Essays of Milton Babbitt*, ed. Stephen Peles (Princeton, NJ: Princeton University Press, 2003), 53; my emphasis. The essay is most often discussed under the editorial title given to it when it first appeared in *High Fidelity* 8, no. 2 (February 1958) as "Who Cares If You Listen?" This latter title gives a much clearer sense of the caricatured portrayal of the essay as simply being about (un)listenability. I consider the original title more productive, particularly in relation to discussion of the pedagogic function of his-

tory discussed below. K. Robert Schwarz chose this same passage to exemplify how Reich, Glass, and other minimalists were the "antithesis" of Babbitt, specifically in how Reich "refuses to alienate himself from the public." See "Steve Reich: Music as a Gradual Process: Part I," *Perspectives of New Music* 19, nos. 1–2 (1980–81): 374.

7. Brian Harker attempts to minimize, via a thickened context, the extremity of Babbitt's pronouncements. See Harker, "Milton Babbitt Encounters Academia (and Vice Versa)," *American Music* 26, no. 3 (2008): 336–77. Joseph Straus has done much the same in an article that challenges the dominance of serialism by counting the number of avowed serialists in music departments at the time. See Straus, "The Myth of Serial 'Tyranny' in the 1950s and 1960s," *Musical Quarterly* 83, no. 3 (1999): 301–43. Both Harker and Straus insist not that Reich's attack on serialism (and less so chance) was *incorrect*, but that it is irrelevant when there were in fact composers of many other stylistic dedications in music departments at the time. Ross refers to this as the police conception of history's weaponization of context; that is, not to counter an argument on its own claims, but to insist that the event was not one because its protagonist did not have a complete, statistical handle on their own present moment. This is a central form by which historians stultify their readers simultaneously with their historical subjects—the insistence that people, in their present, do not understand its causalities. Ross (and Rancière) have each pointed at François Furet's famous argument that the French Revolution did not happen because the French state was already so weakened by 1792 as to have been little more than a phantom: "The revolutionary consciousness, from 1789, was informed by the illusion of defeating a State that has already ceased to exist." François Furet, *Interpreting the French Revolution*, trans. Elborg Forster (Cambridge: Cambridge University Press, 1981), 24–25.

8. It is beyond the scope of this chapter to consider a broader ecology I find important here. Reich's observation that there are no secrets of structure should perhaps be read as intentionally polemical in that, under a particularly cynical reading, we can say that music theory as a discipline is founded on the premise that there *must be secrets of structure*. Saying there aren't any recalls a child shouting, "You can't catch me" before toddling away shoeless. The symbiotic relationship between formalist composition and formalist-positivist music analysis, as I understand it, runs on a contract in which the beauty of the structure needs to be matched by the composers' elegance in its obfuscation. This beauty/obfuscation dynamic gives the theorist something on which to stake arguments about the composers' genius or novel stylistic innovations that simultaneously make the case that the work was worth studying in the first place.

9. John Cage, *Silence: Lectures and Writings* (Middletown, CT: Wesleyan University Press, 1961), 90.

10. Cage, *Silence*, 7.

11. Cage, *Silence*, 7.

12. Ross, in Rancière, *The Ignorant Schoolmaster*, xi.

13. Ross, *May '68*, 11.

14. Chris Stover, "Rancière's Affective Impropriety," in *Rancière and Music*, ed.

João Pedro Cachopo, Patrick Nickleson, and Chris Stover (Edinburgh: Edinburgh University Press, 2020), 231.

15. Despite my contrast here of process and control, Reich did not abandon the importance of control in his own work. As Kerry O'Brien has shown, Reich's relationship to yoga and spirituality during this period refers him to another binary contrast, between the "controls imposed from without" of totalitarian politics, or those controls from within "related to yogic controls of the breath and mind." See O'Brien, "Machine Fantasies into Human Events: Reich and Technology in the 1970s," in *Rethinking Reich*, ed. Sumanth Gopinath and Pwyll ap Siôn (Oxford: Oxford University Press, 2019), 329.

16. O'Brien, "Experimentalisms of the Self," 99.

17. See Ross Cole, "'Sound Effects (O.K., Music)': Steve Reich and the Visual Arts in New York City, 1966–1968," *Twentieth Century Music* 11, no. 2 (2014): 217–44.

18. Wim Mertens, *American Minimal Music* (London: Kahn & Averill, 1983), 54.

19. Keith Potter, *Four Musical Minimalists* (New York: Cambridge University Press, 2000), 174–75 and 210–11.

20. K. Robert Schwarz, *Minimalists* (London: Phaidon, 1996), 227.

21. Edward Strickland, *Minimalism: Origins* (Bloomington: Indiana University Press, 1993), 198.

22. Sumanth Gopinath, "Contraband Children: The Politics of Race and Liberation in the Music of Steve Reich, 1965–1966," PhD diss., Yale University, 2005, 59 n. 78.

23. Michael Nyman in Reich, *Writings on Music*, 95.

24. Martin Scherzinger, "Curious Intersections, Uncommon Magic: Steve Reich's *It's Gonna Rain*," *Current Musicology* 79–80 (2005): 228; Ross Cole, "'Fun, Yes, but Music?' Steve Reich and the San Francisco Bay Area's Cultural Nexus, 1962–65," *Journal of the Society for American Music* 6, no. 3 (2012): 239.

25. Susan McClary, "Rap, Minimalism, and Structures of Time in Late Twentieth-Century Culture," in Cox and Warner, *Audio Culture*, 289–98, and her afterword to Jacques Attali, *Noise: The Political Economy of Music* (Minneapolis: University of Minnesota Press, 1985); Robert Fink, *Repeating Ourselves: American Minimal Music as Cultural Practice* (Berkeley: University of California Press, 2005).

26. Scherzinger, "Curious Intersections," 222.

27. O'Brien, "Experimentalisms of the Self," 14.

28. Scherzinger, "Curious Intersections," 226.

29. I do not engage directly with the psychoanalytic legacy in criticism of minimalism, though it is an important thread in its discursive development. See in particular Mertens, *American Minimal Music*, 113–24 and Fink, *Repeating Ourselves*, 1–22. See also Johan Girard's critique of Fink (as representative of new musicological turns to structural homologies) in *Répétitions: L'esthétique Musicale de Terry Riley, Steve Reich et Philip Glass* (Paris: Presses Sorbonne nouvelle, 2010), 200–212.

30. Richard Taruskin, "Chapter 8: A Harmonious Avant-Garde?," in the *Ox-*

ford History of Western Music, vol. 5: *Music in the Late Twentieth Century* (New York: Oxford, 2005), 351–410.

31. Rancière, *The Ignorant Schoolmaster*, 28.

32. Taruskin, "A Harmonious Avant-Garde?," 373.

33. I should note here that Taruskin is hardly averse to political readings. His long and important career is closely associated with Cold War politics in music. His argument is not against political intrusions into music but *this* politics.

34. Paul Epstein, "Pattern Structure and Process in Steve Reich's 'Piano Phase,'" *Musical Quarterly* 72, no. 4 (1986): 494–502.

35. The relationship between minimalism and high-modernist theoretical methods is well captured in its historical and conceptual complexity by Christophe Levaux in Chapter 19 of *We Have Always Been Minimalist*: "[Richard Cohn] never proved what Reich's music actually was. Instead he carried out a series of manipulations (transpositions or translations, slicing and dicing every which way) on what would perhaps become 'Reich's music,' insofar as others followed suit." Particularly striking is how Levaux reproduces Cohn's graphic analysis of beat-class sets in *Violin Phase* not as an analytic exemplar, but, as I read it, to articulate its strangeness and incoherence. See Levaux, 170–71.

36. Taruskin, "A Harmonious Avant-Garde?," 374; my emphasis.

37. Taruskin is not alone here. I have already traced a similar tone in Scherzinger and Fink. Marcelle Pierson joins them in a recent essay on the role of the voice in Reich's music. In particular, she is concerned for the problematic way that Reich treats the voice, and particularly the Black voice, as "natural." Within a much larger and compelling critique, Pierson nevertheless writes that Reich's failure to properly position her critical language of choice (*technē*) "is all the more insidious in his obliviousness to it." See "Voice, *Technē*, and *Jouissance* in *Music for 18 Musicians*," *Twentieth Century Music* 13, no. 1 (2016): 36.

38. Thank you, Kerry O'Brien, for sharing this observation with me.

39. Rita Felski, *The Limits of Critique* (Chicago: University of Chicago Press, 2015).

40. Joshua Klein, "Steve Reich," *Pitchfork Media*, 22 November 2006; my emphasis. We need not jump so far ahead to find Reich dismissive of such ideas through the language of the "early." In his 1973 essay "Notes on Music and Dance," Reich writes, "The basic idea of the Judson dance group (Steve Paxton, Yvonne Rainer, etc.) as well as the contribution of Simone Forti, could be summed up as: any movement is dance. This is the precise equivalent to the basic idea of the composer John Cage: Any sound is music." He continues, "There is, however, another primary sense of these words, where one can say that all sounds are obviously not music, all movement are not dance, and *most children can usually tell the difference between one and the other*." See *Writings on Music*, 71; my emphasis. My thanks once again to Kerry O'Brien for drawing this connection.

41. As my particular focus is on the poetics of historiography in relation to moments of revolt and dispute, we need to keep in mind the importance of metaphors (in the conclusion I turn to the different work of metonymy) and the historical

work done through them. In *What's the Use: On the Uses of Use* (Durham: Duke University Press, 2019), Sarah Ahmed deals at length with different metaphors of use, commenting, for example, on how a knife, a word, or a critical argument, can be either sharpened or dulled by (over)use depending on the author's poetic needs.

42. Susana Draper, *Mexico 1968: Constellations of Freedom and Democracy* (Durham: Duke University Press, 2008), 41.

Chapter 2

1. Tony Conrad, liner notes to *Early Minimalism: Volume One* (Table of the Elements, AS-33, 1997), 14–15.

2. Joseph, *Beyond the Dream Syndicate*, 27.

3. This is true from the earliest texts on the Theatre of Eternal Music to the most recent. Wim Mertens writes, "The use of long tones is in itself no novelty, but up till recently they were only used as a drone over which a melody was placed. For Young it is precisely these long notes that are the subject of his music." Mertens, *American Minimal Music*, 21. Thirty years later, Barry Shank writes: "Instead of the tamboura ringing behind the improvisations of lead instruments, Young began to compose for a variety of droning sounds as the sole object of audition, not only in the foreground, but unaccompanied." Shank, *The Political Force of Musical Beauty* (Durham: Duke University Press, 2014), 117; my emphasis.

4. See Branden Joseph's liner notes to the 2016 vinyl reissue of *Outside the Dream Syndicate* (Superior Viaduct SV048, 2016).

5. Conrad, *Early Minimalism*, 20.

6. In his interview in *The Wire*, Young says he offered them these contracts around the time of the 1972 performances; in a March 1983 letter to Betty Freeman, Young and Zazeela say that the December 1963 tape "the fire is a mirror" cannot be offered as a gift because they needed permission from the other musicians on the recording, signaling uncertainty around its authorial status. See Young and Zazeela to Betty Freeman, 17 March 1983, UC San Diego Library, Special Collections & Archives, Betty Freeman Papers, MSS 227, Box 11, Folder 5.

7. The full text of his pamphlets and placard is reproduced in Conrad's interview with Brian Duguid of *EST* magazine: http://media.hyperreal.org/zines/est/intervs/conrad.html

8. During the period of their 1990s dispute, interviews were published in *The Wire: Adventures in Modern Music* on Conrad (Issue 170, April 1998) and on Young and Zazeela (Issue 178, December 1998).

9. Robert Fink made this point in the question session after Cecilia Sun's paper at the 2013 meeting of the Society for Minimalist Music in Long Beach, California. Young's eventual willingness to release the tapes—in some form—will likely tender incredible profit for him (or whoever inherits the material).

10. Tony Conrad, *Slapping Pythagoras* (Table of the Elements, V-23, 1995) and *Early Minimalism*.

11. The WKCR broadcast was hosted by Brooke Wentz and featured com-

mentary by a number of collaborators, colleagues, and "disciples" in Young's career, including C. C. Hennix, Alex Dea, Dan Wolf, Henry Flynt, Terry Riley, and Young and Zazeela themselves. The full twenty-four-hour marathon broadcast is available at the British Library as part of the Michael Gerzon tape archive. See Nickleson, "They (Merely) Held Drones."

12. See John Cale / Tony Conrad / Angus MacLise / La Monte Young / Marian Zazeela, *Inside the Dream Syndicate Vol. 1: Day of Niagara (1965)* (Table of the Elements CD W-74, 2000).

13. La Monte Young, "Notes on the Theatre of Eternal Music and *The Tortoise, His Dreams and Journeys*," http://melafoundation.org/theatre.pdf, 2000; Arnold Dreyblatt, "An Open Letter to La Monte Young and Tony Conrad," www.dreyblatt.net/html/music.php?id=68&more=63#more, 2000 and reproduced in part in *The Wire*, 199 (September 2000); Tony Conrad, "Tony Conrad's Response to 'An Open Letter to La Monte Young and Tony Conrad,'" http://www.dreyblatt.de/pdf/Tony%20Conrad%20Response.pdf, September 2000.

14. The most comprehensive and accurate overview to date, though still centered on Young, is Alan Licht, "The History of La Monte Young's Theatre of Eternal Music," *Forced Exposure* 16 (1990).

15. See Nickleson, "They (Merely) Held Drones."

16. Schwarz, *Minimalists*, 37–38; my emphasis. See also Joseph, *Beyond the Dream Syndicate*, 376 n. 66.

17. Mertens, *American Minimal Music*, 27; my emphasis.

18. Mertens, *American Minimal Music*, 28.

19. Potter, *Four Musical Minimalists*, 73–76. Cecilia Sun relies on much the same binary of improvisation and performance. Sun, "Experiments in Musical Performance," 50. On Potter's turn to this binary, Christophe Levaux's discussion of the British reception of Young in the early 1960s in relation to Cardew and the Scratch Orchestra seems relevant: "The Scratch Orchestra's music, like Young's, was concert music in which each of the members was encouraged to contribute accompaniments 'performable continuously for indefinite periods.'" I suspect that in pointing to this binary, and in the terms he does, Potter is calling upon a longer British reception of American minimalism and the performance/improvisation binary. See Levaux, *We Have Always Been Minimalist*, 27.

20. Strickland, *Minimalism: Origins*, 155.

21. The most reliable account of how the group came to be so heavily amplified insists that Conrad and Cale developed the idea together, probably in the spring/summer of 1964. Cale credits Conrad with bringing the pickups; see John Cale and Victor Bockris, *What's Welsh for Zen: The Autobiography of John Cale* (New York: Bloomsbury, 1999), 60. Tim Mitchell suggests the same before becoming unclear: "Conrad bought some cheap contact microphones, the kind of pick-ups that John Cale used and which were available from any street corner electronics store." See *Sedition and Alchemy* (Chester Springs, PA: Peter Owens, 2003), 37. For a potentially relevant account of Cage's use of pickups in a New York Philharmonic concert on 9 February 1964, see Benjamin Piekut's chapter "When Orchestras Attack!"

in *Experimentalism Otherwise*, 20–64. In the available preceding bootleg tape, the "12 I 64 first twelve *Sunday morning blues*," the strings are both unamplified; in the next tape following Cage's (potentially unrelated) philharmonic concert, the "2 IV 64 day of the holy mountain" (the pre-*Tortoise* Dream Music), all players are amplified. See Nickleson, "They (Merely) Held Drones."

22. Strickland, *Minimalism: Origins*, 156; my emphasis.

23. Strickland, *Minimalism: Origins*, 157.

24. Young, "Theatre of Eternal Music," 11; my emphasis.

25. In Jeremy Grimshaw's case, direct and extensive access was given before all reproduction permissions were revoked. See Grimshaw, "Gonzo Musicology," in *Draw a Straight Line*, as well as La Monte Young's critique of the book at https://drawastraightlineandfollowit.com

26. Such revolving membership within a defined community is of central importance throughout the chapters that follow: in the rare cases in which the pieces under discussion have scores, they do not include parts for "saxophone" or for "viola" but for "Jon [Gibson]" or "John [Cale]." As Cornelius Cardew noted of Sylvano Bussotti's *5 Pieces for David Tudor*, Tudor's name is "in no sense a dedication, but rather an instrumental indication, part of the notation." See Cardew, "Notation— Interpretation, Etc.," *Tempo* 58 (1961): 22.

27. Author's conversation with Tony Conrad, Buffalo, August 27, 2015.

28. See liner notes to the CD release by Tony Conrad and Faust, *Outside the Dream Syndicate* (Table of the Elements Li 3, 2002). See also Conrad, "Tony Conrad's Response."

29. "Given the manner in which such groups presented and performed music," Benjamin Piekut has argued, "it makes as much sense to connect them to the Cecil Taylor Unit or the Stooges as to Charles Ives or Arnold Schoenberg." Piekut, *Experimentalism Otherwise*, 16.

30. Young, "Theatre of Eternal Music," 3.

31. Kyle Gann, "The Outer Edge of Consonance: Snapshots from the Evolution of La Monte Young's Tuning Installations," in *Sound and Light: La Monte Young and Marian Zazeela*, ed. William Duckworth and Richard Fleming (Lewisburg, PA: Bucknell University Press, 1996), 163.

32. Richard Kostelanetz, *The Theatre of Mixed Means: An Introduction to Happenings, Kinetic Environments, and Other Mixed-Means Performances* (New York: Dial Press, 1968), 205–6; my emphasis. Young also acknowledges Conrad's role in introducing just intonation to the group in Strickland's interview from *American Composers: Dialogues on Contemporary Music* (Bloomington: Indiana University Press, 1991), 65; Cole Gagne's *Soundpieces 2: Interviews with American Composers* (Metuchen, N.J.: Scarecrow Press, 1993), 498; and William Duckworth, *Talking Music* (New York: Schirmer Books, 1995), 241.

33. I discuss this further in Nickleson, "Transcription, Recording, and Authority," in particular the section "La Monte Young and His Secretaries," 382–86.

34. Joseph, *Beyond the Dream Syndicate*, 101. Cardew was clearly enamored with Young's text-based concerns as early as 1961, when he wrote that Young "dis-

penses with musical notation altogether and 'writes' his pieces in the language of everyday," as an example of following Americans like Cage and Feldman in turning toward being "a composer of human rather than musical situations." See Cardew, "Notation—Interpretation, Etc.," 26. See also Liz Kotz, *Words to Be Looked At: Language in 1960s Art* (Cambridge, MA: MIT Press, 2007), 80. This parallels Taruskin's observation that Reich did not set out to liberate sounds but to liberate people (Chapter 1).

35. Reproduced in Joseph, *Beyond the Dream Syndicate*, 67.

36. Grimshaw, *Draw a Straight Line*, 82.

37. See Joseph, *Beyond the Dream Syndicate*, 111–12. As a further refutation of the modernist insistence upon originality, #10 was itself a restatement of #9, which simply featured a straight, horizontal line printed on a catalog card.

38. The program is reproduced in Henry Flynt, "La Monte Young in New York, 1960–1962," in Duckworth and Fleming, *Sound and Light*, 59–63.

39. Young quoted in Kostelanetz, *Theatre of Mixed Means*, 204.

40. Henry Flynt, quoted in Joseph, *Beyond the Dream Syndicate*, 155.

41. Mertens, *American Minimal Music*, 27; my emphasis.

42. I hesitate to put the word "minimalist" in Mertens's mouth here; Mertens's book's literal English translation would have been "American Repetitive Music."

43. Conrad certainly read Rancière. D. Olivier Delrieu-Schulze reports that once, during a conversation with Conrad about teaching, Conrad went searching for something and came back with a copy of *The Ignorant Schoolmaster*. "'You can have this,' he said as he explained that it was about Joseph Jacotot, who in the 1800s had developed a method of teaching that didn't require the teacher to know the subject. We both agreed that was a pretty good idea." Quoted in Rachel Adams, "Unscripted Pedagogy," in *Introducing Tony Conrad*, ed. Cathleen Chaffee and Rachel Adams (Buffalo: Albright-Knox Art Gallery, 2018), 62. When I visited Conrad in his Buffalo apartment in 2015, while nosily browsing his bookshelf, I noticed a copy of Rancière's *The Politics of Aesthetics*.

44. Rancière, *Disagreement*, x.

45. Rancière, *Disagreement*, 27.

46. Rancière, *Disagreement*, 29.

47. Rancière, *Disagreement*, 29–30.

48. Rancière, *Disagreement*, 28.

49. Rancière, "Good Times, or Pleasure at the *Barrière*," in *Staging the People: The Proletarian and His Double*, trans. David Fernbach (New York: Verso, 2011), 175–232.

50. See Rancière, *Proletarian Nights: The Workers' Dream in Nineteenth-Century France*, trans. John Drury (London: Verso, 2012 [1981]).

51. For accounts of Young's childhood in Bern, see Mertens, *American Minimal Music*, 19; for a more critical perspective on Young's "mytho-biography" see Grimshaw, *Draw a Straight Line*, 178. Young's early biography was most recently examined at length by Maizels, who is interested in how Young's "specific aural memory" of his rural childhood becomes the ground for his "aesthetics of the current." See *In and Out of Phase*, 22.

52. Among other sources, see Tony Conrad, *What Music Did: the Story of Nu-merocracy*, ed. Patrick Nickleson (forthcoming).

53. Conrad, *Early Minimalism*, 11.

54. Conrad, *Early Minimalism*, 12.

55. Conrad, *Early Minimalism*, 9–10.

56. See Benjamin Piekut, "Demolish Serious Culture!," in *Experimentalism Otherwise*, 65–101. See also David Grubbs, "Henry Flynt on the Air," in *Records Ruin the Landscape: John Cage, the Sixties, and Sound Recording* (Durham: Duke University Press, 2014), 19–44.

57. See Watkin, "Rewriting the Death," 44. Social media conversations on the topic very frequently and quickly lead to accusations against Conrad; I have seen prominent American composers call Conrad a "vulture," and many dismiss his claims as parasitic on Young's compositional enterprise.

58. Conrad, *Early Minimalism*, 20; my emphasis. I think here of Alexander Weheliye's writing on phonographies in reflecting the impact of African American music and sound on recording technologies. See *Phonographies*.

59. Though exciting in the context of the post-Cagean avant-garde and Western art music (literate) composition more generally, this ideal was hardly new; George Lewis, Michael Heller, Benjamin Piekut, and others have focused at length on efforts to problematize the improvisation-composition binary, particularly in its post-Cagean, heavily racialized, and hierarchical understanding. Weheliye notes that within orally transmitted Black musical traditions, the historical arrival of sound recording caused much less anxiety than among Euro-Americans who had grounded an entire metaphysics in the division between *logos* and *phoné*. Much of minimalism's historical novelty can perhaps be tied to the arrival of consumer recording technologies into individual composer's (i.e., noninstitutional) studio composition practice. Johan Girard considers the magnetic tape recorder the necessary medium for the realization of the minimalist repetitive aesthetic, or rather, the transfer from tape recorder to live instrumentation; see Girard, *Répétitions*, especially Chapter 1. For my part, the difference in many of these disputes relates in part to the gap between how they understood the potential of that authorial opening in the moment versus how they attempted to narrate it in later decades.

60. Conrad, *Early Minimalism*, 20.

61. I am referring here to Reich's "Music as a Gradual Process." See Chapter 1.

62. Conrad, *Early Minimalism*, 16–17.

63. Conrad, *Early Minimalism*, 21.

64. Conrad, liner notes to *Early Minimalism*, 21–22. Performing—and, equally, listening to—just intonation drones through their difference tones is a unique experience that differs strongly from typical concerns for playing in tune, as it is primarily a rhythmic rather than pitch phenomenon (or perhaps it is an equal "rhythm/pitch interaction," as Joseph suggests in *Beyond the Dream Syndicate*, 73). For a powerful description of Conrad's performances (from someone who has played in many of them) see Grubbs, *Records Ruin the Landscape*, 35–36.

65. Joseph, *Beyond the Dream Syndicate*, 37.

66. Conrad, *Early Minimalism*, 25.

67. Conrad, *Early Minimalism*, 24.

68. Johnson, Wakoski, Riley, and Zazeela quoted in Young, "Theatre of Eternal Music," 19–23.

69. Young, "Theatre of Eternal Music," 26–27.

70. Young refers to the composer and pianist Michael Harrison as a disciple in the letter ("Theatre of Eternal Music," 25), and Diane Wakoski writes that Cale and Conrad, while they contributed original ideas, did so "not as collaborators but as disciples" (20).

71. Young, "Theatre of Eternal Music," 26.

72. Young, "Theatre of Eternal Music," 27.

73. Young, "Theatre of Eternal Music," 25.

74. Young, "Theatre of Eternal Music," 26.

75. Duguid, "Tony Conrad Interview."

76. Conrad quoted in Peter Margasak, "Amid the Drone, a Feud over Who Composed It," *New York Times*, 13 August 2000.

77. There are many instances of such collective nominations having been used in the 1960s and 1970s only to have been abandoned or elided retrospectively under an author's proper name. While a group like the AACM retains its discursive hold (perhaps thanks in part to George Lewis calling his tome *A Power Stronger Than Itself: The AACM and American Experimental Music* (Chicago: University of Chicago Press, 2008) a "collective autobiography"), other names are largely forgotten. Kerry O'Brien pointed, among others, to the original and extensive use of ♀ Ensemble for early presentations of Oliveros's *Sonic Meditations*, and the frequency with which "Sounds Out of Silent Spaces" was the name used for performances of what we now recognize as Philip Corner's music.

78. In calling this structure recursive, I am drawing upon Robert Nichols's writing on dispossession in *Theft Is Property!* as taken up in the conclusion to this book.

79. Zazeela's collaborative light-installation work with Young, which began with the December 1965 Filmmakers Cinematheque concert, has been the focus of some attention, most notably from Henry Flynt in Duckworth and Fleming, *Sound and Light*. Surprisingly, there has been no commentary to date on her calligraphic work. All announcements and invitations mentioned below were sent to Peter Yates by La Monte Young, and are present in the Peter Yates Papers, MSS 14, Special Collections & Archives, UC San Diego Library. A copy of *The Celebration of the Tortoise* invitation is also in Steve Reich's papers at the Paul Sacher Stiftung, sent to him by the artist Larry Poons, and in Terry Riley's archive, courtesy of Vincent de Roguin. I reproduce them here in recognition of their function as public, printed, and widely reproduced concert advertisements. A full list of known public performances is in Nickleson, "They (Merely) Held Drones."

80. Young, "Theatre of Eternal Music," 24; my emphasis.

81. See Cale and Bockris, *What's Welsh for Zen?*, 60–61.

82. Strickland, *Minimalism: Origins*, 159.

83. "A Partial Index of the American Theatre for Poets, Inc. 1961–1965." Avail-

able at http://2011-2014.pastelegram.org/features/282/event/692, accessed 1 November 2021. The website lists the program as being from a 25 February 1965 concert, though this date is not cited anywhere in the existing literature on the ensemble and is more likely the 4 March performance, though if it is February, this would back up Strickland's narrative of the use of the name above (though it would still be late). Many of these dates—as has hopefully been made clear throughout—are still up for question. I very much look forward to future research that draws upon the archive directly to correct many of the dates and titles used throughout this chapter.

84. Grimshaw, *Draw a Straight Line*, 186. The "Ballad of the Tortoise" program is included in the Peter Yates Papers, UCSD Library Special Collections and Archives, Correspondence with La Monte Young, Box 20, Folder 3.

85. I first found one of these cards in Steve Reich's correspondence at the Paul Sacher Foundation in September 2014. I subsequently found others in Peter Yates's correspondence with Young at the UCSD Special Collections. They are also present in Tony Conrad's archives, courtesy of Jeff Hunt.

86. The works list that Young sent to Peter Yates in late 1965 suggests that the middle of 1965, while it may have been active for rehearsals, saw few public performances; none are listed between the 7 March performance at Geldzahler's loft and the 16 October performance at the Theatre Upstairs. Peter Yates Papers, MSS 14, Special Collections & Archives, UC San Diego Library.

87. The invitation also includes an ornate calligraphic map of the region directing attendees to the proper location, in Zazeela's hand, above the fold.

88. All [*sic*]. Terry Riley to Steve Reich [2 August 1966]. Paul Sacher Stiftung, Sammlung Steve Reich, Correspondence. Many thanks to Terry Riley for his generous permission to directly cite from the letter, and to Vincent de Roguin for making the connection.

89. Piekut, *Experimentalism Otherwise*, 17–18. Ned Sublette has commented on the same issue: "Cage's work may have radically undermined the function of the score, but the position of the score in his work was primary. . . . All of Cage's work was scored, that I can recall. And it was not only scored; the scores were published by C.F. Peters and dutifully purchased by university libraries everywhere, where we bookish young composition students imbibed them." Ned Sublette, quoted in Tim Lawrence, "Pluralism, Minor Deviations, and Radical Change: The Challenge to Experimental Music in Downtown New York, 1971–85," in *Tomorrow Is the Question: New Directions in Experimental Music Studies*, ed. Benjamin Piekut (Ann Arbor: University of Michigan Press, 2014), 73. Brigid Cohen draws on similar comparisons to highlight the novelty of Yoko Ono's contribution to the New York downtown scene in *Musical Migration*. Liz Kotz, in *Word to be Looked At*, pays much attention to the materiality of Cage's 1960 scores.

90. Potter recognizes this problem in his contribution to Potter, Gann, and ap Siôn, *Ashgate Research Companion*. See Keith Potter, "Mapping Early Minimalism," 19–38.

91. The score is reproduced in Potter, *Four Musical Minimalists*, 75. Young's

layout and column titles are strikingly similar to a chart from one of Conrad's notebooks that Joseph reproduces. See Tony Conrad, "Table of Harmonics" and "Harmonics in Octal and Binary" from 1 July 1964 in Joseph, *Beyond the Dream Syndicate*, 32–33.

92. Potter, *Four Musical Minimalists*, 76; my emphasis.

93. Tony Conrad in *Film Culture* 41 (1966): 1–8, reprinted in *Tony Conrad Writings*, ed. Constance DeJong and Andrew Lampert (New York: Primary Information, 2019), 302–10.

94. There is a single use of the first-person singular: "I don't want to seem to represent that everyone should use the new scale, but it's hard to throw light on the scene without coloring my tone."

95. Conrad, "Inside the Dream Syndicate," in *Tony Conrad Writings*, 307.

96. Conrad, "Inside the Dream Syndicate," 308.

97. Conrad, "Inside the Dream Syndicate," 309. Young's strongest critique from his open letter is that when Dreyblatt's bootleg tape was made from Young's archives, it was accidentally sped up such that the 60 Hz drone is made 80—in Conrad's words, then, *Day of Niagara* "fall[s] less resonantly on the city ear."

98. Peter Yates, "Music," *Arts & Architecture*, October 1965, 35. Yates also gives a thorough description of the performance, which he calls "Young's *Dream Tortoise*." He continues: "The small audience sat without shuffling its feet or coughing, seemingly as relaxed as I became; and the two hours I sat there paid tribute to a unique musical experience—no tribulation. At 11 p.m. we were invited to enjoy a 15-minute break and return for another 1 ½ hours of the same thing. Regretfully—I mean it—I apologized to the performers that I must leave."

99. Conrad, "Inside the Dream Syndicate," 309. The mention of "the rock 'n roll orchestra" references Cale's daytime work with the Velvet Underground before heading to Young and Zazeela's loft for their nightlong rehearsals and concerts.

100. Grimshaw, *Draw a Straight Line*, 193 n. 27. This "unknown" status is extremely important: Grimshaw had access to Young and Zazeela's archives, and this is the only case in which he marks an important document as unknown or missing.

101. La Monte Young and Marian Zazeela, *Selected Writings* (Munich: Heiner Friedrich, 1969); republished online by ubuweb.com (2004); *Aspen No. 9: The Psychedelic Issue* (1971), ed. Angus and Hetty MacLise (New York: Roaring Fork Press).

102. East End Theatre program: http://2011-2014.pastelegram.org/features/282/event/692, accessed 1 November 2021. Also available in Peter Yates Papers, MSS 14, Special Collections & Archives, UC San Diego Library.

103. Young, "Theatre of Eternal Music," 17; my emphasis. Young acknowledges his appreciation of Conrad's, Cale's, and MacLise's work in the following duties: carpentry, painting, Hoovering, polishing, archiving, carpentry, and repairs. In the context, Young is suggesting that they were there and of course did *stuff*, but it was not the *stuff* of authorship. His claim that their disagreement was *temporarily* ameliorated is misleading as well: even as late as the July 1966 concerts at Christof de Menil's home in Long Island, the four names Young, Zazeela, Conrad, and Riley are presented in the same diamond figuration.

104. Young, "Theatre of Eternal Music," 17; my emphasis.

105. My thinking on the manifesto as a genre has been influenced by Martin Puchner, *Poetry of the Revolution: Marx, Manifestos, and the Avant-Garde* (Princeton, NJ: Princeton University Press, 2006). For more on the collective nominations that so often sign the manifesto as a genre, see Marco Deseriis, *Improper Names: Collective Pseudonyms from the Luddites to Anonymous* (Minneapolis: University of Minnesota Press, 2015).

106. Marianne DeKoeven, *Utopia Limited: The Sixties and the Emergence of the Postmodern* (Durham: Duke University Press, 2004), 130.

107. Shank, *Political Force*, 123–28. Zazeela, as in all cases, is not explicitly discussed here. However, as I discuss in "They (Merely) Held Drones," Zazeela was a central figure in the social scene around not only Young and Conrad, but also Jack Smith, Amiri Baraka, and others; she and Young have, by all accounts, rarely been apart since meeting.

108. Program notes to East End Theatre and Pocket Theatre performances. In his discussion of the original impetus for amplification leading Conrad to attaching a contact microphone, Cale mentions that Conrad had described how vividly he heard difference tones in his left ear, while the rest of the ensemble could not hear them. See Cale and Bockris, *What's Welsh for Zen?*, 60.

109. Young to Yates, 16 January 1965, Peter Yates Papers, MSS 14, Special Collections & Archives, UC San Diego Library. Importantly, Young uses the term "improvisation" in the letter and prioritizes the contributions of Young and Conrad over those of the other members, both in the music and in the essay.

110. Tony Conrad to Peter Yates, November 1965, Peter Yates Papers, MSS 14, Special Collections & Archives, UC San Diego Library; Conrad's letter to Yates is reprinted in Conrad, *Tony Conrad Writings*, 298–301. Tony Conrad, conversation with the author, 27 August 2015.

Chapter 3

1. Duckworth, *Talking Music*, 301.

2. Duckworth, *Talking Music*, 239.

3. Walter Zimmerman speaks at length to Glass, with no mention of the others; Reich and Young are only included in the book jokingly, as neither responded positively to interview requests. See Walter Zimmerman, *Desert Plants: Conversations with 23 American Composers* (Vancouver: A.R.C. Publications, 1976). Cole Gagne and Tracey Caras speak to Glass and Reich without bringing up either of them, let alone Riley or Young. See Cole Gagne and Tracey Caras, *Soundpieces: Interviews with American Composers* (Metuchen, NJ: Scarecrow Press, 1982). Michael Nyman interviewed Reich twice, in 1971 and 1976; neither includes questions about the other minimalists. See Reich, *Writings on Music*. Similarly, a 1980 "Dialogue with Philip Glass and Steve Reich" led by Tim Page does not raise the issue of their interrelated influence. See *Writings on Glass: Essays, Interviews, Criticism*, ed. Richard Kostelanetz (New York: Schirmer, 1997).

4. This is particularly true when he mentions, in both the chapter on Young

and the one on Riley, their collaborative work together with Ann Halprin. See Mertens, *American Minimal Music*, 20 and 35. Throughout the chapter on Riley, he and Young are written about as equals in a way entirely uncommon in much subsequent literature: "While La Monte Young's early compositions were influenced by Schoenberg, Terry Riley was initially influenced by Stockhausen. . . . During 1959 and 1960, Riley's and La Monte Young's improvisations, which gave their great stop for experiment and accident, served as accompaniment to Ann Halprin's dance. . . . Though both Young and Riley were interested in the physiological and psychical effects of music, they both had very different attitudes to these effects," and so on (Mertens, 36). In all following publications, as will be shown below in the interviews, Riley's career would be narrated as subsequent to Young's, rather than simultaneous and parallel. Potter makes a similar point regarding *Music with Changing Parts in Four Musical Minimalists*, 306.

5. Mertens, *American Minimal Music*, 77; my emphasis. On the metaphysical narrative, see Joseph, *Beyond the Dream Syndicate*, and Chapter 2 of this book.

6. Strickland, *Minimalism: Origins*, 211.

7. Conrad, *Early Minimalism*.

8. Indeed, Young, Riley, Reich and Glass were frequently lumped together by astute critics. Keith Potter calls Tom Johnson's "La Monte Young, Steve Reich, Terry Riley, Philip Glass," *Village Voice*, 6 April 1972, the first instance of this in criticism. See Potter, *Four Musical Minimalists*, xiii. For another example, see Joan La Barbara's 1974 essay "Philip Glass and Steve Reich: Two from the Steady State School," in Kostelanetz, *Writings on Glass*, 39–45. La Barbara begins, "La Monte Young, Terry Riley, Steve Reich, and Philip Glass have been linked together in a school of composition based on repetitions and exploration of minimal amounts of material." La Barbara was a member of both Reich's and Glass's early ensembles and a composer and critic. For more on La Barbara, see David Chapman, "Collaboration, Presence, and Community: The Philip Glass Ensemble in Downtown New York, 1966–1976," PhD diss., Washington University, 2013.

9. See Rancière, "On the Theory of Ideology: Althusser's Politics," in *Althusser's Lesson*, 125–54.

10. Ross in Rancière, *The Ignorant Schoolmaster*, xvi; see also Louis Althusser, "Student Problems (1964)," *Radical Philosophy* 170 (2011): 14.

11. Rancière, *The Method of Equality*, 90–91.

12. Rancière, *The Ignorant Schoolmaster*, 28.

13. Ross in Rancière, *The Ignorant Schoolmaster*, xiv.

14. Rancière, *The Ignorant Schoolmaster*, 3.

15. Rancière, *The Ignorant Schoolmaster*, 6.

16. Rancière, *The Ignorant Schoolmaster*, 8.

17. Rancière, *The Ignorant Schoolmaster*, 7. Stultification has become a major focus for secondary English work on Rancièrian pedagogy, without having considered this problem of translation. See, for example, Jason E. Smith and Annette Weisser, eds., *Everything Is in Everything: Jacques Rancière between Intellectual Emancipation and Aesthetic Education* (Pasadena: Art Center Graduate Press, 2011); and Charles

Bingham and Gert J. J. Biesta, eds,. *Jacques Rancière: Education, Truth, Emancipation* (London: Continuum, 2010). For a second consideration of the term within Rancière's broader oeuvre, see my own "A Lesson in Low Music," in Cachopo, Nickleson, and Stover, *Rancière and Music* .

18. Mertens, *American Minimal Music*, 44.

19. Robert Carl, *Terry Riley's "In C"* (New York: Oxford University Press, 2009), 36.

20. Strickland, *American Composers*, 112. See also Veniero Rizzardi, "The Complete Birth of the Loop: Terry Riley in Paris, 1962–63," in *Crosscurrents: American and European Music in Interaction, 1900–2000*, ed. Felix Meyer, Carol J. Oja, Wolfgang Rathert, and Anne C. Shreffler (Rochester: Boydell Press, 2014).

21. Carl, *Terry Riley's "In C"*, 37.

22. Strickland, *American Composers*, 113.

23. Strickland, *American Composers*, 114. For more on the Mime Troupe, see Sumanth Gopinath, "Reich in Blackface: *Oh Dem Watermelons* and Blackface Minstrelsy in the 1960s," *Journal of the Society for American Music* 5, no. 2 (2011): 139–93; and Cole, "Fun, Yes, but Music?"

24. Strickland, *American Composers*, 114.

25. Potter, *Four Musical Minimalists*, 170.

26. Duckworth, *Talking Music*, 274.

27. See Patrick Nickleson, "Terry Riley in New York, 1965–1969," in *Ecstatic Aperture: The Life and Music of Terry Riley*, ed. Vincent de Roguin (forthcoming).

28. Strickland, *Minimalism: Origins*, 194; my emphasis.

29. Potter, *Four Musical Minimalists*, 117.

30. On the road trip, see O'Brien, "Experimentalisms of the Self," 62.

31. Strickland, *American Composers*, 41.

32. Duckworth, *Talking Music*, 300.

33. Duckworth, *Talking Music*; my emphasis.

34. Riley quoted in Carl, *Terry Riley's "In C"*, 18.

35. The widespread popularity of this connective logic, perhaps compounded with a desire for supposed reconciliation, was well capitalized on when Reich and Glass performed a series of "reunion" concerts together at the Brooklyn Academy of Music in 2015.

36. Duckworth, *Talking Music*, 282–83; my emphasis. Riley's pedagogic theory came up in a later conversation with Robert Ashley for his series *Music with Roots in the Aether*: "Guruji [Pran Nath] says this too: teaching and learning are the same thing. Teaching is a learning experience because in order to teach you have to examine a thing very closely, so you're learning what its nature is."

37. Strickland, *American Composers*, 41.

38. Strickland, *American Composers*, 41; my emphasis.

39. Strickland, *American Composers*, 41–42; my emphasis.

40. Paul Sacher Stiftung, Sammlung Steve Reich, Textmanuskripte, Eigene Texte; my emphasis.

41. Mark Alburger clarifies that the program of the Pulsa concert featured Ri-

ley's *Dorian Reeds,* Reich's *Melodica,* and Glass's *Strung Out* alongside Young's work. See Alburger, "Philip Glass: String Quartet to Strung Out," *21st Century Music* 10, no. 7 (July 2003): 7.

42. Strickland, *American Composers,* 204. Glass also mentions Young in his 1975 interview with Walter Zimmerman: "I was very much at the time, very much alone. . . . When I was living in Paris I had no contact with any other musicians. I knew Alla Rakha. But the Indian music developed so clearly along different lines. It could be important in inspiration, but they didn't offer new models for my music. Because the instruments were too different. The raga system demanded a kind of perception of intonation, which I'm not particularly gifted at. Someone like La Monte, who works with intonation in a very precise way, could be attracted to that. But for me personally, my strong point was not that kind of precise hearing to hear microintervals." See Zimmerman, *Desert Plants.* Glass's interview is available online at http://home.snafu.de/walterz/biblio/06_phil_glass.pdf, accessed 23 February 2018.

43. Duckworth, *Talking Music,* 110–11.

44. Duckworth, *Talking Music,* 111.

45. Young has held onto the capacity to impel writers toward hagiography even when we would expect everyone involved to know better. See M. H. Miller, "The Man Who Brian Eno Called 'the Daddy of Us All,'" *New York Times,* 22 July 2020.

46. Ev Grimes, "Interview: Education (1989)," in Kostelanetz, *Writings on Glass,* 12–36.

47. Potter, *Four Musical Minimalists,* 112. Potter does not give a concrete example of these "all too frequent" performances or their specific performance problems.

48. Carl, *Terry Riley's "In C",* 41.

49. Carl, *Terry Riley's "In C",* 44.

50. Potter, *Four Musical Minimalists,* 108–9. Martin had drawn little attention in histories up to 2000, but he has subsequently become visible as a major artistic figure of the period for his innovations in projected light. See Gregory Zinman, *Making Images Move: Handmade Cinema and the Other Arts* (Oakland: University of California Press, 2020).

51. Carl, *Terry Riley's "In C",* 44.

52. Richard Landry, interview by Clifford Allen, August 2010, http://www.paristransatlantic.com/magazine/interviews/landry.html

53. Carl, *Terry Riley's "In C",* 46.

54. Carl, *Terry Riley's "In C",* 50.

55. Duckworth, *Talking Music,* 297.

56. Carl, *Terry Riley's "In C",* 296.

57. Steve Reich, interview by Seth Colter Walls, 2014, http://www.timeout.com/newyork/music/steve-reich-interview-whos-the-best-do-it-yourselfer-in-history-if-not-johann-sebastian-bach. There is something decidedly Trumpian in Reich's discussion here, in that any discussion of *In C* turns into a kind of gift economy. It seems that for Reich, his proprietary claims on *In C* are tempered if he also turns it into a comment about how much he received in turn. The meaning

of "zero sum" here becomes strange, in that no matter what, the narration of that back-and-forth turns each back and each forth into his victory—a symbol either of benevolent generosity or of modest reception.

58. *It's Gonna Rain* is the first piece discussed in Reich's essay "Early Works (1965–1968)" in Reich 2000, 19–21. It is also on the 1989 Nonesuch CD *Steve Reich—Early Works*.

59. See Strickland, *Minimalism: Origins*, 185; and Potter, *Four Musical Minimalists*, 164.

60. Potter, *Four Musical Minimalists*, 165.

61. On Riley's activities during his New York years, see Nickleson, "Terry Riley in New York."

62. Lloyd Whitesell, "White Noise: Race and Erasure in the Cultural Avant-Garde," *American Music* 19, no. 2 (2001): 169.

63. Whitesell, "White Noise," 176.

64. Whitesell, "White Noise," 177.

65. Gopinath, "Contraband Children," 125–93.

66. Scherzinger, "Curious Intersections," 219.

67. Siarhei Biareishky, "Come Out to Show the Split Subject: Steve Reich, Whiteness, and the Avant-Garde," *Current Musicology* 93 (2012): 88.

68. John Pymm has taken a rather different approach to *It's Gonna Rain* in examining the source material that Reich originally recorded in June 1964 in San Francisco's Union Square. Most of this focuses on Reich (seemingly—he edited himself out of the tapes) interviewing people in the square on what Pymm asserts was probably a Sunday; these included not only Brother Walter, but also another preacher named Ray, a shoeshine man, several "winos," and people Reich labels as "Spanish women." See Pymm, "Minimalism and Narrativity," in Potter, Gann, and ap Siôn, *Ashgate Research Companion*, 279–96.

69. Duckworth, *Talking Music*, 296.

70. Gopinath, "Contraband Children," 155.

71. Strickland, *American Composers*, 41.

72. Crawley, *The Lonely Letters*, 42.

73. Strickland, *American Composers*, 116.

74. Potter, *Four Musical Minimalists*, 117.

75. Strickland, *Minimalism: Origins*, 188.

76. Potter, *Four Musical Minimalists*, 165.

77. Duckworth, *Talking Music*, 300.

78. Potter, *Four Musical Minimalists*, 287.

79. Strickland, *Minimalism: Origins*, 211.

80. Strickland, *Minimalism: Origins*, 211. The internal quotation is from Strickland, *American Composers*, 157.

81. Chapman, "Collaboration, Presence, and Community," 5.

82. Chapman, "Collaboration, Presence, and Community," 46.

83. Duckworth, *Talking Music*, 337.

84. Philip Glass, *Music by Philip Glass* (New York: Harper & Row, 1987), 13.

85. Chapman, "Collaboration, Presence, and Community," 66.

86. Chapman, "Collaboration, Presence, and Community," 94–95. See also Benjamin Piekut's discussion of "the hidden history of loudness" in the New York scene at the time—among the Theatre of Eternal Music, the Velvet Underground and Stooges, Robert Ashley, Philip Glass Ensemble, and so on. See Piekut, *Experimentalism Otherwise*, 193.

87. Chapman "Collaboration, Presence, and Community," 5.

88. The first and most visible of these close collaborations is of course with Robert Wilson and Lucinda Childs on *Einstein on the Beach*, as Leah Weinberg has shown. See "Opera behind the Myth: An Archival Examination of *Einstein on the Beach*," PhD diss., University of Michigan, 2016, especially Chapter 4, "Playing Together: Modeling Authorship of a Downtown Opera."

89. As Jeremy Grimshaw perceptively did when he discussed the role of sound engineer Kurt Munkacsi as a full-time part of the Philip Glass Ensemble. See "High, 'Low,' and Plastic Arts: Philip Glass and the Symphony in the Age of Postproduction," *Musical Quarterly* 86, no. 3 (2002): 472–507.

90. See Steve Reich, "The Phase Shifting Pulse Gate—Four Organs—Phase Patterns—an End to Electronics (1968–1970)," in Reich, *Writings on Music*, 38–51. Kerry O'Brien's dissertation, "Experimentalisms of the Self," deals extensively with Reich's relationship to electronics during this period, including archival work on his time working with Owens and the Bell Labs.

91. Rare exceptions exist here—*The Desert Music* and *Variations for Winds, Strings, and Keyboards* each include a full brass section.

92. Sumanth Gopinath, "Departing to Other Spheres," in *Rethinking Reich*, ed. Sumanth Gopinath and Pwyll ap Siôn (Oxford University Press, 2019), 37n95.

93. Chapman, "Collaboration, Presence, and Community," 251.

94. Glass, in Kostelanetz, *Writings on Glass*, 47.

95. Despite the official date of January 1970, Reich had already been developing the piece in rehearsal in December with Art Murphy and Jon Gibson; sketches first appear in an entry dated 10 November 1969.

96. Russell Hartenberger, *Performance Practice in the Music of Steve Reich* (New York: Cambridge University Press, 2016), 131–32.

97. Cardew, "Notation, Interpretation, Etc.," 22.

98. Let alone that it is technically the first commercial recording made of what would come to be known as minimalism, predating the recording of *In C* by a few months. Histories that aspire to make it the first rock/minimalism crossover thus far have failed to contend with other complexities: that perhaps the *first* commercial LP from one of the "big four" was in fact a "crossover," or that Cale, a "rocker" had a more conventional art music pedigree than Riley. Indistinctions abound.

Chapter 4

1. Quoted in John Rockwell, "The Evolution of Steve Reich," *New York Times*, 14 March 1982.

2. Quoted in Lawrence, *Hold On to Your Dreams*, 80.

3. Rancière, *The Names of History*, 35.

4. Rockwell, "Evolution of Steve Reich."

5. Tim Page, "Framing the River: A Minimalist Primer," *High Fidelity*, November 1981.

6. Joan La Barbara, "New Music," *High Fidelity / Musical America*, November 1977.

7. Peter Goodman, "Minimalist Music: Is Less More—or a Bore?," *Newsday*, 1 April 1984.

8. *Time*, 3 January 1983, 80. The statement is part of a review of Steve Reich, *Tehillim* (ECM 1215, 1982).

9. I think here of one of the first key critical takes on minimalism, which asked whether the term designates an "aesthetic, style, or technique" before setting out to distinguish and classify among possible uses. Johnson, "Minimalism."

10. Rancière, *The Names of History*, 3.

11. Rancière, *The Names of History*, 3.

12. Rancière, *The Names of History*, 8.

13. I consider Christophe Levaux's *We Have Always Been Minimalist* as an ideal exemplar of such distinctions. Levaux is very concerned to construct minimalism as a "fact" and music history as a science that works toward its discovery. Alongside the remarkable archival and disciplinary contributions to minimalist scholarship, then, I read in Levaux's framing a real anxiety around (music) history's proximity to literature and fiction. For Levaux, this is all about calling upon a Latourian framework of science; I believe Donna Haraway is correct, however, when she notes that followers of Latour too often risk reifying a transcendent ideal of Science where, in fact, Latour consistently anchors his writing in the minute workings of various *sciences*. See Christophe Levaux, *We Have Always Been Minimalist* and Haraway, *Staying with the Trouble*, 41.

14. In the course of final revisions of this book, I attended a screening of John Akomfrah's 1986 *Handsworth Songs*, which presents differing accounts of an uprising that occurred in a predominantly Black neighborhood of Birmingham, UK. Akomfrah's depiction is remarkable for how little it addresses the historical "fact" of the riot (or its possible generic distinction as a rebellion, an uprising, and so on) but for how it tracks the narrative efforts to articulate what precisely happened. That is, the film accounts for both Black and Muslim residents of the community articulating what happened and its reason, while media, police, and local politicians insist that nothing in particular happened or, if something did happen, it was incoherent, senseless violence by people who do not understand.

15. Rancière, "The Use of Distinctions," 218.

16. Rancière, "The Use of Distinctions," 208.

17. Rancière, "The Use of Distinctions," 208.

18. Rancière, "The Use of Distinctions," 218. He does much the same for music, writing "Music . . . is the concern of the Muses before it is that of the instrumentalists." See "Metamorphosis of the Muses," in *Sonic Process: A New Geography of Sounds* (Barcelona: Actar, 2002), 23.

19. Rancière, "The Use of Distinctions," 211.

20. Girard, *Répétitions*.

21. Strickland, *Minimalism: Origins*, 241–53; Potter, *Four Musical Minimalists*, 2–3; Peter Shelley, "Rethinking Minimalism: At the Intersection of Music Theory and Art Criticism," PhD diss., University of Washington, 2013, 16–71; most recently, Levaux, *We Have Always Been Minimalist*. I will focus primarily on Strickland's initial overview as it was first and has remained the benchmark in relation to which later ones have developed.

22. Barbara Rose, "ABC Art," *Art in America*, October–November 1965, 57–69.

23. Jill Johnston, "Music: La Monte Young," *Village Voice*, 19 November 1964; see Chapter 2.

24. John Perreault, "La Monte Young's Tracery: The Voice of the Tortoise," *Village Voice*, 22 February 1970.

25. Donal Henahan, "Steve Reich Presents a Program of Pulse Music at the Guggenheim," *New York Times*, 9 May 1970); quoted in Strickland, *Minimalism: Origins*, 241–45.

26. "First Interview with Michael Nyman (1970)," in Reich, *Writings on Music*, 52–54; Wasserman, "Interview with Composer Steve Reich," 48, quoted in Strickland, *Minimalism: Origins*, 241.

27. Johnson, "La Monte Young, Steve Reich, Terry Riley, Philip Glass," quoted in Strickland, *Minimalism: Origins*, 242, and Shelley, "Rethinking Minimalism," 21.

28. Tom Johnson, "Meditating and on the Run," *Village Voice*, 31 January 1974, quoted in Strickland, *Minimalism: Origins*, 244.

29. John Rockwell, "There's Nothing Quite Like the Sound of Glass," *New York Times*, 26 May 1974, quoted in Strickland, *Minimalism: Origins*, 244.

30. Strickland, *Minimalism: Origins*, 244; my emphasis.

31. Strickland, *Minimalism: Origins*, 244.

32. Strickland, *Minimalism: Origins*, 241.

33. Hillier in Reich, *Writings on Music*, 4. Hillier highlights 1976 for his own collection of pieces well beyond my own scope, but that again points to the desire to return "minimalism" to a traditional (and European) direction: in his narrative, *Music for 18 Musicians* and *Einstein* are paired with Andriessen's *De Staat*, Pärt's early tinntinnabuli style, and Górecki's *Symphony of Sorrowful Songs*. For further reading on this period from scholars eager to set it as the beginning of a new trajectory rather than falling into the "end of the 1960s" trope, see Timothy Rutherford-Johnson, *Music after the Fall: Modern Composition and Culture since 1989* (Oakland: University of California Press, 2017) and William Robin, *Industry: Bang on a Can and New Music in the Marketplace* (New York: Oxford University Press, 2020).

34. This is true whether we consider a book like Wim Mertens's, written during the period in question, or Keith Potters from two decades later. Mertens's chapter on Reich ends with *Music for a Large Ensemble* (1978) and *Octet* (1980) as expansions of the forces used in *Music for 18 Musicians* (1976)—the last works available to him. He also concludes his chapter on Glass with *Northstar* and *Satyagraha*. See Mertens, *American Minimal Music*, 83–86. Potter, decades later, concludes on the exact same pieces for Reich, despite having two decades more material to poten-

tially comment upon. See Potter, *Four Musical Minimalists*, 246–47. While K. Robert Schwarz in *Minimalists* discusses Reich's 1990s opera *The Cave*, he prioritizes *Large Ensemble* and *Octet* as increasing his instrumental forces as connection between *18 Musicians* and *Tehillim*. Robert Fink uses works from around this period in *Repeating Ourselves* as well, including comparing Donna Summers's "Love to Love You Baby" to *Music for 18 Musicians* as an example of the "culture of repetition," and then centrally analyzes *Octet* in relation to his argument about the media sublime. See Fink, *Repeating Ourselves*, 49–55 and 145–52, respectively. For more on this period's historiography, see Joseph, *Beyond the Dream Syndicate*, 39.

35. Ross, "Historicizing Untimeliness," 16.

36. See Levaux, *We Have Always Been Minimalist*, 43–50, 92–97, and 55, respectively.

37. For example, when he writes of Johnson's 30 December 1974, piece on David Behrman; see Shelley, "Rethinking Minimalism," 23.

38. As when Shelley outlines Johnson's use of the term "hypnotic school" for Young, Riley, Reich, and Glass; see Shelley, "Rethinking Minimalism," 22.

39. This methodological fault is particularly clear in Peter Shelley's work, in that he cites all of his readings of Tom Johnson from Johnson's volume of selected writings, *The Voice of New Music: New York City, 1972–1982* (Paris: Editions 75, 1989), rather than directly from the pages of the *Village Voice*. Some notable omissions result, both in Shelley's research and in Johnson's clear effort to flawlessly narrate his prophetic vision of minimalism in that volume.

40. Tom Johnson, "A Surprise under the Piano," *Village Voice*, 9 March 1972. Johnson suggests that his 30 March 1972 article "The Minimal Slow-Motion Approach: Alvin Lucier and Others" marks the "first time that the new music was described critically as 'minimal.'" See Johnson, *Voice of New Music*, n.p.

41. Tom Johnson, "Steve Reich's 'Drumming,'" *Village Voice*, 9 December 1971.

42. Tom Johnson, "Charlemagne Palestine: Electronics, Voice, and Piano," *Village Voice*, 31 January 1974.

43. In his edited collection of criticism Johnson follows Strickland and others in placing his first uses of "minimal" later than was actually the case. Johnson, *Voice of New Music*.

44. Gendron, *Montmartre*, 233–34.

45. Gendron, *Montmartre*, 238; my emphasis. Gendron cites Strickland here in his historical overview of the discourse of minimalism, though not when he comes around to discussion of punk at the CBGB scene.

46. For an examination of Iggy Pop's relationship with the 1960s avant-garde, see Piekut, *Experimentalism Otherwise*, 177–98.

47. Gendron, *Montmartre*, 255.

48. For a consideration of the racialized implications of the split between the various downtown musics of the late 1970s—downtown and punk on the one hand, disco and hip-hop on the other—see Gendron, *Montmartre*, 254–57. Court, "Racialising Amateurism," addresses many of these same issues through considering the racialized distinctions of amateurism. The best-known contemporary criti-

cal take on racism in the 1970s punk scene is by Bangs himself. See Lester Bangs, "The White Noise Supremacists," in *White Riot: Punk and the Politics of Race* (New York: Verso, 2011); the article was originally published in the 30 April 1979 issue of the *Village Voice*. I only very belatedly became interested in the ostensibly more positive relationship between (white) punk artists and (Black) reggae musicians in late 1970s England, but I hope to pursue this dynamic in the future.

49. Tommy Ramone, quoted in Clinton Heylin, *From the Velvets to the Voidoids: A Pre-punk History for a Post-punk World* (London: Penguin, 1993), 210; quoted in Gendron, *Montmartre*, 258.

50. Gendron, *Montmartre*, 258. Gendron develops this claim in "The Downtown Music Scene," in *The Downtown Scene: The New York Art Scene, 1974–1984*, ed. Marvin J. Taylor (Princeton, NJ: Princeton University Press, 2006), 55.

51. Michael Watts, "So Shock Me, Punks," *Melody Maker*, 11 September 1976.

52. James Wolcott, "A Conservative Impulse in the New York Rock Underground," *Village Voice*, 18 August 1975.

53. Nick Kent, "Talking Heads: Are These Guys Trying to Give Rock a Bad Name?," *New Musical Express*, 25 June 1977.

54. Farren, "Notes on Minimalism."

55. Patrick Humphries, "In Search of the Lost Chord," *Melody Maker*, 11 October 1980.

56. Most music historians have suggested that LeWitt's work was influential on Reich; however, less self-conscious about music's possibility to influence other arts, the art historian Michael Maizels makes a compelling case for Reich's conceptual work having had an impact on LeWitt. Maizels's reading is especially compelling for how he tracks the influence of Milton Babbitt among minimalist visual artists, not particularly for his music, but for analyses of serialism appearing in *Die Reihe*. See Maizels, *In and Out of Phase*.

57. Rancière, "The Use of Distinctions," 210.

58. For more on Riley's performance and the Electric Ear, see Nickleson, "Terry Riley in New York."

59. Harold C. Schonberg, "Music: The Medium Electric, the Message Hypnotic," *New York Times*, 15 April 1969.

60. John Rockwell, "Rhys Chatham: Classical Road to Rock," *New York Times*, 17 April 1981.

61. Author's conversation with Rhys Chatham, Skype, September 2014.

62. Author's conversation with Rhys Chatham, Skype, September 2014.

63. Author's conversation with Rhys Chatham, Skype, September 2014.

64. Author's conversation with Rhys Chatham, Skype, September 2014.

65. The Kitchen press release for "An Evening of Music by Tony Conrad." Available at http://archive.thekitchen.org/wp-content/uploads/2011/12/PR_Conrad_72.pdf. The recording was released in 2017 as Tony Conrad, *Ten Years Alive on the Infinite Plain* (Superior Viaduct SV-049, 2017).

66. Tony Conrad, "Inside the Dream Syndicate," *Film Culture* 41 (1966): 7.

67. See Tony Conrad, "On 60 Cycles [1972]," in *Tony Conrad Writings*, 104–6.

68. Schonberg, "Music."

69. Conrad, "On 60 Cycles," 106.

70. The album was released with almost no notice and remained, as Jeff Hunt has said, of extreme fringe interest even for fans of the avant-garde. Hunt subsequently released it on his record label, Table of the Elements, in 1993 with twenty minutes of extra material. In 2003, Table of the Elements also released a two-CD thirtieth-anniversary edition. For further context, see liner notes by Branden Joseph and Jim O'Rourke to the Superior Viaduct 2016 vinyl reissue of *Outside the Dream Syndicate*. See also Branden Joseph, *The Roh and the Cooked: Tony Conrad and Beverly Grant in Europe* (Cologne: Buchhandlung Walter Konig, 2012).

71. Alan Licht, "Rhys Chatham," http://bombmagazine.org/article/3206/rhys-chatham, 17 October 2008.

72. Tom Johnson, "Someone's in the Kitchen—with Music," *New York Times*, 8 October 1972.

73. Chatham was, even more precociously, only nineteen at the time. It's unclear whether Chatham and the Kitchen had lied to Johnson about his age in an effort to be taken more seriously, or whether this was a simple mistake.

74. "One-man" here requires qualification. The Kitchen, and indeed the downtown scene of this period, did a relatively good job for the time of representing women in their programming. The no wave bands examined below featured something resembling gender parity across many groups, with women like Nina Canal, Pat Place, Ikue Mori, Barbara Ess, Christine Hahn, and many others playing key roles. Still, the 1979 New Music New York festival at the Kitchen featured fifty-three composers, only about 20 percent of whom were women.

75. Gordon is one of the scene's more astute commentators: "Punk rock was in the nascent stages, and was literally just around the corner, at CBGB's and other clubs. The punk aesthetic (*not unrelated to minimalism*) extended to the visual artists and writers, as well as composers. I took Rhys Chatham to see the Ramones in 1975, and he never looked back. Brian Eno showed up in 1978, and handpicked a few bands for his 'No New York' anthology, garnering attention for certain *noise bands*, Talking Heads first appeared as a trio at St. Mark's Church Parish Hall, and David Byrne appeared on recordings by Arthur Russell and myself. Rhys Chatham and Glenn Branca began writing ringing guitar pieces, with their influence extending to Sonic Youth. There was a whole group of musicians who made their own instruments, others found connections with the loft-jazz scene. Disco and dance music was in its heyday." Peter Gordon quoted in *New York Noise* (New York: Soul Jazz Publishing, 2007), 92; my emphasis. Notably Gordon says the show was in 1975—it has been difficult to pin down the precise date on which the two saw the concert, but Chatham's recollection that it was for the album release seems likely. See Lawrence, *Hold On to Your Dreams*.

76. Author's conversation with Rhys Chatham, September 2014. There is of course a jocular sarcasm in his referring to the Ramones as "highly complex": he is well aware of the discourse of the Ramones as the height of musical simplicity, while simultaneously pointing up the fact that his music at the time was even more

"minimal," as understood by a "minimum of means" type definition. I do not mean by this latter point that it was a contest—who's more minimal—but that within mainstream commentary on the Ramones, arguments about harmonic complexity surely miss the point and are out of touch with the broader context in downtown New York City.

77. Author's conversation with Rhys Chatham, September 2014.

78. Following the breakup of the Gynecologists, Chatham took a job as guitarist in the short-lived band Arsenal to learn rudimentary guitar progressions.

79. Rockwell, "Rhys Chatham." I have directly asked Chatham about this claim—which he has made in many interviews and in his writing—because I find it surprising that, in the break he took from programming at the Kitchen, he never heard any of the rock bands that Arthur Russell programmed, including the Modern Lovers. It is possible he has forgotten, that they had no impact on him, or that he entirely avoided the Kitchen once Russell took over.

80. See Robinson, *Hungry Listening*.

81. Russell's role of bringing together a variety of scenes at the Kitchen is well documented. See Lawrence, *Hold On to Your Dreams*.

82. "Voice Choices," *Village Voice*, 8 May 1978. The descriptor "arty and empty" inspired the Mars song "RTMT."

83. https://artistsspace.org/history/ (accessed 20 April 2022)

84. Michael Heller, *Loft Jazz: Improvising New York in the 1970s* (Oakland: University of California Press, 2017), 34–35.

85. Douglas Eklund, *The Pictures Generation, 1974–1984* (New York: Metropolitan Museum of Art, 2009), 196. One such event can be seen on the DVD *135 Grand Street, 1979* (Soul Jazz Films SJR DVD226), which features, among others, the Static, Chatham performing *Guitar Trio*, Jill Kroesen, and Ut.

86. "For Immediate Release—BANDS at Artists Space." Available online at http://artistsspace.org/programs/bands.

87. Branca quoted in Marc Masters, *No Wave* (London: Black Dog, 2007), 20; my emphasis.

88. Masters, *No Wave*, 20.

89. Masters, *No Wave*, 20.

90. Masters, *No Wave*, 20.

91. Masters, *No Wave*, 20.

92. Conrad, "Inside the Dream Syndicate," *Film Culture*, 7–8.

93. Masters, *No Wave*, 20.

94. Masters, *No Wave*, 20.

95. See various artists, *No New York* (Antilles AN-7067, 1978); reissued (Lilith Records LR102, 2005).

96. Brandon Stosuy, "Various Artists—*No New York*," Pitchfork.com, 12 November 2005.

97. Gendron, *Montmartre*, 292.

98. Simon Reynolds, *Rip It Up and Start Again: Postpunk, 1978–1984* (London: Faber and Faber, 2005), 155.

99. John Rockwell, "Rock: Underground," *New York Times*, 8 May 1978.

100. Rockwell, "Rock: Underground"; my emphasis.

101. John Rockwell, "The Pop Life: The Rock World and Visual Arts," *New York Times*, 2 June 1978.

102. Masters includes posters for performances at the Kitchen. On 9 April 1978, Daily Life, The Gynecologists, Theoretical Girls, and Arsenal played. Another Theoretical Girls concert poster is dated 21 May—probably also 1978. See Masters, *No Wave*, 110–11.

103. Rockwell, "The Pop Life"; my emphasis. This piece continues, with more clarity, some of the ideas he first wrote up in "When the Punks Meet the Progressives," *New York Times*, 23 October 1977. There he focused on distinguishing European art-rock from New York punk. Toward the end of the article, he undercuts the earlier distinction by noting a zone of indistinction between the two: "When the punks get minimal and the progressive get austere, the two can become one—as Patti Smith and Talking Heads, in their own different ways, have already shown." The article also highlights the ever-present grouping of Brian Eno–David Bowie–Iggy Pop–Robert Fripp, writing that "the basic idiom of leaden, driving, minimal art-rock goes back to such London progressives of the early 1970's as the original Roxy Music," which included Eno, whose work is highlighted in relation to Bowie's recently released *Heroes* (featuring Fripp on guitar), and more peripheral involvement (via Bowie) on Iggy Pop's new *Lust for Life*. Fripp and Eno also released *No Pussyfooting* around this time using a system identical to Riley's time-lag accumulator, which they dubbed Frippertronics.

104. Robert Palmer, "Philip Glass Comes to Carnegie Hall—at Last," *New York Times*, 28 May 1978. The integration of the "minimalist aesthetic" and trends in punk music was of course nothing new for Glass. In June 1973 John Rockwell wrote of Glass "the avant-garde composer" (no mention is made of minimalism) as "making an effort to broaden his audience beyond the 'in' crowd" by performing at Max's Kansas City and doing a five-boroughs park tour. See John Rockwell, "Philip Glass Works to Broaden Scope beyond 'In' Crowd," *New York Times*, 28 June 1973.

105. John Rockwell, "Music: Philip Glass," *New York Times*, 2 June 1978.

106. John Rockwell, "Music and Theatre Offered at Kitchen in a 3-Part Concert," *New York Times*, 21 February 1973.

107. Rockwell, "Music: Philip Glass."

108. This last image appears in a website cataloging the early chronology of no wave concerts. See http://www.fromthearchives.com/ll/chronology4.html, accessed 9 June 2021.

109. The earliest available recording is from the "audio cassette magazine" *Tellus*. Issue 1 includes a performance of *Guitar Trio (1977)* from May 1979 performed by Chatham, Branca, Nina Canal, and Wharton Tiers. https://www.ubu.com/sound/tellus_1.html, accessed June 2021.

110. Gendron, *Montmartre*, 161–67.

111. John Rockwell, "Rock: 2 of the No-Wave," *New York Times*, 28 June 1979.

112. Rockwell, "2 of the No-Wave."

113. John Rockwell, "Music: 53 Composers in 9-Day Festival," *New York Times*, 18 June 1979.

114. Rockwell, "Music: 53 Composers."

115. Tom Johnson, "Contradictions and Glenn Branca's Static," *Village Voice*, 24 September 1979.

116. John Rockwell, "Avant-Garde: 2 New-Music Concerts," *New York Times*, 5 November 1979.

117. Glenn Branca, "Rhys Chatham," *New York Rocker*, November 1979. Branca's appeal to *Metal Machine Music* again highlights the central place—all but forgotten throughout the 1980s and most of the 1990s—of the 60 Hz hum of the Theatre of Eternal Music. In a 1975 profile in which he was provoked about his new feedback-oriented release, Lou Reed reportedly said, "Outrageous? You should have heard the Dream Syndicate." Quoted at https://www.tableoftheelements.org/tcc-10-day-of-niagara, accessed 9 June 2021.

118. Gregory Sandow, "Classical Music for Loud Guitars," *Village Voice*, 25 February 1980.

119. Kim Gordon makes a similar comment in her article on Chatham for *Real Life* magazine. See Gordon, "Trash Drugs and Male Bonding," in *Real Life Magazine: Selected Projects and Writing, 1979–1994* (New York: Primary Information, 2006), 47.

120. Sandow, "Classical Music for Loud Guitars."

121. Gregory Sandow, "The New New Music," *Village Voice*, 13–19 May 1981.

122. Sandow, "The New New Music."

123. Kyle Gann, "Metametrics as an Illiteracy Solution," *Postclassic* blog, 1 March 2006, https://www.artsjournal.com/postclassic/2006/03/metametrics_as_an_illiteracy_s.html

124. John Rockwell, "Music: Glenn Branca, Avant-Gardist," *New York Times*, 19 July 1981.

125. Rockwell, "Music: Glenn Branca."

126. Of course, Palmer and Rockwell are notable in this period for having (perhaps necessarily) reviewed both popular and new musics. For a more nuanced handling of the popular musical reception of minimalism, see Levaux, *We Have Always Been Minimalist*, Chapters 17 and 20.

127. Robert Palmer, "Nine Guitars: Symphony by Glenn Branca," *New York Times*, 8 May 1982.

128. Palmer, "Nine Guitars."

129. John Rockwell, "His Forte Is Massive Sonic Grandeur," *New York Times*, 2 May 1982.

130. Rockwell, "Massive Sonic Grandeur."

131. Branca became best known in 1982 when the performance of his piece *Indeterminate Activity of Resultant Masses* at the Chicago edition of the New Music America festival (which grew out of New Music New York) drew the intense criticism of John Cage. The event was a major piece of downtown mythology for years, but the entire interview was released on CD by Branca as "So That Each Person Is

In Charge of Himself (1982 interview with John Cage)" on *Indeterminate Activity of Resultant Masses* (Atavistic Records, 2007). Notably, the person interviewing John Cage is Wim Mertens in the year prior to the English publication of *American Minimal Music*.

132. As far as I know, Branca has not been included in any survey style textbook, with the notable exception of Kyle Gann, *American Music in the Twentieth Century* (Belmont: Schirmer Books, 1997), 301–4. There are of course any number of choices the editors of these books can make about what is representative of a period, but it is important to recognize that the "later" era of minimalism into the 1980s is most often represented in these contexts by the Romantic leaning and notated work of John Adams or something like *Tehillim* by Reich. That is, there is a distinct effort to fold minimalism's later developments back onto earlier styles rather than continuing to follow its thread outward to someone like Branca (or Fullman, Eastman, Amacher, Chatham, Oliveros . . .).

133. Alain Badiou, "The Lessons of Jacques Rancière: Knowledge and Power after the Storm," in Rockhill and Watts, *Jacques Rancière*, 35.

134. Goodman, "Minimalist Music."

135. John Rockwell, "Kitchen Plans 2 Fund-Raising Concerts," *New York Times*, 4 June 1981.

136. Jon Pareles, "The Avant-Garde in the Kitchen," *Listener, Player, Audience*, August 1981.

137. Jon Panish, quoted in Lewis, *Power Stronger Than Itself*, 31.

138. George E. Lewis, "Experimentalism in Black and White: The AACM in New York, 1970–1985," *Current Musicology* nos. 71–73 (Spring 2001–Spring 2002): 127–28.

139. For more on the relationship between Young, Coleman, Shepp, and the Theatre of Eternal Music, see Nickleson, "They (Merely) Held Drones."

140. Robert Palmer, "Pop Jazz; Brian Eno, New Guru of Rock, Going Solo," *New York Times*, 13 March 1981.

Conclusion

1. Author's conversation with Rhys Chatham, September 2014.

2. "Rhys Chatham Interviewed by Rob Young," *The Wire*, February 1999, available online at http://www.rhyschatham.net/nintiesRCwebsite/wire.html

3. Author's conversation with Rhys Chatham, September 2014.

4. Glenn Branca interviewed by David Todd in *Feeding Back: Conversations with Alternative Guitarists* (Chicago: Chicago Review Press, 2012), 217.

5. I think here of Ashon Crawley's writing about minimalism, or how the minimalism of Reich's *Music for 18 Musicians* reminds him of James Baldwin: "There is always a beat beneath the beat, another music beneath the music, and beyond." James Baldwin, quoted in Crawley, *The Lonely Letters*, 42.

6. The reference to Rancière's often-ignored 1995 book on historiography aside.

7. Rancière, "The Use of Distinctions," 208–9; see the Introduction to this book.

8. I am drawing here on the list of technical characteristics used by Potter, Gann, and ap Siôn, *Ashgate Research Companion*.

9. Nichols, *Theft Is Property!*

10. Nichols, *Theft is Property!*, 145.

11. Such lines of argument have been best explored in Glen Sean Coulthard's critique of colonial practices of "recognition" in *Red Skin, White Masks: Rejecting the Colonial Politics of Recognition* (Minneapolis: University of Minnesota Press, 2014). I think as well, in a much different context, of the methods by which global sonic practices are internalized into "music" with the assumption that this is an unmarked gesture of benevolent inclusion.

12. Robin Gray, "Repatriation and Decolonization: Thoughts on Ownership, Access, and Control," in *The Oxford Handbook of Musical Repatriation*, ed. Frank Gunderson, Rob Lancefield, and Bret Woods (Oxford: Oxford University Press, 2018).

13. Robinson, *Hungry Listening*, especially 47–54.

14. Robinson, *Hungry Listening*, 50–51.

15. Hence Conrad's important position, at least in the last decade and especially since his death in 2016, in art history while remaining all but irrelevant in music histories.

16. Nichols, *Theft Is Property!*, 146.

17. Rancière, *The Names of History*, 35.

18. Sebastian Matzner, *Rethinking Metonymy: Literary Theory and Poetic Practice from Pindar to Jakobson* (Oxford: Oxford University Press, 2016), 5. Matzner describes Trypho's definition as "not only bewilderingly obscure, certainly on first reading, but one that also, on reflection, turns out to assert little more than that metonymy is some sort of indirect expression that draws on terms which are somehow related."

19. Gary Tomlinson, *The Singing of the New World: Indigenous Voice in the Era of European Contact* (New York: Cambridge University Press, 2007).

20. Tomlinson, *Singing of the New World*, 30.

21. Tomlinson, *Singing of the New World*, 30.

22. Tomlinson, *Singing of the New World*, 40.

23. See Coulthard, *Red Skin White Masks*, 60–61. I think here as well of Dylan Robinson's writing on nonrepresentation in *Hungry Listening* as well as the "agglutinating" work of affect (*Hungry Listening*, 205).

24. Another musicological discussion of metonymy is in Phil Ford, *Dig: Sound and Music in Hip Culture* (Oxford: Oxford University Press, 2013). Ford's direct discussion of metonymy in relation to handshakes (64–67) to my mind falls back into the problem of treating parts of things as representative of wholes. Nevertheless, his concluding discussion of the work of John Benson Brooks and "musical practice" is, to my mind, precisely about metonymy. There he writes about "find[ing] ourselves in a space defined by a logic of participation, not causality" and about "consubstantiality" (213).

25. Warren Montag, *Louis Althusser* (New York: Palgrave, 2003), 14. Along the same lines, Chambers calls *Reading "Capital"* "collective in spirit," and a work to be read "as a large quilt [rather] than a singular, coherent whole." See Chambers, *Bearing Society in Mind: Theories and Politics of the Social Formation* (London: Rowman & Littlefield International, 2014), 139–42.

26. Louis Althusser, *The Future Lasts a Long Time and the Facts* (London: Chatto & Windus, 1993), 208–9.

27. Jacques Rancière, "The Concept of Critique and the Critique of Political Economy: From the *1844 Manuscripts* to *Capital*," in Louis Althusser et al., *Reading "Capital": The Complete Edition*, trans. Ben Brewster (New York: Verso, 2016 [1965]), 73–174. The book has had a complex publication history. See Chambers, *Bearing Society in Mind*, 139–42. See also Rancière, *The Method of Equality*, 8–12.

28. Althusser, *Reading "Capital*,*"* 344.

29. Althusser, *The Future*, 209.

30. Peter Hallward and Knox Peden, eds., *Concept and Form*, vol. 2: *Interviews and Essays on the "Cahiers pour l'Analyse"* (New York: Verso, 2012), 28 n. 97; my emphasis.

31. Rok Benčin, "Metaphorical and Metonymical Equality: From a Rhetoric of Society to an Aesthetics of Politics," *Maska* 185–86 (Autumn 2017): 60.

32. Benčin, "Metaphorical and Metonymical Equality," 60.

33. Rancière, *The Emancipated Spectator* (New York: Verso, 2009), 97.

34. Panagia, *Rancière's Sentiments*, 36–37. I have cited Panagia, Chambers, and especially Ross extensively throughout this book. Their work in aesthetics, politics, and history, respectively, enlivens the goals and value of Rancière's work, particularly at key moments in which he refuses to explicitly state the achievements of his own discourse. To my mind, a complete reading of Rancière's work must register the texts of these three as standing in yet another contiguous relationship with it, rather than as "secondary literature" commenting on his work. Where Rancière often refuses to draw out the efficacy of his discourse, these scholars stand out for having done so within a decidedly Rancièrian style and/as method.

35. Crawley, *The Lonely Letters*, 41.

36. Rancière, *The Method of Equality*, 25.

37. See Jacques Rancière, "Autonomy and Historicism: The False Alternative," trans. Patrick Nickleson, *Perspectives of New Music* 57, nos. 1–2 (2019): 330–31.

Works Cited

Adams, Rachel. "Unscripted Pedagogy." In *Introducing Tony Conrad: A Retrospective*, edited by Cathleen Chaffee, 58–63. Buffalo: Albright-Knox Gallery, 2018.

Ahmed, Sara. *On Being Included: Racism and Diversity in Institutional Life*. Durham: Duke University Press, 2012.

Ahmed, Sara. *What's the Use: On the Uses of Use*. Durham: Duke University Press, 2019.

Alburger, Mark. "Philip Glass: String Quartet to Strung Out." *21st Century Music* 10, no. 7 (July 2003).

Althusser, Louis. *The Future Lasts a Long Time and the Facts*. London: Chatto & Windus, 1993.

Althusser, Louis. "Student Problems (1964)." *Radical Philosophy* 170 (2011): 11–15.

Austin, Larry and Douglas Kahn, eds. *Source: Music of the Avant-Garde, 1966–1973*. Berkeley: University of California Press, 2011.

Babbitt, Milton. "The Composer as Specialist (1958)." In *The Collected Essays of Milton Babbitt*, edited by Stephen Peles, 48–54. Princeton, NJ: Princeton University Press, 2003.

Badiou, Alain. *The Communist Hypothesis*. London: Verso, 2010.

Badiou, Alain. "The Lessons of Jacques Rancière: Knowledge and Power after the Storm." In *Jacques Rancière: History, Politics, Aesthetics*, edited by Gabriel Rockhill and Philip Watts, 30–54. Durham: Duke University Press, 2009.

Bangs, Lester. "The White Noise Supremacists." In *White Riot: Punk and the Politics of Race*, edited by Stephen Duncombe and Maxwell Tremblay, 105–13. New York: Verso, 2011.

Benčin, Rok. "Metaphorical and Metonymical Equality: From a Rhetoric of Society to an Aesthetics of Politics." *Maska*, Autumn 2017, 58–63.

Biareishky, Siarhei. "Come Out to Show the Split Subject: Steve Reich, Whiteness, and the Avant-Garde." *Current Musicology* 93 (2012): 73–93.

Bingham, Charles and Gert J. J. Biesta, eds. *Jacques Rancière: Education, Truth, Emancipation*. London: Continuum, 2010.

Boutwell, Brett. "Terry Jennings, the Lost Minimalist." *American Music* 32, no. 1 (Spring 2014): 82–107.

Branca, Glenn. "Rhys Chatham." *New York Rocker*, November 1979.

Cage, John. *Silence: Lectures and Writings*. Middletown, CT: Wesleyan University Press, 1961.

Cale, John and Victor Bockris. *What's Welsh for Zen? The Autobiography of John Cale*. New York: Bloomsbury, 1999.

Cardew, Cornelius. "Notation—Interpretation, Etc." *Tempo* 58 (1961): 21–33.

Cardew, Cornelius. *Stockhausen Serves Imperialism*. London: Latimer New Directions, 1974. Reprinted by Primary Information, 2020.

Carl, Robert. *Terry Riley's "In C"*. New York: Oxford University Press, 2009.

Chambers, Samuel. *Bearing Society in Mind: Theories and Politics of the Social Formation*. London: Rowman & Littlefield International, 2014.

Chambers, Samuel. *The Lessons of Rancière*. New York: Oxford University Press, 2013.

Chapman, David. "Collaboration, Presence, and Community: The Philip Glass Ensemble in Downtown New York, 1966–1976." PhD diss., Washington University, 2013.

Cohen, Brigid. *Musical Migration and Imperial New York: Early Cold War Scenes*. Chicago: University of Chicago Press, 2022.

Cohen, Michael, ed. *Tony Conrad: Doing the City / Urban Community Interventions*. New York: 80WSE, 2014.

Cole, Ross. "'Fun, Yes, but Music?' Steve Reich and the San Francisco Bay Area's Cultural Nexus, 1962–65." *Journal of the Society for American Music* 6, no. 3 (2012): 315–48.

Cole, Ross. "'Sound Effects (O.K., Music)': Steve Reich and the Visual Arts in New York City, 1966–1968." *Twentieth Century Music* 11, no. 2 (2014): 217–44.

Conrad, Tony. *Early Minimalism: Volume One*. Liner notes. Table of the Elements AS-33, 1997.

Conrad, Tony. "Inside the Dream Syndicate." In *Tony Conrad Writings*, edited by Constance DeJong and Andrew Lampert, 302–10. New York: Primary Information, 2019. Originally printed in *Film Culture* 41 (1966): 1–8.

Conrad, Tony. *Slapping Pythagoras*. Liner notes. Table of the Elements, V-23, 1995.

Conrad, Tony. *Ten Years Alive on the Infinite Plain*. Liner notes. Superior Viaduct SV-049, 2017.

Conrad, Tony. "Tony Conrad's Response to 'An Open Letter to La Monte Young and Tony Conrad.'" September 2000. http://www.dreyblatt.de/pdf/Tony%20C onrad%20Response.pdf.

Conrad, Tony. *What Music Did*. Edited by Patrick Nickleson. Forthcoming.

Coulthard, Glen Sean. *Red Skin, White Masks: Rejecting the Colonial Politics of Recognition*. Minneapolis: University of Minnesota Press, 2014.

Court, Benjamin. "Racialising Amateurism: Punk and Rap." *Third Text* 34, no. 1 (2020): 49–61.

Cox, Christopher and Daniel Warner, eds. *Audio Culture: Readings in Modern Music*. New York: Bloomsbury Academic, 2017.

Crawley, Ashon T. *Blackpentecostal Breath: The Aesthetics of Possibility*. New York: Fordham University Press, 2017.

Crawley, Ashon T. *The Lonely Letters*. Durham: Duke University Press, 2020.

DeKoeven, Marianne. *Utopia Limited: The Sixties and the Emergence of the Postmodern*. Durham: Duke University Press, 2004.

Deseriis, Marco. *Improper Names: Collective Pseudonyms from the Luddites to Anonymous*. Minneapolis: University of Minnesota Press, 2015.

Dohoney, Ryan. "Julius Eastman, John Cage, and the Homosexual Ego." In *Tomorrow Is the Question: New Approaches to Experimental Music Studies*, edited by Benjamin Piekut, 39–62. Ann Arbor: University of Michigan Press, 2014.

Draper, Susana. *Mexico 1968: Constellations of Freedom and Democracy*. Durham: Duke University Press, 2008.

Dreyblatt, Arnold. "An Open Letter to La Monte Young and Tony Conrad." 2000. https://static1.squarespace.com/static/56d5b65df850827e476cb1f9/t/5770c78 9cd0f68ce8dd7a63a/1467008905359/Letter+to+the+Wire.pdf, 20 April 2022.

Duckworth, William. *Talking Music*. New York: Schirmer Books, 1995.

Duguid, Brian. "Tony Conrad Interview." *EST* 7 (Summer 1996). http://media.hyp erreal.org/zines/est/intervs/conrad.html.

Eklund, Douglas. *The Pictures Generation, 1974–1984*. New York: Metropolitan Museum of Art, 2009.

Epstein, Paul. "Pattern Structure and Process in Steve Reich's 'Piano Phase.'" *Musical Quarterly* 72, no. 4 (1986): 494–502.

Farren, Mick. "Notes on Minimalism (or Learning to Live with the Ramones)." *New Musical Express*, 21 May 1977.

Felski, Rita. *The Limits of Critique*. Chicago: University of Chicago Press, 2015.

Fink, Robert. "(Post-)minimalisms 1970–2000: The Search for a New Mainstream." In *The Cambridge History of Twentieth-Century Music*, edited by Nicholas Cook and Anthony Pople, 539–56. Cambridge: Cambridge University Press, 2004.

Fink, Robert. *Repeating Ourselves: American Minimal Music as Cultural Practice*. Berkeley: University of California Press, 2005.

Flynt, Henry. "La Monte Young in New York, 1960–1962." In *Sound and Light: La Monte Young and Marian Zazeela*, edited by William Duckworth and Richard Fleming, 44–97. Lewisburg, PA: Bucknell University Press, 1996.

Ford, Phil. *Dig: Sound and Music in Hip Culture*. Oxford: Oxford University Press, 2013.

Foucault, Michel. "The Subject and Power." *Critical Inquiry* 8, no. 4 (Summer 1982): 777–95.

Furet, François. *Interpreting the French Revolution*. Translated by Elborg Forster. Cambridge: Cambridge University Press, 1981.

Gagne, Cole. *Soundpieces 2: Interviews with American Composers*. Metuchen, NJ: Scarecrow Press, 1993.

Gagne, Cole and Tracey Caras. *Soundpieces: Interviews with American Composers*. Metuchen, NJ: Scarecrow Press, 1982.

Gann, Kyle. *American Music in the Twentieth Century*. Belmont: Schirmer Books, 1997.

Gann, Kyle. "Metametrics as an Illiteracy Solution." *Postclassic* blog, 1 March 2006. https://www.artsjournal.com/postclassic/2006/03/metametrics_as_an_illitera cy_s.html, accessed 9 June 2021.

Gann, Kyle. "The Outer Edge of Consonance: Snapshots from the Evolution of La Monte Young's Tuning Installations." In *Sound and Light: La Monte Young and Marian Zazeela*, edited by William Duckworth and Richard Fleming, 152–90. Lewisburg, PA.: Bucknell University Press, 1996.

Gann, Kyle. "Reconstructing *November*." *American Music* 28, no. 4 (Winter 2010): 481–91.

Gendron, Bernard. *Between Montmartre and the Mudd Club: Popular Music and the Avant-Garde*. Chicago: University of Chicago Press, 2002.

Gendron, Bernard. "The Downtown Music Scene." In *The Downtown Book: The New York Art Scene, 1974–1984*, edited by Marvin J. Taylor, 41–65. Princeton, NJ: Princeton University Press, 2006.

Girard, Johan. *Répétitions: L'esthétique Musicale de Terry Riley, Steve Reich et Philip Glass*. Paris: Presses Sorbonne nouvelle, 2010.

Glass, Philip. *Music by Philip Glass*. New York: Harper & Row, 1987.

Goldman, Jonathan. "'How I Became a Composer': An Interview with Vinko Globokar." *Tempo* 68 (267): 22–28.

Goodman, Peter. "Minimalist Music: Is Less More—or a Bore?" *Newsday*, 1 April 1984.

Gopinath, Sumanth. "'Black Forces': Julius Eastman Against Minimalism." In *We Have Delivered Ourselves from the Tonal—Of, Towards, On, For Julius Eastman*, edited by Bonaventure Soh Bejeng Ndikung et al. Berlin: Savvy Contemporary, 2020.

Gopinath, Sumanth. "Contraband Children: The Politics of Race and Liberation in the Music of Steve Reich, 1965–1966." PhD diss., Yale University, 2005.

Gopinath, Sumanth. "Reich in Blackface: *Oh Dem Watermelons* and Blackface Minstrelsy in the 1960s." *Journal of the Society for American Music* 5, no. 2 (2011): 139–93.

Gordon, Kim. "Trash Drugs and Male Bonding." In *Real Life Magazine: Selected Projects and Writing, 1979–1994*, edited by Miriam Katzeff, Thomas Lawson, and Susan Morgan, 47. New York: Primary Information, 2006.

Gray, Robin. "Repatriation and Decolonization: Thoughts on Ownership, Access, and Control." In *The Oxford Handbook of Musical Repatriation*, edited by Frank Gunderson, Rob Lancefield, and Bret Woods. Oxford: Oxford University Press, 2018.

Greer, Allan. *The Patriots and the People: The Rebellion of 1837 in Rural Lower Canada*. Toronto: University of Toronto Press, 1993.

Grimes, Ev. "Interview: Education (1989)." In *Writings on Glass: Essays, Interviews, Criticism*, edited by Richard Kostelanetz, 12–36. New York: Schirmer, 1997.

Grimshaw, Jeremy. *Draw a Straight Line and Follow It: The Music and Mysticism of La Monte Young*. New York: Oxford University Press, 2011.

Grimshaw, Jeremy. "High, 'Low,' and Plastic Arts: Philip Glass and the Symphony in the Age of Postproduction." *Musical Quarterly* 86, no. 3 (2002): 472–507.

Grubbs, David. *Records Ruin the Landscape: John Cage, the Sixties, and Sound Recording*. Durham: Duke University Press, 2014.

Hallward, Peter and Knox Peden, eds. *Concept and Form*. Vol. 2: *Interviews and Essays on the "Cahiers pour l'Analyse"*. New York: Verso, 2012.

Haraway, Donna. *Staying with the Trouble: Making Kin in the Chthulucene*. Durham: Duke University Press, 2016.

Harker, Brian. "Milton Babbitt Encounters Academia (and Vice Versa)." *American Music* 26, no. 3 (2008): 336–77.

Harris, Cheryl I. "Whiteness as Property." *Harvard Law Review* 106, no. 8 (1993): 1707–91.

Hartenberger, Russell. *Performance Practice in the Music of Steve Reich*. New York: Cambridge University Press, 2016.

Heller, Michael. *Loft Jazz: Improvising New York in the 1970s*. Oakland: University of California Press, 2017.

Henahan, Donal. "Steve Reich Presents a Program of Pulse Music at the Guggenheim." *New York Times*, 9 May 1970.

Heylin, Clinton. *From the Velvets to the Voidoids: A Pre-punk History for a Post-punk World*. London: Penguin, 1993.

Hicks, Darren. *Artistic License: The Philosophical Problem of Copyright and Appropriation*. Chicago: University of Chicago Press, 2017.

Hisama, Ellie. "'Diving into the Earth': The Musical Worlds of Julius Eastman." In *Rethinking Difference in Music Scholarship*, edited by Olivia Bloechl, Melanie Lowe, and Jeffrey Kallberg, 260–86. Cambridge: Cambridge University Press, 2015.

Humphries, Patrick. "In Search of the Lost Chord." *Melody Maker*, 11 October 1980.

Iddon, Martin. "The Haus That Karlheinz Built: Composition, Authority, and Control at the 1968 Darmstadt Festival." *Musical Quarterly* 87, no. 1 (2004): 87–118.

Johnson, Timothy A. "Minimalism: Aesthetic, Style, or Technique." *Musical Quarterly* 78, no. 4 (1994): 742–73.

Johnson, Tom. "Charlemagne Palestine: Electronics, Voice, and Piano." *Village Voice*, 31 January 1974.

Johnson, Tom. "Contradictions and Glenn Branca's Static." *Village Voice*, 24 September 1979.

Johnson, Tom. "La Monte Young, Steve Reich, Terry Riley, Philip Glass." *Village Voice*, 7 September 1972.

Johnson, Tom. "Meditating and on the Run." *Village Voice*, 31 January 1974.

Johnson, Tom. "The Minimal Slow-Motion Approach: Alvin Lucier and Others." *Village Voice*, 30 March 1972.

Johnson, Tom. "Someone's in the Kitchen—with Music." *New York Times*, 8 October 1972.

Johnson, Tom. "Steve Reich's 'Drumming.'" *Village Voice*, 9 December 1971.

Johnson, Tom. "A Surprise under the Piano." *Village Voice*, 9 March 1972.

Johnston, Jill. "Music: La Monte Young." *Village Voice*, 19 November 1964.

Joseph, Branden W. *Beyond the Dream Syndicate: Tony Conrad and the Arts after Cage*. New York: Zone Books, 2008.

Joseph, Branden W. *Outside the Dream Syndicate*. Liner notes. *Superior Viaduct* SV048, 2016.

Joseph, Branden W. *The Roh and the Cooked: Tony Conrad and Beverly Grant in Europe.* Cologne: Buchhandlung Walter Konig, 2012.

Kent, Nick. "Talking Heads: Are These Guys Trying to Give Rock a Bad Name?" *New Musical Express,* 25 June 1977.

Klein, Joshua. "Steve Reich." *Pitchfork Media,* 22 November 2006.

Kostelanetz, Richard. *The Theatre of Mixed Means: An Introduction to Happenings, Kinetic Environments, and Other Mixed-Means Performances.* New York: Dial Press, 1968.

Kostelanetz, Richard, ed. *Writings on Glass: Essays, Interviews, Criticism.* New York: Schirmer, 1997.

Kotz, Liz. *Words to Be Looked At: Language in 1960s Art.* Cambridge, MA: MIT Press, 2007.

La Barbara, Joan. "New Music." *High Fidelity / Musical America,* November 1977.

Lawrence, Tim. *Hold On to Your Dreams: Arthur Russell and the Downtown Music Scene, 1973–1992.* Durham: Duke University Press, 2009.

Lawrence, Tim. "Pluralism, Minor Deviations, and Radical Change: The Challenge to Experimental Music in Downtown New York, 1971–85." In *Tomorrow Is the Question: New Directions in Experimental Music Studies,* edited by Benjamin Piekut, 63–85. Ann Arbor: University of Michigan Press, 2014.

Leach, Mary Jane and Renee Levine Packer, eds. *Gay Guerilla: Julius Eastman and His Music.* Rochester: University of Rochester Press, 2015.

Levaux, Christophe. *We Have Always Been Minimalist: The Construction and Triumph of a Musical Style.* Berkeley: University of California Press, 2020.

Lewis, George E. "Experimentalism in Black and White: The AACM in New York, 1970–1985." *Current Musicology* nos. 71–73 (Spring 2001–Spring 2002): 100–157.

Lewis, George E. *A Power Stronger Than Itself: The AACM and American Experimental Music.* Chicago: University of Chicago Press, 2008.

Licht, Alan. "The History of La Monte Young's Theatre of Eternal Music." *Forced Exposure* 16 (1990): 60–69.

Macciocchi, Maria-Antonietta. *Letters from Inside the Communist Party to Louis Althusser.* Translated by Stephen M. Hellman. London: New Left Books 1973.

Mackey, Eva. "Unsettling Expectations: (Un)certainty, Settler States of Feeling, Law, and Decolonization." *Canadian Journal of Law and Society* 29, no. 2 (2014): 235–52.

Maizels, Michael. *In and Out of Phase: An Episodic History of Art and Music in the 1960s.* Ann Arbor: University of Michigan Press, 2020.

Mansfield, Corey. "Animating the Periphery: Studio of the Streets and the Politicizing of the Buffalo Community through Public Access Television and Media Literacy." MA thesis, University of Southern California, 2014.

Margasak, Peter. "Amid the Drone, a Feud over Who Composed It." *New York Times,* 13 August 2000.

Masters, Marc. *No Wave.* London: Black Dog, 2007.

Matzner, Sebastian. *Rethinking Metonymy: Literary Theory and Poetic Practice from Pindar to Jakobson.* Oxford: Oxford University Press, 2016.

McClary, Susan. "Rap, Minimalism, and Structures of Time in Late Twentieth-

Century Culture." In *Audio Culture: Readings in Modern Music*, edited by Christopher Cox and Daniel Warner, 289–98. New York: Bloomsbury Academic, 2017.

McKittrick, Katherine. *Dear Science and Other Stories*. Durham: Duke University Press, 2021.

Mertens, Wim. *American Minimal Music*. London: Kahn & Averill, 1983.

Meyer, James. *Minimalism: Art and Polemics in the Sixties*. New Haven: Yale University Press, 2001.

Miéville, China. *October: The Story of the Russian Revolution*. New York: Verso, 2018.

Miller, M. H. "The Man Who Brian Eno Called 'the Daddy of Us All.'" *New York Times*, 22 July 2020.

Mitchell, Tim. *Sedition and Alchemy: A Biography of John Cale*. Chester Springs, PA: Peter Owens, 2003.

Montag, Warren. *Louis Althusser*. New York: Palgrave, 2003.

Moreton-Robinson, Aileen. *The White Possessive: Property, Power, and Indigenous Sovereignty*. Minneapolis: University of Minnesota Press, 2015.

Morrison, Matthew D. "Race, Blacksound, and the (Re)making of Musicological Discourse." *Journal of the American Musicological Society* 72, no. 3 (2019): 781–823.

Nichols, Robert. *Theft Is Property! Dispossession and Critical Theory*. Durham: Duke University Press, 2020.

Nickleson, Patrick. "A Lesson in Low Music." In *Rancière and Music*, edited by João Pedro Cachopo, Patrick Nickleson, and Chris Stover, 71–93. Edinburgh: Edinburgh University Press, 2020.

Nickleson, Patrick. "On Which They (Merely) Held Drones: Fugitive Tapes from the Theatre of Eternal Music Archive, 1962–1966." *Journal of the Royal Musical Association*, 147/2 (2022).

Nickleson, Patrick. "Terry Riley in New York, 1965–1969." In *Ecstatic Aperture: The Life and Work of Terry Riley*, edited by Vincent de Roguin. Shelter Press, forthcoming.

Nickleson, Patrick. "Transcription, Recording, and Authority in 'Classic' Minimalism." *Twentieth Century Music* 14, no. 3 (2017): 361–98.

O'Brien, Kerry. "Burning Pianos and Whispering Rivers: A Composer's Journey." *New York Times*, 8 November 2019.

O'Brien, Kerry. "A Composer and Her (Very) Long String Instrument." *New York Times*, 1 May 2020.

O'Brien, Kerry. "Experimentalisms of the Self: Experiments in Art and Technology, 1966–1971." PhD diss., Indiana University, 2018.

O'Brien, Kerry. "Machine Fantasies into Human Events: Reich and Technology in the 1970s." In *Rethinking Reich*, edited by Sumanth Gopinath and Pwyll ap Siôn, 323–39. Oxford: Oxford University Press, 2019.

Page, Tim. "Framing the River: A Minimalist Primer." *High Fidelity*, November 1981.

Palmer, Robert. "Nine Guitars: Symphony by Glenn Branca." *New York Times*, 8 May 1982.

Palmer, Robert. "Philip Glass Comes to Carnegie Hall—at Last." *New York Times*, 28 May 1978.

Palmer, Robert. "Pop Jazz: Brian Eno, New Guru of Rock, Going Solo." *New York Times*, 13 March 1981.

Panagia, Davide. *Rancière's Sentiments*. Durham: Duke University Press, 2018.

Panagia, Davide. *Ten Theses for an Aesthetics of Politics*. Minneapolis: University of Minnesota Press, 2016.

Pareles, Jon. "The Avant-Garde in the Kitchen." *Listener, Player, Audience*, August 1981.

Perreault, John. "La Monte Young's Tracery: The Voice of the Tortoise." *Village Voice*, 22 February 1970.

Piekut, Benjamin. *Experimentalism Otherwise: The New York Avant-Garde and Its Limits*. Berkeley: University of California Press, 2011.

Piekut, Benjamin. *Henry Cow: The World Is a Problem*. Durham: Duke University Press, 2019.

Pierson, Marcelle. "Voice, *Technē*, and *Jouissance* in *Music for 18 Musicians*." *Twentieth Century Music* 13, no. 1 (2016): 25–52.

Potter, Keith. *Four Musical Minimalists: La Monte Young, Terry Riley, Steve Reich, Philip Glass*. New York: Cambridge University Press, 2000.

Potter, Keith, Kyle Gann, and Pwyll ap Siôn, eds. *The Ashgate Research Companion to Minimalist and Postminimalist Music*. Burlington, VT: Ashgate, 2013.

Pritchett, James. "David Tudor as Composer/Performer in Variations II." *Leonardo Music Journal* 14 (2004): 11–16.

Puchner, Martin. *Poetry of the Revolution: Marx, Manifestos, and the Avant-Garde*. Princeton, NJ: Princeton University Press, 2006.

Pymm, John. "Minimalism and Narrativity." In *The Ashgate Research Companion to Minimalist and Postminimalist Music*, edited by Keith Potter, Kyle Gann, and Pwyll ap Siôn, 279–96. Burlington, VT: Ashgate, 2013.

Rancière, Jacques. "A Few Remarks on the Method of Jacques Rancière." *parallax* 15, no. 3 (2009): 114–23.

Rancière, Jacques. *Aisthesis: Scenes from the Aesthetic Regime of Art*. Translated by Zakir Paul. New York: Verso, 2013.

Rancière, Jacques. *Althusser's Lesson*. Translated by Emiliano Battista. New York: Verso, 2011 [1974].

Rancière, Jacques. "Autonomy and Historicism: The False Alternative." Translated by Patrick Nickleson. *Perspectives of New Music* 57, nos. 1–2 (Winter–Summer 2019): 329–51.

Rancière, Jacques. "The Concept of Critique and the Critique of Political Economy: From the *1844 Manuscripts* to *Capital*." In Louis Althusser et al., *Reading "Capital": The Complete Edition*, translated by Ben Brewster. New York: Verso, 2016.

Rancière, Jacques. "The Death of the Author or the Life of the Artist? (April 2003)." In *Chronicles of Consensual Times*, translated by Steven Corcoran, 101–5. London: Continuum, 2010.

Rancière, Jacques. *Disagreement: Politics and Philosophy*. Translated by Julie Rose. Minneapolis: University of Minnesota Press, 1998.

Rancière, Jacques. *The Emancipated Spectator*. Translated by Gregory Elliott. New York: Verso, 2009.

Rancière, Jacques. "Good Times, or Pleasure at the *Barrière*." In *Staging the People: The Proletarian and His Double*, 175–232, translated by David Fernbach. New York: Verso, 2011.

Rancière, Jacques. *The Ignorant Schoolmaster: Five Lessons in Intellectual Emancipation*. Translated by Kristin Ross. Stanford: Stanford University Press, 1991.

Rancière, Jacques. *La Mésentente: Politique et Philosophie*. Paris: Galilée, 1995.

Rancière, Jacques. "Metamorphosis of the Muses." In *Sonic Process: A New Geography of Sounds*, 17–29. Barcelona: Actar, 2002.

Rancière, Jacques. *The Method of Equality: Interviews with Laurent Jeanpierre and Dork Zabunyan*. Translated by Julie Rose. Cambridge: Polity Press, 2016.

Rancière, Jacques. *The Names of History: On the Poetics of Knowledge*. Translated by Hassan Melehy. Minneapolis: University of Minnesota Press, 1994.

Rancière, Jacques. *The Philosopher and His Poor*. Translated by John Drury, Corinne Oster, and Andrew Parker. Durham: Duke University Press, 2004.

Rancière, Jacques. *Proletarian Nights: The Workers' Dream in Nineteenth-Century France*. Translated by John Drury. London: Verso, 2012 [1981].

Rancière, Jacques. "Ten Theses on Politics." Translated by Rachel Bowlby with Davide Panagia. *Theory & Event* 5, no. 3 (2001): n.p.

Rancière, Jacques. "The Use of Distinctions." In *Dissensus: On Politics and Aesthetics*, edited and translated by Steve Corcoran, 205–18. New York: Continuum, 2010.

Rancière, Jacques and Danielle Rancière. "The Philosophers' Tale: Intellectuals and the Trajectory of Gauchisme" In *The Intellectual and His People*, vol. 2 of *Staging the People*, translated by David Fernbach, 75–100. New York: Verso, 2012.

Reich, Steve. *Writings on Music, 1965–2000*. New York: Oxford University Press, 2002.

Reynolds, Simon. *Rip It Up and Start Again: Postpunk, 1978–1984*. London: Faber and Faber, 2005.

Rizzardi, Veniero. "The Complete Birth of the Loop: Terry Riley in Paris, 1962–63." In *Crosscurrents: American and European Music in Interaction, 1900–2000*, edited by Felix Meyer, Carol J. Oja, Wolfgang Rathert, and Anne C. Shreffler, 353–63. Rochester: Boydell Press, 2014.

Robin, William. *Industry: Bang on a Can and New Music in the Marketplace*. New York: Oxford University Press, 2020.

Robinson, Dylan. *Hungry Listening: Resonant Theory for Indigenous Sound Studies*. Minneapolis: University of Minnesota Press, 2020.

Robinson, Dylan. "To All Who Should Be Concerned." *Intersections* 39, no. 1 (2019): 137–44.

Rockwell, John. "Avant-Garde: 2 New-Music Concerts." *New York Times*, 5 November 1979.

Rockwell, John. "The Evolution of Steve Reich." *New York Times*, 14 March 1982.

Rockwell, John. "His Forte Is Massive Sonic Grandeur." *New York Times*, 2 May 1982.

Rockwell, John. "Kitchen Plans 2 Fund-Raising Concerts." *New York Times*, 4 June 1981.

Rockwell, John. "Music: 53 Composers in 9-Day Festival." *New York Times*, 18 June 1979.

Rockwell, John. "Music: Glenn Branca, Avant-Gardist." *New York Times*, 19 July 1981.

Rockwell, John. "Music: Philip Glass." *New York Times*, 2 June 1978.

Rockwell, John. "Music and Theatre Offered at Kitchen in a 3-Part Concert." *New York Times*, 21 February 1973.

Rockwell, John. "Philip Glass Works to Broaden Scope beyond 'In' Crowd." *New York Times*, 28 June 1973.

Rockwell, John. "The Pop Life: The Rock World and Visual Arts." *New York Times*, 2 June 1978.

Rockwell, John. "Rhys Chatham: Classical Road to Rock." *New York Times*, 17 April 1981.

Rockwell, John. "Rock: 2 of the No-Wave." *New York Times*, 28 June 1979.

Rockwell, John. "Rock: Underground." *New York Times*, 8 May 1978.

Rockwell, John. "There's Nothing Quite Like the Sound of Glass." *New York Times*, 26 May 1974.

Rockwell, John. "When the Punks Meet the Progressives." *New York Times*, 23 October 1977.

Rose, Barbara. "ABC Art." *Art in America*, October–November 1965.

Ross, Kristin. *Communal Luxury: The Political Imaginary of the Paris Commune*. New York: Verso, 2015.

Ross, Kristin. *The Emergence of Social Space: Rimbaud and the Paris Commune*. New York: Verso, 2008 [1988].

Ross, Kristin. "Historicizing Untimeliness." In *Jacques Rancière: History, Politics, Aesthetics*, edited by Gabriel Rockhill and Philip Watts, 15–29. Durham: Duke University Press, 2009.

Ross, Kristin. *May '68 and Its Afterlives*. Chicago: University of Chicago Press, 2002.

Rutherford-Johnson, Timothy. *Music after the Fall: Modern Composition and Culture since 1989*. Oakland: University of California Press, 2017.

Sandow, Gregory. "Classical Music for Loud Guitars." *Village Voice*, 25 February 1980.

Sandow, Gregory. "The New New Music." *Village Voice*, 13–19 May 1981.

Sarlin, Paige. "In Person, on Screen, in Context, on Tape." In *Introducing Tony Conrad: A Retrospective*, edited by Cathleen Chaffee, 247–51. Buffalo: Albright-Knox Art Gallery, 2019.

Scherzinger, Martin. "Curious Intersections, Uncommon Magic: Steve Reich's *It's Gonna Rain*." *Current Musicology* 79–80 (2005): 207–44.

Schonberg, Harold C. "Music: The Medium Electric, the Message Hypnotic." *New York Times*, 15 April 1969.

Schwarz, K. Robert. *Minimalists*. London: Phaidon, 1996.

Schwarz, K. Robert. "Steve Reich: Music as a Gradual Process: Part I." *Perspectives of New Music* 19, nos. 1–2 (1980–81): 373–92.

Shank, Barry. *The Political Force of Musical Beauty.* Durham: Duke University Press, 2014.

Shelley, Peter. "Rethinking Minimalism: At the Intersection of Music Theory and Art Criticism." PhD diss., University of Washington, 2013.

Smith, Jason E. and Annette Weisser, eds. *Everything Is in Everything: Jacques Rancière between Intellectual Emancipation and Aesthetic Education.* Pasadena: Art Center Graduate Press, 2011.

Stosuy, Brandon. "Various Artists—No New York." Pitchfork.com, 12 November 2005.

Stover, Chris. "Rancière's Affective Impropriety." In *Rancière and Music,* edited by João Pedro Cachopo, Patrick Nickleson, and Chris Stover, 230–61. Edinburgh: Edinburgh University Press, 2020.

Straus, Joseph. "The Myth of Serial 'Tyranny' in the 1950s and 1960s." *Musical Quarterly* 83, no. 3 (1999): 301–43.

Strickland, Edward. *American Composers: Dialogues on Contemporary Music.* Bloomington: Indiana University Press, 1991.

Strickland, Edward. *Minimalism: Origins.* Bloomington: Indiana University Press, 1993.

Sun, Cecilia Jian-Xuan. "Experiments in Musical Performance: Historiography, Politics, and the Post-Cagean Avant-Garde." PhD diss., University of California Los Angeles, 2004.

Taruskin, Richard. "Chapter 8: A Harmonious Avant-Garde?" In *The Oxford History of Western Music,* vol. 5: *Music in the Late Twentieth Century,* 351–410. New York: Oxford, 2005.

Thompson, E. P. *The Making of the English Working Class.* New York: Vintage, 1966.

Tilbury, John. *Cornelius Cardew (1936–1981): A Life Unfinished.* Essex: Copula, 2008.

Todd, David. *Feeding Back: Conversations with Alternative Guitarists.* Chicago: Chicago Review Press, 2012.

Tomlinson, Gary. *The Singing of the New World: Indigenous Voice in the Era of European Contact.* New York: Cambridge University Press, 2007.

Tucker, Marcia and James Monte. *Anti-illusion: Procedures/Materials.* New York: Whitney Museum of Art, 1969.

Wasserman, Emily. "An Interview with Composer Steve Reich." *Artforum,* May 1972.

Watkin, Christopher. "Rewriting the Death of the Author: Rancièrian Reflections." *Philosophy and Literature* 39, no. 1 (2015): 32–46.

Watts, Michael. "So Shock Me, Punks." *Melody Maker,* 11 September 1976.

Weheliye, Alexander. *Phonographies: Grooves in Sonic Afro-Modernity.* Durham: Duke University Press, 2005.

Weinberg, Leah. "Opera behind the Myth: An Archival Examination of *Einstein on the Beach.*" PhD diss., University of Michigan, 2016.

Weiss, Piero and Richard Taruskin, eds. *Music in the Western World: A History in Documents.* Belmont: Thomson/Schirmer, 2008.

Whitesell, Lloyd. "White Noise: Race and Erasure in the Cultural Avant-Garde." *American Music* 19, no. 2 (2001): 168–89.

Wolcott, James. "A Conservative Impulse in the New York Rock Underground." *Village Voice*, 18 August 1975.

Woodard, Josef. "Hail! Hail! Gunther Schuller." *Musician Magazine*, October 1991.

Yates, Peter. "Music." *Arts & Architecture*, October 1965.

Young, La Monte. "Notes on the Theatre of Eternal Music and *The Tortoise, His Dreams and Journeys*." 2000. http://melafoundation.org/theatre.pdf, accessed 16 March 2022.

Young, La Monte and Marian Zazeela. *Selected Writings*. Munich: Heiner Friedrich, 1969.

Zimmerman, Walter. *Desert Plants: Conversations with 23 American Composers*. Vancouver: A.R.C. Publications, 1976.

Zinman, Gregory. *Making Images Move: Handmade Cinema and the Other Arts*. Oakland: University of California Press, 2020.

Index

Branca, Glenn, 5, 24, 133–135, 142–143,
151, 152, 153, 154, 155, 157, 159–169, 170,
171, 174, 176, 178–179, 202n59, 225n75,
228n117, 228n131, 229n132; *5 Lessons for
Electric Guitar*, 163, 164; *Instrumental
for Six Guitars*. 159–160, 163; *Symphonies 1–3*, 164, 166–167, 174; *(Untitled)
1979*, 163, 162
Brother Walter, 108–115, 126, 172,
219n68
Bush Tetras, the (band), 171

Cage, John, 14, 15, 23, 25, 30, 32, 33, 36,
40, 41, 42, 58, 79, 98, 100, 124, 199n21,
206n40, 208n21, 210n34, 211n59,
213n89, 228n131; critique of authorship, 64–67
Cale, John, 1, 46–54, 64, 68–74, 77, 79,
85–88, 90, 97, 127, 153, 155. 208n21,
209n26, 212n70, 214n99, 214n103,
215n108; *The Church of Anthrax* LP,
125, 220n98
Canal, Nina, 158, 225n74, 227n109
Cardew, Cornelius, 1, 58, 124, 195n4,
208n19, 209n26, 209n34
Carnegie Hall, 134, 158–159, 171
Carl, Robert, 96, 105, 107
Caras, Tracey, 89, 215n3
CBGB, 134, 139, 141, 153, 154, 157, 158,
223n45, 225n75
Chambers, Samuel, 61, 196n8, 231n25,
231n34
Chambers, Steve, 121, 124
Chance, James, 154, 157
Chapman, David, 118, 119, 197n11
Chatham, Rhys, 5, 24, 122, 133–135, 138,
142, 143–151, 152, 154, 155, 157, 159–164,
166, 168, 169, 170, 174, 176–178, 202n59,
225n73, 225n75, 225n76, 226n78,
227n109, 228n119, 229n132; *Guitar
Trio*, 155, 160, 162, 163, 168, 226n85,
227n109
Choi, Jung Hee, 54
Christgau, Robert, 151, 158

citation, 89, 99, 108, 111–112, 126, 128,
198n20
Cohen, Brigid, 25, 213n89
Coleman, Ornette, 14, 15, 23, 25, 46, 152,
172, 229n129; and Artists House (131
Prince Street), 152
collaboration, 1, 3–6, 8–11, 13, 14, 16, 18,
21, 47, 49, 50, 51, 53–57, 60, 63, 65–66,
68–70, 72, 82, 85, 87, 88, 89–91, 95–100,
104, 105, 107–108, 115, 116, 118, 119, 120,
124, 126, 127, 128, 133, 143, 153, 159, 160,
161, 170, 173, 176–178, 179, 199n20,
212n70, 212n79, 216n4, 220n88
collectivism, 1, 3, 4, 5, 6, 9, 12–13, 47, 48–
50, 51, 53–55, 60, 63, 65–68, 71, 72, 73–
88, 90, 106, 107, 117, 120, 127, 155, 161,
171, 173, 177, 179, 180, 189, 192, 199n20,
212n77, 215n105, 231n25
Coltrane, John, 14, 15, 111, 192n12
commons, common sensorium, 3, 61,
66, 95, 114, 118, 190
Communists (band), 151
complexity, 1, 6, 38–39, 41, 99, 135, 150,
185, 226n76
composer, the, 4, 5, 8, 11, 13, 21, 23, 24,
26, 28–35, 38–40, 41, 42, 44, 45, 54, 55,
65, 66, 67, 69–70, 72, 73, 74, 85, 89, 115,
118–120, 126, 129, 130, 138–139, 144, 149,
155–156, 160–169, 177–179, 192; and
intervention in the sound, 138, 159;
and privilege, 8–9, 16–17, 28–29, 33–35,
42, 44, 65, 66, 72, 110, 119, 120, 172, 179,
184–185
composition, art music, 10, 14, 16, 25,
30–36, 50–51, 55, 56–59, 64–70, 73, 115–
117, 128, 138, 155, 160, 172, 179, 183, 192,
201n35, 211n59
Conrad, Tony, 1–4, 15, 56–58, 60, 63–71,
145, 147–148, 149, 153, 155, 176–178,
183, 195n1, 199n20, 208n21, 209n32,
210n43, 211n57, 211n64, 214n91, 214n97,
214n103, 215nn107–110, 230n15; *Early
Minimalism, Vol. 1.*, 48, 64, 70, 82;
Film Culture essay, 81–84; *Flicker,*

Nahuatl language. *See* Aztec song
names and nominations, 18, 25–27,
54, 60–81, 71–77, 80–82, 85–86, 89,
94–95, 126–128, 176, 179–180, 182, 185,
192–193; collective nomination (and
band names), 55, 71–73, 86, 155, 157,
161, 163, 212n77; improper names, 132,
180, 193, 199n20, 215n105; in Reich's
work, 108–115, 116, 126; Young's titling
practice, 55–57, 60
narrative/narratology/emplotment, 6,
9–15, 18–20, 47, 49, 52–54, 60, 63–64,
66, 90–92, 99–105, 121, 128, 131, 137,
175, 179, 181, 183, 185, 192–193, 199n23,
201n41, 211n59, 213n83, 216n4, 216n5,
219n57
Napster. *See* file-sharing
New Music, New York (festival), 161–
162
Niblock, Phill, 162
Nichols, Robert, 181–185, 212n78
No New York (compilation album), 134,
151, 154–155, 225n75
notation, 5, 8, 42, 57, 67, 126, 171, 179,
193, 201n35, 209n26, 210n34, 213n89,
229n132; Branca and 160, 164, 166–
168, 178; scores as delegation, 16,
22–23, 49, 54, 64, 67–68, 74, 79–80, 83,
87, 114, 177

O'Brien Kerry, 36, 38, 205n15, 206n38,
206n40, 212n77

Palestine, Charlemagne, 136, 138, 149,
151, 176, 177
Palmer, Robert, 158, 166–167, 228n126
Panagia, Davide, 9, 15, 21, 61, 190,
200n33, 231n34
Pareles, Jon, 170–171, 173
pedagogy, 4, 8, 12, 16, 30, 40–42, 99, 102,
105, 112, 128, 217n36; pedagogic myth
or relation, 89–95, 103, 120–121, 125,
216n17
phasing. *See* tape (magnetic)

Piekut, Benjamin, 64, 150–151, 196n7,
209n29, 211n59, 220n86
Place, Pat, 153
Pocket Theatre (New York venue),
74–76, 84
police, police order of history. *See*
Rancière
Potter, Keith. 37, 50–51, 52, 68, 79–81,
97, 105–106, 113–114, 116, 126, 208n19,
222n34
Pran Nath, Pandit, 47, 217n36
prolepsis. *See* historiography
proper names, 72, 82, 95, 108, 110–114,
115–116, 126–128, 130, 142, 155, 161, 179–
180, 183, 193, 199n20, 212n77
property, 3–4, 8–9, 10, 14, 26, 47, 60–63,
70, 71, 87, 114, 179–182, 193, 197n11,
199n20
protest, 1–4, 86, 131, 183
purity. *See* (im)purity

Ramones, The, 22, 134–5, 139–141, 149–51,
157–160, 225nn75–6
Rancière, Jacques, 15, 19, 21, 33–34, 60,
92–93, 180, 185, 189–191, 202n56,
231n34; *abrutir* and stultification, 40,
42, 44, 92–95, 104, 119–120, 175, 177,
179, 181, 192, 204n7, 216n17; *Althusser's
Lesson*, 92–95, 200n28; and Danielle
Rancière, 12; *Disagreement* (French:
La Mésentente), 61, 131, 132, 196n8;
dissensus, 5–6, 17–18, 24, 28, 71, 90,
131, 185, 190–191, 196n8; distribution
of the sensible, 17, 19, 22, 25, 29, 35–36,
62, 111, 125, 132–133, 184, 191; *histoire*
and history, 11–15, 19, 25, 129, 131–132,
184–186, 196n8; homonymy in, 5–6,
17–18, 25, 61, 63, 70, 73, 130–134, 181,
185, 190–191, 196n8, 199n20; *Ignorant
Schoolmaster, The*, 40, 92–93, 210n43;
logos, 131, 211n59; and Marxism 12,
180, 189–192; *Names of History, The*
(and the "primeval legislator"), 25,
129, 131, 185, 196n8, 229n6; poetics of